Negotiation

The City Law School, City University, London

OXFORD
UNIVERSITY PRESS

OXFORD
UNIVERSITY PRESS

Great Clarendon Street, Oxford OX2 6DP

Oxford University Press is a department of the University of Oxford.
It furthers the University's objective of excellence in research, scholarship,
and education by publishing worldwide in

Oxford New York

Auckland Cape Town Dar es Salaam Hong Kong Karachi
Kuala Lumpur Madrid Melbourne Mexico City Nairobi
New Delhi Shanghai Taipei Toronto

With offices in

Argentina Austria Brazil Chile Czech Republic France Greece
Guatemala Hungary Italy Japan Poland Portugal Singapore
South Korea Switzerland Thailand Turkey Ukraine Vietnam

Oxford is a registered trademark of Oxford University Press
in the UK and in certain other countries

Published in the United States
by Oxford University Press Inc., New York

British Library Cataloguing in Publication Data
Data available

Typeset by Laserwords Private Limited, Chennai, India
Printed in Great Britain on acid-free paper by
Ashford Colour Press Ltd., Gosport, Hampshire

ISBN 978-0-19-955349-5

10 9 8 7 6 5 4 3 2 1

Negotiation

Author

Margot Taylor, Solicitor, Principal Lecturer, The City Law School

Contributors

Susan Blake, Barrister, Associate Dean, The City Law School
Susannah Leahy, Barrister, former Senior Lecturer, ICSL

Editor

Margot Taylor, Solicitor, Principal Lecturer, The City Law School

Series Editor

Julie Browne, Barrister, Senior Lecturer, The City Law School

FOREWORD

I am delighted to write this Foreword to the manuals which are written by practitioners and staff of the Inns of Court School of Law (ICSL [now The City Law School]).

The manuals are designed primarily to support training on the Bar Vocational Course (BVC). They now cover a wide range, embracing both the compulsory and the optional subjects of the BVC. They provide an outstanding resource for all those concerned to teach and acquire legal skills wherever the BVC is taught.

The manuals for the compulsory subjects are updated and revised annually. The manuals for the optional subjects are revised every two years. To complement the Series, the publishers will maintain a website for the manuals which will be used to keep them up-to-date throughout the academic year.

The manuals, continually updated, exemplify the practical and professional approach that is central to the BVC. I congratulate the staff of The City Law School who have produced them to an excellent standard, and Oxford University Press for its commitment in securing their publication. As my predecessor the Hon. Mr Justice Gross so aptly said in a previous Foreword, the manuals are an important ingredient in the constant drive to raise standards in the public interest.

The Hon. Mr Justice Etherton
Chairman of the Advisory Board of the Institute of Law
City University, London
May 2008

PREFACE

Negotiation is a vital skill for all lawyers to have. With changes in the civil litigation process it is becoming increasingly important that lawyers understand and recognise the skills which underpin negotiation and how those build on advocacy skills but differ from them. This manual explains the underlying psychological influences and how they are used by experienced negotiators to manipulate their opponent. It then gives practical guidance on how to prepare to deal with every aspect of a negotiation effectively, including how to counter and use psychological influences. Ten chapters are devoted to preparation, looking at each stage in detail.

The first two chapters consider the importance of understanding the context of the negotiation and the way in which you can use the objectives of the parties to achieve more for your client.

The next chapter looks at how negotiators seek to persuade their opponent to compromise, first considering some of the more simplistic approaches of traditional 'bargaining' negotiators and then looking at more sophisticated and effective methods of persuasion. A whole chapter is then devoted to guidance on how to analyse the case, formulate and evaluate argument to use it effectively.

The role of and tactics used in information exchange are then examined and tips are given as to how to ensure that you get all the information you need and how to give information to your opponent in order to assist the negotiation to proceed but avoid the risks of giving information which may be harmful to your case.

Concession planning, one of the most difficult aspects of negotiation, is also the subject of a whole chapter. It explains the traditional ways of using concession in negotiations, including explanation of a number of specific tactics used. It then gives guidance on how to prepare to use concessions effectively to ensure that you obtain the best achievable settlement for your client.

Consideration is then given to the different overall strategies that can be adopted, looking at what influences any one person to adopt a particular strategy and the advantages and disadvantages of each strategy.

The next chapter deals with the extent to which you can plan how to open and structure a negotiation, given the lack of any formalities and the uncertainties. It highlights considerations to bear in mind when planning this aspect of a negotiation.

A chapter is then devoted to an explanation of the full range of tactics which may be used in a negotiation and how to deal with them. Another chapter gives tips on how to present and respond effectively.

Finally, two chapters give detailed guidance on how to put your preparation and planning into effect and conduct a successful negotiation. One chapter deals with matters that you are likely to encounter in any negotiation. The other gives specific guidance on how to deal with particularly difficult situations.

OUTLINE CONTENTS

Foreword v
Preface vii

1 Introduction to negotiation 1
2 The essentials of negotiation 6
3 Style, strategy and tactics 15
4 Legal negotiations 24
5 Preparation and planning—an overview 37
6 Understanding the context 54
7 Analysis—objectives 60
8 Persuasion—the role of argument 71
9 Analysis—formulating arguments 83
10 Information exchange 100
11 Preparation—concessions 111
12 Planning your strategy 126
13 Planning the structure 134
14 Considering possible tactics 143
15 Communicating effectively 152
16 Conducting an effective negotiation 162
17 Dealing with difficulties 177
18 Recording and enforcing a negotiated agreement 187
19 Assessing negotiation skills 200
20 Adapting skills for Alternative Dispute Resolution 213

APPENDIX: Case studies 220

Suggested reading 250
Index 251

DETAILED CONTENTS

Foreword v
Preface vii

1 Introduction to negotiation 1
1.1 The importance of negotiation skills 1
1.2 Learning negotiation skills 2

2 The essentials of negotiation 6
2.1 What does negotiation mean? 6
2.2 Types of negotiation 8
2.3 Issues to be negotiated 11
2.4 The negotiation process 13

3 Style, strategy and tactics 15
3.1 Introduction 15
3.2 Style 15
3.3 Strategy overview 16
3.4 Competitive strategy 18
3.5 Cooperative strategy 19
3.6 Collaborative/principled/problem-solving 20
3.7 Tactics—an overview 22

4 Legal negotiations 24
4.1 Generally 24
4.2 Why cases settle 24
4.3 Negotiations by solicitors and barristers 28
4.4 The role and influence of the lay client 31
4.5 'Without prejudice' negotiations 33
4.6 Effective legal negotiators 34
4.7 Preparing to be an effective legal negotiator 35

5 Preparation and planning—an overview 37
5.1 The importance of preparation and planning 37
5.2 What preparing and planning to negotiate entails 37
5.3 Summary 41
5.4 Case studies 41

6 Understanding the context 54
6.1 Putting the negotiation into context 54
6.2 Check you have complete instructions 58
6.3 Application to Case Study A 58
6.4 Application to Case Study B 59

7 Analysis—objectives 60
7.1 Objectives of the negotiation—strategies compared 60
7.2 Useful collaborative techniques 60
7.3 Using these techniques in your preparation 63
7.4 What your client wants from a settlement 65
7.5 What the opponent may want from a settlement 68
7.6 Shared and opposing objectives 69
7.7 Application to Case Study A 69
7.8 Application to Case Study B 70

8 Persuasion—the role of argument 71
8.1 The role of persuasion in negotiation 71
8.2 Persuasive techniques of the three strategies 71
8.3 The use of argument to persuade 75
8.4 Using merit-based argument in legal negotiations 79
8.5 Summary of persuasion and argument 82

9 Analysis—formulating arguments 83
9.1 Introduction 83
9.2 Analysis to formulate argument 84
9.3 Formulating persuasive arguments 91
9.4 Evaluating the arguments 93
9.5 Be ready to respond to your opponent's arguments 93
9.6 Summary 93
9.7 Application to Case Study A 94
9.8 Application to Case Study B 99

10 Information exchange 100
10.1 The role in negotiation 100
10.2 Factors which may distort information 100

10.3 Information exchange in the three strategies 102
10.4 Tactics on information exchange 104
10.5 Preparing to exchange information 106
10.6 Summary 109
10.7 Application to Case Study A 109
10.8 Application to Case Study B 110

11 Preparation—concessions 111

11.1 Introduction 111
11.2 Psychological influences of concessions 111
11.3 Use of concessions in the three strategies 112
11.4 Concessions distinguished from clarification; statements of law; admissions of fact 117
11.5 Concession planning strategy 118
11.6 The whole list/thinking laterally 119
11.7 Evaluating your case/what is achievable 120
11.8 Using your evaluation to plan concessions—justifying your proposals 121
11.9 Reviewing and using your client's priorities 122
11.10 Making a note 122
11.11 Summary 123
11.12 Application to Case Study A 123
11.13 Application to Case Study B 125

12 Planning your strategy 126

12.1 Introduction 126
12.2 Behavioural aspects of negotiation—dealing with differences 126
12.3 Negotiation strategies 127
12.4 Summary of strategies 133

13 Planning the structure 134

13.1 Can a negotiation be structured? 134
13.2 Planning how to start 135
13.3 Planning the structure 138
13.4 Summary 141
13.5 Application to Case Study A 141
13.6 Application to Case Study B 142

14 Considering possible tactics 143

14.1 Introduction 143
14.2 Specific tactics 143
14.3 Dubious tactics 149
14.4 General attitude/preparation for tactics 151

15 Communicating effectively 152

15.1 Introduction 152
15.2 Behavioural and psychological influences 152
15.3 Speaking, questioning and listening effectively 154
15.4 Presenting argument and information visually 157
15.5 Effective presentation and response 157
15.6 Summary 161

16 Conducting an effective negotiation 162

16.1 Introduction 162
16.2 Acting professionally 162
16.3 Recognising the impact of stress 164
16.4 The context of the negotiation 164
16.5 Dealing with the different phases of the negotiation 165
16.6 Summary 176

17 Dealing with difficulties 177

17.1 An overview 177
17.2 Techniques for getting past no 177
17.3 How to deal with competitive negotiators 180
17.4 Dealing with the weak/ill-prepared opponent 181
17.5 Dealing with failure to move/deadlock 182
17.6 Emotions interfering 184
17.7 Summary 186

18 Recording and enforcing a negotiated agreement 187

18.1 Introduction 187
18.2 Methods of recording 188
18.3 Advising the client and seeking approval 198
18.4 Informing/seeking permission of the court 199

19 Assessing negotiation skills 200

19.1 Learning lawyers' negotiation skills 200
19.2 The negotiation course 201
19.3 The negotiation criteria 202
19.4 Checklist for preparation 209
19.5 Your written plan 211
19.6 Reviewing your conduct of a negotiation 212

20 Adapting skills for Alternative Dispute Resolution 213

20.1 Alternatives in civil dispute resolution 213
20.2 Mediation 214
20.3 How the different processes influence the skills used 217

APPENDIX: Case studies 220
Case Study A 220
Case Study A: Plans and Notes of the Law 224
Case Study B 232
Case Study B: Preparation Notes 237
Case Study B: Plans and Notes of the Law 246

Suggested reading 250
Index 251

1

Introduction to negotiation

1.1 The importance of negotiation skills

1.1.1 Is courtroom advocacy the prime skill?

The word 'barrister' produces for most people the picture of an advocate in court on his or her feet either addressing the court or questioning a witness. It is generally recognised that this work is highly skilled and that the skill lies in being able to put the case persuasively. We have all seen it either in the courtroom or on the screen: just the right question asked of the witness, just the right phrase used to convince the jury.

However, a barrister's role extends well beyond this scene of courtroom drama. One could say it only represents the tip of the iceberg. Most cases never get to trial. A very high percentage of civil cases settle (estimates differ but it is probably around 80 to 90 per cent) and these settlements are achieved by negotiation. Many cases settle at the court door. For most people trial is the last resort. Thus, any barrister who has been briefed for trial will frequently find himself or herself negotiating the case to try to reach a settlement outside the courtroom. Lawyers, barristers and solicitors spend a substantial part of their time negotiating.

Most civil cases settle. Negotiation skills are therefore used more in the determination of civil cases than courtroom advocacy.

1.1.2 How does negotiation differ from courtroom advocacy?

Trials occur because two parties cannot agree. There is a dispute and they cannot agree how to resolve it aside from taking the case to a third party (ie, to court) to determine the dispute for them. There are two basic aspects of good courtroom advocacy. First, there is the ability to address the court using argument to persuade the court to see the case your way. Secondly, there is the ability to ask the right questions of witnesses to elicit information which strengthens your case or weakens your opponent's in the eyes of the court. While there are differing levels of sophistication in the use of these two abilities, basically these are the two tasks of an advocate in court. In both circumstances the advocates on both sides of the case are seeking to persuade a third party, the court, to see the facts and law from their point of view—ie, to find in their favour.

Although not all negotiations are about matters which are actually disputed (for example, two people may negotiate the terms on which they will operate a partnership), negotiation is a process by which people try to reach agreement or settlement where there are differences either real or perceived. Negotiation could be said to include any situation where a decision is sought which takes into account more than one person's point of view. Unlike courtroom advocacy, where the advocates are trying to persuade a third party who will make a final determination of any differences, in negotiation the negotiators are trying to persuade each other about how they can, between them, resolve differences. Like advocacy, negotiation is about the use of information and persuasion. Negotiations involve questioning and discussion. In questioning, each negotiator will be seeking information to assess what the differences are and how best they can be resolved in a way that he or she wants. In discussing the case, each negotiator will be attempting to persuade the other negotiator to resolve the differences in the manner that he or she wants.

Persuasion can be defined as causing a person to have a belief of fact or that a thing is so or as inducing a person to do something. The word 'persuade' is used in this broad sense and, as you will see when considering strategies and tactics in negotiation, there are a variety of methods of 'persuading' used in negotiations. The ability to persuade is an essential skill of a good advocate and a good negotiator. The prime difference is that advocates are seeking to persuade a third party and negotiators are seeking to persuade each other.

1.2 Learning negotiation skills

1.2.1 Can negotiation skills be learned?

'Can we discuss this case and see if we can settle it?' may be the first thing which is said to you on your first day at court. The frequency with which court cases settle means that when you are briefed for a hearing you will take on two roles: negotiator and courtroom advocate. There will almost invariably be discussion between counsel of any case prior to a hearing, even if this discussion is not to settle the whole case. You have arrived fully prepared to present the case in court but are you prepared for this discussion which may obviate the need for trial (the very thing you have prepared for)?

Can you learn to negotiate outside the courtroom in the same way you can learn to present a case in court effectively?

(a) There are set procedures and rules for the conduct of court hearings which you can find out by reading books on advocacy or asking colleagues so that you go into court at least understanding the process and your role in it. What procedures apply to negotiations and where can you find out about them? How do you decide the order in which matters should be discussed? How do you learn to structure and take control of the proceedings and what is covered?

(b) In a trial the court determines the outcome on its assessment of the merits of the parties' cases. In a negotiation you have to decide whether the settlement suggested is a good one for your client. How do you judge it? What standards do you use? You are not an impartial judge weighing up both sides. Your duty is owed to the client. On the other hand, in preparing for trial, you should have assessed the merits of the case. How do you use this assessment?

(c) In court there are rules of evidence and procedure which determine what information is made available to the court. Again you can look these up in a book or find out from colleagues so you know what is expected. What information should you exchange in a negotiation?

(d) Court etiquette sets certain standards of behaviour for the various parts played in a courtroom trial. Although personality still does play a part in this, to a degree, courtroom behaviour has been ritualised and you can learn the conventions by watching others in court or reading books on advocacy. Are there any rules of etiquette in negotiation? How much does behaviour and personality influence what happens in a negotiation and the ultimate settlement reached?

It is now well accepted that legal skills such as legal research, interviewing, drafting, etc can be learned. The concept that some skills used by lawyers are innate and cannot be learned clings more heavily to advocacy and negotiation than to others. This myth is perhaps being eroded more quickly in respect of courtroom advocacy than in negotiation.

Advocacy in the courtroom is done according to set rules with both the process and the result being observed and open to analysis and assessment by a variety of people including the decision makers (judge, magistrate or jury), the advocates, the parties, the witnesses and members of the public (where the case is heard in public). It is therefore possible for there to be discussion and possible consensus about what constitutes good advocacy. For obvious reasons (ie, the main players are lawyers) the characteristics of a good advocate have largely been defined from a legal point of view (although there is huge crossover with general presentation skills). Courtroom advocacy has been the province of lawyers until recently. However, the monopoly of lawyers in providing this service is breaking down and much time and resources are being spent on analysing both the elements of good advocacy and how these skills can be learned.

Negotiation, on the other hand, is done privately; only those participating know what happened in the course of the negotiation and the terms of the settlement. Any later discussion about the negotiation will usually be confined to the outcome and whether or not it was what was sought. Although people know what they need to achieve in a negotiation (ie, get a good outcome), they are much less clear about how to do it. How does negotiation work? What is the process and how can one do it to achieve a good outcome?

While courtroom advocacy is seen as the province of lawyers, everyone negotiates. Thus, our concepts of both the process of negotiation and the characteristics of a good negotiator and a good settlement come from a much broader range of transactions and participants than our concepts about advocacy.

We have all been negotiating since infancy when our main task was to try to control the feeding schedule. As adults we negotiate in a more sophisticated way using a broader range of tactics (hopefully!). We negotiate every day both in our working lives, eg, seeking a pay rise, and in our personal lives, eg, deciding what movie to see, what to have for dinner, etc, through a vast list of everyday situations. As a skill used by professionals, however, we probably associate negotiation more with trade union negotiations or commercial transactions and salespeople than with the legal profession. This has influenced the concepts of what good negotiation is all about. Two classic pictures of successful negotiators are: first, the brash, hard-nosed born negotiator who basically gets what he or she wants by bullying and, secondly, the golden-tongued, charming negotiator who gets what he or she wants by clever manipulation. People who see negotiation in these terms tend to think that negotiation is a skill which comes naturally to some and cannot be learned by others. They think that being a good negotiator depends on your personality. While personality does play a part, good negotiation skills can be learned.

1.2.2 How can negotiation skills be learned?

Given the number of interactions you have each day, you frequently 'negotiate' without being conscious of doing so. In many interactions which are in fact negotiations, you do not analyse what you are doing and why. You may be conscious that you are being more successful in getting what you want sometimes than others and you will already have some individuality in how you negotiate and the tactics you use. However, you need to learn to build on the skills you have and adapt them to negotiating in a legal context. To do this you need to understand the process and your part in it, and you need to know what is and what is not effective.

Lawyers have come later than some professions to skills training. Until very recently they 'learned' their skills 'sitting with Nelly', ie, watching others on the assumption that they would be able to distinguish the good from the bad habits, the effective from the ineffective techniques, and then somehow adopt the good and effective and reject the bad and ineffective. Much of the learning for barristers was focused on courtroom advocacy, and the experience of observing negotiations in process was very limited both in time and in the range of people observed, as it would be restricted to one's pupil master or pupil mistress (or others in chambers to whom one might from time to time be assigned). What one observed about negotiation was therefore completely arbitrary and done without any context of what one should be looking for, what, if any, research or theories existed about the process, effective and ineffective strategies, tactics, behaviour, etc or how to judge a settlement or a negotiator's performance.

Salespeople are taught how to sell and part of the training is learning how to negotiate within the commercial context. They have training programmes and there are scores of books written on successful negotiation techniques for salespeople.

There is a large body of literature on negotiation in a variety of contexts beyond those of the world of commercial selling. These include the more general business environment and the world of international relations. Some of this work draws on theories which have been debated for much longer: for example, dispute theory (how disputes arise, are dealt with and settled) and game theory (what people do in highly structured games which require them to decide a strategy against an opponent). There is a smaller but growing body of literature on negotiation in the legal context which draws on some of the other disciplines and covers a wide variety of issues including: attempts to categorise the different types of negotiations; discussion of different strategies and tactics and the factors which influence the effectiveness and choice of strategy; analysis of the process of negotiation; factors which influence whether people settle a case or take it to trial; and where negotiation fits in the judicial system, particularly given the development of alternatives to litigation. There is some empirical research on negotiation but it is limited both in the number of research projects done and in the manner in which they were done.

Negotiation is now part of legal professional skills training in many jurisdictions. There appears to be a similar basis to the training across jurisdictions which has been heavily influenced by some of the literature and theories which focus on analysis of negotiation, strategy and tactics.

Learning negotiation is about learning to understand the process and theories and how to apply these to your situation, *not* about learning a formula or rules which will guarantee a perfect negotiation. To learn to negotiate effectively you need to understand the process, the strategies and tactics used, and have some criteria against which to judge in what ways a performance is and is not effective and to determine whether and why an outcome is a good or a bad settlement. With this understanding you are able to assess and critique your own and others' performance in negotiations.

1.2.3 The purpose of the manual

Negotiation is a complex and challenging skill and a fundamental part of the work of all lawyers. To succeed as a lawyer, you must be able to negotiate effectively. To be effective, you must understand the psychology which underpins the various strategies and tactics used when negotiating. You must also be able to use this understanding effectively.

This manual is a comprehensive guide to negotiating effectively based on an understanding of the factors that influence legal negotiations and research on what is and is not effective. It explains the underlying psychological influences and how they are used in the different strategies and the different aspects of the negotiation. Within this context, it then gives practical guidance on how to prepare to deal with every aspect of a negotiation: how to persuade your opponent to compromise, how to use and respond to argument persuasively, how to make and respond to concessions effectively, how to use, recognise and deal with different strategies and tactics, and how to structure and conduct a negotiation to achieve the best for your client.

Chapters 2 to **5** give you the necessary background about the skill of negotiation. **Chapters 2** and **3** set out some of the essentials of negotiation and the basics of the different strategies. **Chapter 4** explains the particular influences on legal negotiations. **Chapter 5** gives an overview of what preparation entails.

Chapters 6 to **15** give practical guidance on how to prepare effectively, from identifying the context of the negotiation, through planning how to be persuasive and deal with concessions, to tactics and guidance on how to use your presentation skills effectively in the negotiation.

Chapters 16, 17 and **18** deal with how to conduct the negotiation generally, how to identify where particularly difficult situations arise in the negotiation, and how to record and enforce a negotiated agreement.

Chapter 19 explains how to assess negotiation skills. It sets out criteria used to assess performance. It also gives you checklists to assist you to review your preparation, plans and conduct of the negotiation.

Chapter 20 explains where negotiation fits into the various methods of dispute resolution, looking at the full range of methods used.

2

The essentials of negotiation

2.1 What does negotiation mean?

The term 'negotiation' can cover a wide range of activities. It is difficult to give a single definition. *The Concise Oxford Dictionary* (1982) defines negotiate as 'confer (with another) with a view to compromise or agreement'.

2.1.1 Compromise/concessions

Negotiation is about communication and compromise. However, just conferring with a view to compromise will not necessarily get you to agreement. Negotiation is also about movement: making and seeking concessions.

Many people consider negotiation to be the same as simple bargaining. The classic example is haggling in a market over the price of an item. The only issue is how much will be paid and both the buyer and the seller have a figure in mind which differs. The 'bargaining' process is about how far each side will move toward the other to reach an agreed price. While such bargaining is a form of negotiation, the term negotiation includes much more complex scenarios (eg, international negotiations or a divorce settlement), and involves more sophisticated considerations.

2.1.2 Shared, compatible and conflicting interests

Two definitions by writers on legal negotiation take on board that it is more complex than just simple bargaining:

(a) Donald G Gifford in his book *Legal Negotiation Theory and Applications* defines negotiation in the introduction as 'a process in which two or more participants attempt to reach a joint decision on matters of common concern in situations where they are in actual or potential disagreement or conflict'.

(b) Roger Fisher and William Ury (Harvard Negotiation Project) define negotiation in the preface to their book *Getting to Yes: Negotiating Agreement Without Giving In* as follows: 'Negotiation is a basic means of getting what you want from others. It is back-and-forth communication designed to reach an agreement when you and the other side have some interests that are shared and others that are opposed.'

These definitions recognise that negotiations can include a broad range of issues, including shared interests or common concerns, together with those on which there maybe disagreement, opposition or conflict. The first of these definitions also recognises that the disagreement may be actual or potential.

2.1.3 Exchange of information

Although the principal purpose of a negotiation is for both parties to accept something different from what they *ideally* want in order to reach agreement on what each will get, it is also about exchanging information on a variety of matters including what the parties want, the facts they allege, the evidence they have, etc.

2.1.4 Persuading by argument

Negotiation is not just haggling or arguing in the sense of exchanging rhetoric. However, argument is a fundamental part of negotiating. Negotiation is about persuading the other side to your view by the use of reasoned argument based on rational analysis. Most books and articles on negotiation fail to address this aspect of negotiation. Those who see negotiation as a battle or a straight competition focus on manipulative tactics which involve coercion rather than rational, persuasive argument. Those who see negotiation as a more collaborative process with both parties working together to reach settlement tend to duck the issue with a slight tendency to treat the use of argument as 'impolite'. Good argument is about advancing reasons to persuade and persuasion is an important part of negotiation.

2.1.5 Dynamic, interactive process

Any negotiation is a dynamic, interactive process. The negotiators' behaviour, expectations and analysis of what is possible are all influenced by the process and by each other's behaviour, expectations and statements of what is possible. During the negotiation, both parties' perceptions and judgements, strategy and tactics will change. Negotiation can be compared to a game of chess where the move of one party influences how the other party will move, and where one is looking several moves ahead all the time.

2.1.6 Getting what you want

Finally and most importantly, negotiation is about getting what you want. For a lawyer this means achieving the client's objectives as far as possible. While it may involve a variety of issues, shared or conflicting, exchange of information, the use of argument, etc, the focus of the negotiation, the reason for the discussion, argument, etc is to achieve the parties' goals as far as possible.

2.1.7 Why is the definition important?

How you define negotiation may influence how you negotiate. If you see it as simple bargaining then you will tend to use simple bargaining strategies. If you see it as a more complex process with a greater range of possibilities, you will extend your strategies to include more sophisticated analysis and behaviour and use a much wider range of methods to achieve compromise.

Negotiation could be described as a process of trying to find a positive, realistic and wide-ranging solution to a problem which offers as much as possible to both sides. At its best it is a creative process in which both sides look as objectively as possible at a whole problem and try to find a joint solution.

2.2 Types of negotiation

The study of negotiation involves consideration of how people seek to and do reach agreement in a huge range of contexts on a wide variety of issues, from simple sales transactions, through more complex business deals and legal transactions (eg, agreeing a lease or settling a claim), to resolving international disputes. Analysing negotiations to see how they differ and whether and how these differences influence the negotiation and the negotiators assists people to understand the process of negotiation. Understanding how the process works is one of the steps in learning how to do it effectively.

Although there is an infinite variety of contexts and issues negotiated, they can be classified in different ways. There is some overlap in the classifications and you may find that some books classify them differently. Set out below are some different contrasting types of negotiation which are relevant to the work of a barrister.

2.2.1 Dispute resolution versus transactional

The principal purpose of a negotiation can be to resolve a dispute (ie, to deal with events which have already happened) or to regulate future transactions (ie, to be forward-looking, setting out the rules for an envisaged future relationship between the parties).

(a) In a dispute settlement, such as a personal injury claim, the purpose of the negotiation is to reach agreement on how the parties should resolve differences resulting from past behaviour, eg, an accident. The parties are not negotiating out of choice. They must deal with each other to resolve the dispute which has arisen, either through the courts or some other process of dispute resolution, eg, negotiation. They probably have little if any interest in future dealings with each other. Their behaviour in the negotiation may reflect this in that they will feel no real need to be conciliatory.

(b) In a transactional negotiation (also called deal-making or rule-making), such as negotiating a lease or partnership agreement, the principal objective is to agree on rules for regulating the future dealings between the parties within that context. Unless one party has a monopoly, the parties are not compelled to negotiate. They have chosen to do business together. They are negotiating together by choice because they wish to set up an agreement by which they can operate in the future. Their behaviour in the negotiation will reflect a consciousness that they will have to build a working relationship.

Not all negotiations fall neatly into one or other of these two categories. Thus, for example, you may be asked to negotiate a settlement for breach of contract where both parties wish to continue their contractual relationship or you may be asked to act for a party in dispute with his or her neighbour. While neither party would choose to maintain a continuing relationship, necessity dictates this. Principally dispute resolving negotiations, they also include a transactional element.

2.2.2 Single issue versus multiple issue

A negotiation can be about a single issue, for example the price of an item in a market, or about a number of issues, for example the terms a of divorce settlement. Clearly, a negotiation involving a number of issues is a more sophisticated interaction and has much greater scope for imaginative problem-solving or trade-offs than one in which only a single issue is at stake. However, few negotiations are genuinely about a single issue. Even a dispute which may appear to be a single issue, eg, a claim for a debt, contains several issues such as: whether it is due at all, how much is to be paid, when payment will be made, whether instalment payments are possible, whether interest was or should be payable, etc.

2.2.3 Distributive/zero-sum versus integrative

This classification overlaps with the one at **2.2.2**.

(a) In a distributive or 'zero-sum' negotiation, one party always gains at the expense of the other party. It is a 'win/lose' situation on the assumption that both parties want equally and exclusively the subject matter being negotiated, usually money. In a genuinely distributive or 'zero-sum' negotiation, the parties are likely to be more competitive as they really are 'competing' to achieve gains.

(b) In an integrative negotiation, one party's gain is not necessarily at the expense of the other party. It is potentially a 'win/win' situation based on the assumption that the parties have some underlying interests which are not in conflict, either because they are shared or because they put differing values on different aspects of the subject matter. An integrative negotiation gives more scope for trade-offs which benefit both parties. There is therefore much more incentive for the parties to be more cooperative and conciliatory in an attempt to find the compatible interests.

The classification is not rigid. Although a case may at first sight appear to be a single issue, distributive negotiation, careful analysis of the facts, law and objectives will usually reveal a variety of issues and potential underlying interests where parties are not in direct conflict. A negotiation which appears initially to be distributive or 'zero-sum' may have integrative elements. Thus, for example, if the claimant in an action puts more value on the actual sum received, and the defendant on the period over which payments can be made, the settlement can reflect these differing priorities.

2.2.4 Impersonal versus personal matters

The subject matter of a negotiation can range from a contract which is 'strictly business' (eg, between two large corporations), to one which affects the whole of a person's life (eg, a divorce settlement with children involved or a personal injury claim where the person has been permanently disabled). The issues being negotiated can therefore be quite impersonal, for example, resolving the matter of delivery dates or level of interest on a commercial contract. Alternatively, they can be very personal with high emotional content, for example, who has custody of the children. The arguments used to support one's position in the negotiation will reflect the issues being negotiated. Clearly, where the issues are more personal, there is much more possibility of the negotiation becoming personalised and emotion-charged and descending into an argument about rights and wrongs rather than a negotiation to resolve the matter.

The issues in any negotiation can range through the spectrum: eg, in a divorce the parties may have no personal attachment to certain assets and may be able to divide them in a very impersonal manner but feel very strongly over other assets which have high sentimental value. A negotiation which appears to be quite impersonal on the face of it may in fact be highly personal: eg, a person may feel that his or her job depends on the outcome of a negotiation of a very commercial matter.

2.2.5 Repeat players versus one-off players

Any single negotiation is ostensibly only about those issues on which settlement is being sought in that negotiation and we generally therefore assume that the negotiators are only concerned with the factors affecting those issues and this negotiation. However, in some cases the parties are repeat players and see any individual negotiation within the wider context. Thus, for example, insurance companies negotiate huge numbers of claims. The way in which they deal with any one claim (eg, one for personal injury), will take on board their experience of dealing with these claims, the fact that they can spread the cost of any individual claim over a huge number of claims and the effect of settlement of this claim on other claims they may have. They will be less anxious about losses in any one claim than about their losses overall. Their overall strategy will be to maximise their profits over the whole of their business. They may adopt a highly competitive stance or 'play hardball' in which they just refuse to budge in the knowledge that they have a leeway on each individual negotiation that the claimant (who is almost invariably a one-off player) does not. Alternatively they may adopt an alternative strategy, recognising that the overall costs of litigation is one factor they can control by settling claims early in the process. Although most claimants are one-off players, lawyers who specialise in the field are, like insurance companies, repeat players. Some of these lawyers will use their knowledge of insurance companies to 'squeeze out something extra' for their client in the knowledge that time is money for insurance companies and that they might settle to avoid the risk of costs. Both of these are examples of a repeat player using the fact that the psychological and financial costs of litigation often push the opponent into settling at a lower value.

2.2.6 Representative versus for oneself

A person can negotiate on their own behalf or on behalf of another person (eg, a client), or on behalf of a group of people (eg, a trade union). Negotiating on behalf of others introduces a whole new set of dynamics into the negotiation.

(a) The person or persons on whose behalf the negotiation is undertaken will know what they want out of the negotiation and have expectations about the outcome and what can be achieved.

(b) They will also have their own ideas about how the negotiation should be conducted.

(c) The relationship between the party represented and the negotiator may affect the negotiation. The involvement of the party represented in the negotiation may be substantial or minimal depending on the degree of trust placed in the negotiator, the relative positions of power and the personalities involved.

(d) The negotiator will be seeking approval from the party represented both in the outcome and the process. Some studies show that, when people negotiate as representatives for someone else, they tend to be more competitive, particularly when they negotiate where the represented party can see them.

2.2.7 Multiple party versus two party

Much of the literature and discussion about negotiation considers it in the context of interaction between two parties. However, a negotiation may involve a number of parties: for example, a company reorganisation or insolvency will involve a variety of types of creditors and shareholders all with slightly different interests. In litigation, there may be several defendants who may in turn add third parties.

Negotiations involving a number of different parties are more complex. They are likely to involve more issues and more possibilities for settlement including settling with some but not all of the other parties. They also alter the dynamics by allowing the development of coalitions by which some of the parties band together to attain their own goals or block those of others. This manual does not attempt to cover the complications produced by additional parties. However, there is a good section in Donald G Gifford, *Legal Negotiation Theory and Practice* (St Paul MN: West Publishing, 1989) at Chapter 10, pp 174–83.

2.2.8 Other types of negotiation

Negotiations can be categorised in a number of other ways to distinguish factors which may affect the negotiation process. Thus, for example, there has been quite a lot written on the dynamics of international negotiations, on cross-cultural negotiations and on negotiations within the field of labour relations. These are quite specialist areas and not covered here. However, should your practice develop to include any of these areas, you should be aware of the impact this may have on the negotiations you do and be conscious that there are books and articles which can give you an insight into the additional factors involved.

2.2.9 Which categories concern barristers?

The work of a litigation advocate principally involves dispute resolution negotiations in which the number of issues and the scope for integrative solutions vary enormously. Barristers conduct negotiations as representatives across the spectrum, from the very impersonal to the highly personal, and may be acting for a repeat player (eg, an insurance company) or a one-off player (eg, the injured party). The negotiation may be two-party (just claimant and defendant) or multi-party (where there are a number of defendants and/or third parties are joined in proceedings).

2.3 Issues to be negotiated

Negotiation is about dealing with the substantive issues on which agreement is sought. However, it is also about procedural matters. Both parties to a negotiation will be seeking agreement not only on the issues they are concerned with but also how the negotiation is actually conducted. There are a variety of procedural or non-substantive issues which form part of the negotiation.

2.3.1 How, where, when and who?

Negotiations can take place in a variety of ways: by letter or fax, telephone, or face-to-face discussion. The way in which the negotiation is conducted clearly has influences on the negotiation.

Negotiating by letter or fax means that the information, offers and responses are written down and can be reviewed in detail. Although it removes the need for instantaneous responses, it means that it is more important to be careful in the wording of what is proposed. Some of the behavioural aspects of negotiation, such as tone of voice, ability to think quickly, use of silence, which are part of oral negotiations (by phone or face-to-face discussions), are absent. While this may mean it is less stressful for the participants, it also means they get less information about each other.

Face-to-face negotiations give the negotiators much more information about each other in that they can assess the personality and feelings of the other side better and use this knowledge in the negotiation, either to build rapport or to use against their opponent.

The timing, location and participants in a face-to-face negotiation may be factors which influence the process. Many international negotiations have pre-negotiations to determine where the negotiations will be held to avoid the power imbalance which might result from one party controlling the location. Everyone recognises the psychological impact of playing a home game as opposed to an away game, and similar considerations apply to negotiations. In addition, the person on whose premises the negotiation takes place can control the physical layout of the location and put the opponent in a disadvantageous position, eg, by sitting oneself at the head of the table (in the position of power).

Finally, the number and status of those attending the negotiation can affect the process and will often be discussed to ensure equality of power.

2.3.2 The agenda

Deciding what will be discussed, the order in which matters will be considered and who starts the negotiation are all matters which themselves are subject to negotiation as they can influence both the conduct and the outcome of the negotiation.

2.3.3 Exchange of information

Although the aim of the negotiation is to reach agreement on the issues being negotiated, much of the process of negotiation involves exchanging information. Some people use negotiations purely as a method of getting information: a fishing expedition to find out the strengths and weaknesses of their opponent's position. They then use that information in another context, eg, to plan their case for the trial. The amount of information the negotiators seek and are prepared to disclose will have a real impact on the negotiation process, and much is written about this element of negotiation in the literature about different strategies and in many 'How To Do It' guides for commercial negotiations.

2.3.4 Interpretation of facts/rules/norms/law

In a negotiation, each party puts his or her case, what is being sought and the arguments for that, from his or her own perspective. But this is just one person's perception of what happened, the facts and any relevant rule, norm or law being used to support his or her argument. No two people see an event in the same way. Perception and reality are different. Disagreement or conflict can stem from different interpretations of events or circumstances. Discussion about these different interpretations or perceptions to see whether any agreement can be reached will form part of the negotiation.

2.3.5 Settlement standard

The purpose of the negotiation is to reach agreement. But the need for negotiation has arisen at least partially because the parties have not been able to agree. Against what criteria do the negotiators measure the proposals and decide to settle? Do they each have their own criteria or do they discuss the criteria to be used and try to reach agreement on it? What kind of criteria are appropriate to consider? There are a great variety of potential criteria, eg, social norms, legal standards, the concept of 'fairness'. In considering the criteria one needs to be clear about what one means. Thus, for example, if the concept of 'fairness' is invoked, what does this mean: fair to whom? Is one speaking of equity (to each according to the contribution made) or equality (split it down the middle)?

2.3.6 Strategies/tactics/behaviour

There is a large and growing body of literature on the different strategies and tactics used in negotiation, some directed specifically at legal negotiations. Any negotiation invariably involves the use of strategy and tactics. Those involved in the negotiation will recognise this and deal with it without expressly commenting on it. Discussion expressly about strategy and tactics in a negotiation is rare. However, the strategy, tactics and behaviour of the negotiators can be negotiated implicitly, by the response to the strategy or tactic, or expressly, by labelling the behaviour and insisting on discussing its use in the negotiation.

2.4 The negotiation process

Consideration of the process of negotiation involves looking at what happens and in what order, from the very beginning of the negotiation to the very end.

Although there are no set rules for the order in which a negotiation should be conducted, a number of people who have studied negotiation have found a recognisable pattern which most negotiations follow; a series of developmental stages through which most pass. As with most research on human behaviour, the writers do not use exactly the same terminology nor do they take a completely uniform approach, with some dividing it into more phases than others. However, there is a great degree of similarity in their descriptions.

It is important, however, to understand that the following fairly simplistic division into four basic phases is merely a description of a general pattern which has been identified and not a rigid structure which all negotiations must follow or necessarily will follow. Each negotiation is unique. Many involve a number of issues and discussion of the different issues may fall in different phases. The phases of any negotiation may overlap and may in fact be repeated. Understanding the process helps one to recognise what may be happening at any particular stage and why certain behaviour may be more prevalent at some stages than others.

2.4.1 Opening/orientation/positioning

In this phase the negotiators set the scene. They assess each other's style and approach and set out their positions, how they expect the negotiation to proceed, their view of the merits of the case and what they are seeking out of the negotiation.

Both negotiators will use this phase to assess the opponent's style and strategy. The behaviour of the two negotiators in this phase will 'set the tone' and have a strong impact on the overall orientation of the negotiation (eg, whether it is cooperative or competitive). The exchanges enable the negotiators to learn to interpret the words, language and non-verbal cues of their opponent before the dynamics of negotiation become more intense.

The negotiators are also likely to set out their 'opening positions', ie, what they want out of the negotiation. Exactly what that 'opening position' is will depend on the strategy which the negotiator is adopting.

In this phase the negotiators will generally be fairly guarded and more competitive than cooperative, unless one or other of the negotiators is specifically setting out to put the negotiation on a very collaborative path.

2.4.2 Exploration/discussion

In this phase the negotiators exchange information, explore the legal and factual issues, try to determine the strengths and weaknesses of the two sides and see how the differences in the positions initially stated can be resolved. There will also be some attempt to narrow the differences by making and/or encouraging concessions. As in the initial stage, unless consciously adopting a collaborative approach, the negotiators are likely to be wary of each other. They are likely to be relatively selective in the information they reveal and concessions they make, using this stage to gather and assimilate information from the other side to enable them to reassess the case.

2.4.3 Bargaining/convergence

In this phase the parties realise that movement is essential to reach agreement and serious efforts are made to resolve differences. This stage may be precipitated by an approaching deadline. The negotiators are likely to be more cooperative in this stage than in the previous two stages. A number of experiments have shown that concession-making increases as the deadline approaches.

2.4.4 Settlement or breakdown

This final phase is the one in which the negotiators either reach settlement or end the negotiation. If they do reach agreement, the details of it must be agreed, including the mechanics for ensuring it is fulfilled. Alternatively, the negotiation may break down for a variety of reasons and, in a legal case for example, the matter proceeds to trial.

2.4.5 Conclusion

Recognising the phases of a negotiation and that competitive behaviour is more likely at the start and cooperative behaviour more likely later in the negotiation can assist you both to understand your opponent's behaviour and to adapt your own. Cooperative behaviour at the start may later be met by competitive behaviour. However, it is worth reiterating that the above pattern is not one which is religiously followed in all negotiations. While many negotiations will move from a basically competitive phase to a more cooperative or collaborative one, this is not always so. Do not assume that all negotiators will become more cooperative over time.

Many negotiations take place over a period of time with different parts of the process involving different people. It is important to be conscious of what has happened previously. This will enable you to at least attempt to assess what stage the negotiation has reached at the point you become involved.

3

Style, strategy and tactics

3.1 Introduction

Any negotiation involves not only the substance of what is said (ie, the content of any discussion about the differences), but also how it is said (ie, the person's behaviour or demeanour). It is important to be able to distinguish between these two, and to be able to identify and understand the difference between the different strategies, styles and tactics used.

Strategy is the overall approach taken to achieve a good settlement. It involves decisions about how to open, what concessions to make and seek and when and how to make them, what information will be sought and given, the order in which matters will be discussed, any tactics to be used, etc. Style is the manner of delivery: a negotiator's attitude and demeanour. Tactics are specific actions used by negotiators to achieve particular ends. They can be either part of the strategy (ie, what is said) or part of the style (how it is said).

This chapter gives you a brief introduction to the different styles and strategies that have been identified as being used in negotiations and why and how they are used. It also explains what tactics are and how they differ from strategies.

3.2 Style

Style is the manner of delivery and attitude taken, the negotiator's behaviour or demeanour. A person's style includes a whole range of factors including the particular language used, tone and volume of voice and physical presence (eg, the way he or she sits or stands). Style can extend to particular types of statements, eg, making personal remarks about the opponent or being sarcastic or condescending are hallmarks of a competitive style.

While people's styles vary enormously, two types which can be relatively readily categorised and identified are the competitive and the cooperative styles. A competitive style is argumentative, using emphatic language, and attempts to wear the opponent down. It could include bullying or demeaning the opponent to undermine him or her. A cooperative style is friendly, courteous, tactful, and conciliatory and attempts to gain trust by using good manners and charm. These two describe styles at either end of the spectrum and many people will fall in the middle, eg, speak fairly forcefully without bullying or demeaning or be very friendly but also very assertive.

A person's style does not always match his or her strategy. A person with a very cooperative style, who is charm itself, may be employing a highly competitive strategy.

It is important therefore to separate the substance of what is being said about the negotiation from the way in which it is delivered: to separate style from strategy and deal with both.

3.3 Strategy overview

3.3.1 Introduction

A negotiation strategy is the way in which the negotiator plans to manage the interaction in the negotiation, including the exchange of information, the making and seeking of concessions and the overall structure of the negotiation to achieve his or her objectives. Strategic behaviour is complex and varies from person to person and case to case. However, specific patterns of strategic behaviour have been identified and labelled as comprising particular negotiation strategies. It is important that you understand the different patterns of behaviour which underlie these strategies at least in outline before starting your preparation. In this chapter we therefore consider the basic components of the three strategies most frequently identified. While there is general consensus about what the different strategies involve, there is not total agreement on terminology. The three classifications are:

(a) The 'competitive' strategy (which is the term almost universally used for this strategy).

(b) The 'cooperative' strategy (alternatively called 'compromising').

(c) What is sometimes termed the 'collaborative' strategy which is derived from two similar but differing strategies promulgated by different schools of thought, namely:

   (i) the 'principled' approach developed by Roger Fisher and William Ury of the Harvard Negotiation Project; and

   (ii) the 'problem-solving' approach which Carrie Menkel-Meadow of UCLA set out in her paper 'Toward Another View of Legal Negotiation: The Structure of Problem Solving' (1984) 31 *UCLA Law Review* 754–842.

Some writers only distinguish two strategies: the competitive (as we describe it) and the cooperative (in which they collapse the two which we have labelled 'cooperative' and 'collaborative' into one which generally leans more towards the 'collaborative').

3.3.2 The underlying theories

Basically, the underlying theories of the strategies are as follows:

(a) Competitive strategy: seeks to maximise one's own gains by taking a strong stance (eg, high opening demands, making few concessions, giving little information) on the basis that this will force the opponent to move towards one. The goal is victory.

(b) Cooperative strategy: assumes that there must be concessions on both sides and seeks, by demonstrably being 'reasonable' in the demands and concessions made and sharing information, to engender trust and reciprocal behaviour in the opponent. The goal is agreement.

(c) Collaborative strategy: assumes the parties can work together (ie, collaborate) to reach agreement by exploring the underlying interests of the parties, sharing information, being creative in the options considered and judging any settlement against some agreed test or criteria. The goal of the problem-solving and principled approaches differ:

(i) In problem-solving strategy, the goal is to achieve a settlement which is fair and reflects both parties' real needs or interests with the lowest transaction costs relative to desirability of the result.

(ii) In principled strategy, the goal is to achieve a settlement which is objectively fair by some external authoritative norm.

One could categorise the three strategies as 'hard bargaining' (competitive negotiator who is after victory and cares little about the relationship), 'soft bargaining' (cooperative negotiator who seeks agreement and does care about the relationship) and 'rationale bargaining' (principled or problem-solving negotiator whose approach is more complex, who seeks an agreement which is based on rational assessment).

3.3.2.1 Win/lose

The competitive and cooperative strategies are based on similar assumptions about what happens in a negotiation. The underlying assumption is that a negotiation is a win/lose situation. One party can win (ie, gain something) only at the expense of the other party (ie, his or her loss). Thus the two parties (eg, claimant and defendant and their lawyers) have analysed the case and determined:

- the most they can get (their opening position);
- the least they will accept (their bottom line);
- the size and frequency of the steps they are prepared to make to get from their opening position to settlement (their concessions).

There will be settlement if there is an 'area of agreement', ie, overlap between the two. Thus in the following situation:

Claimant's opening position: £4,000 bottom line: £2,000
Defendant's opening position: £1,000 bottom line: £3,000
The area of agreement is:

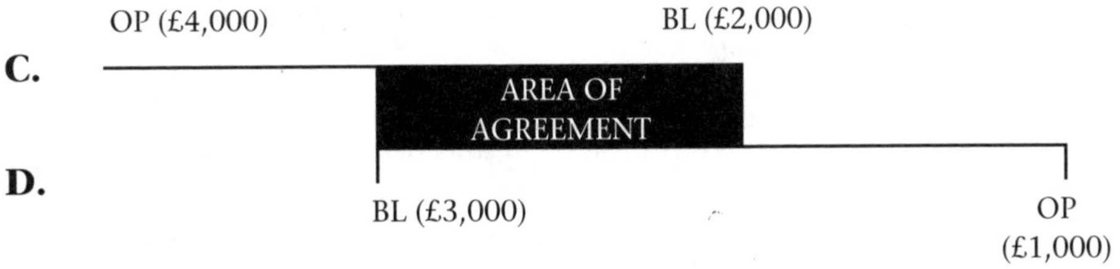

OP = opening position BL = bottom line

There is an 'area of agreement' or overlap here of £1,000 so they should reach settlement. Both competitive and cooperative negotiators will probably assume that they will not get what they state in their opening position. The big question is where along the line will the settlement be? Will it be closer to the claimant's or the defendant's bottom line? Both will try during the negotiation to ascertain what the other's bottom line is so they can aim for that. Both use the concession-making process to seek agreement. It is the approaches taken to seek agreement which differ between competitive and cooperative negotiators (eg, concessions and information).

3.3.2.2 Win/win

There is a different underlying ethos to both the principled and problem-solving strategies. The underlying assumption is that a negotiation can be a win/win situation. One party's gain is not necessarily achieved at the expense of the other party. Effective negotiators can reach settlement where both parties win. While the above two strategies tend to see negotiation as swapping concessions and exchanging information largely to determine the opponent's position, these 'collaborative' strategies view it as a more complex interaction in which interests are explored and solutions sought jointly. They tend to use different language and concepts from competitive or cooperative ones.

It is worth noting that any particular negotiator will not necessarily use one strategy throughout the whole negotiation. A negotiator may take a predominantly competitive or predominantly cooperative approach. Alternatively, he or she might be competitive on concessions but cooperative on information, or might start out being competitive and move to being cooperative. A negotiator may take a collaborative approach on one aspect (eg, future trading arrangements), and a competitive approach on another aspect (eg, how to deal with past losses). The following analysis is done purely to try to give you some understanding of the basic characteristics of the strategies.

3.4 Competitive strategy

Sometimes called positional bargaining or hard bargaining because of the extreme position and tough stance taken, this is perhaps the most identifiable strategy. It is the one promoted in most commercial 'How To Do It' guides for business or salespeople. It is also the one most people expect a lawyer to adopt. It is basically adversarial and the barrister works in an adversarial system.

3.4.1 Underlying assumptions and ethos

The competitive strategy is based on the assumption that all negotiations are distributive, zero-sum (ie, each side wants equally and exclusively what the other side wants). By definition, one side's gains are the other's losses. The competitive negotiator genuinely sees the other party as his or her 'competitor' or 'opponent' with a similar mindset (ie, out to compete, to win).

The competitive negotiator has high expectations and the overall aim is to maximise his or her own gain, to come out ahead, to do better than the opponent, to claim victory. It is a win/lose approach. The underlying theory of the strategy is that taking a firm stance with fairly extreme positions, making few and small concessions and withholding information will reduce the opponent's expectations or cause loss of confidence, thereby manipulating him or her into moving towards the competitive negotiator.

3.4.2 General tactics

Competitive negotiators will:

(a) open at the most extreme position maintainable, stay high and sometimes increase demands. They will demand concessions from the opponent but be slow to make them themselves. Any concessions made will be small, unimportant and possibly false;

(b) use information exchange as a tool to win, pressing for information from the opponent but revealing little, being selective in what is revealed and possibly giving inaccurate information (which raises ethical points—see later);

(c) take a strong stance, want to be seen as tough, determined, unyielding. They will maintain pressure throughout the negotiation. They will take every advantage, concentrating on achieving their own objectives exclusively. They will use a variety of techniques to confuse or divert the opponent from obtaining information. They distrust their opponent and think that all effective negotiators are competitive. Their manner may also be argumentative, using emphatic language and tone of voice and employing tactics to make the opponent feel uncomfortable and intimidated.

3.4.3 Measuring success

A competitive negotiator usually defines success by reference to how much he or she has won, possibly by comparison with how well the other side has done, ie, has he or she come out ahead? Thus success is defined fairly narrowly and may well disregard a variety of important aspects such as whether any shared interests have been identified, what the outcome might do to future relationships between the parties, etc.

3.5 Cooperative strategy

Cooperative strategy can also be called soft bargaining or 'cordial' bargaining (see Robert Condlin, 'Bargaining in the Dark: The Normative Incoherence of Lawyer Dispute Bargaining Role' (1992) 51 *Maryland Law Review* 1–104 at pp 16–22). Most discussions of this particular strategy are in the context of comparing the effectiveness of the different techniques used in competitive and cooperative strategies. Many articles, books and materials for negotiation courses tend to mix characteristics of pure cooperative strategy with those of the more 'collaborative' (principled and problem-solving), some not really distinguishing between the two (eg, Williams' research on effective negotiators (see **4.6.1**) compared only competitive and cooperative without distinguishing the additional 'collaborative' techniques as a separate strategy). While use of some of the techniques are effective, few people would recommend a purely cooperative strategy.

3.5.1 Underlying assumptions and ethos

The underlying assumption is that a negotiator can create an open, trusting atmosphere by making concessions, sharing information, etc, and that the other negotiator will respond to this by being open and trusting too, ie, reciprocating concessions and information exchange. A cooperative negotiator focuses on the principle that, to reach agreement, both sides must give. The main goal is agreement, not victory; cooperative negotiators are more concerned with reaching agreement than precisely what they get out of the agreement. They are concerned with both sides, either genuinely or because they have to be to get something from them. They compromise as a matter of principle or necessity.

Cooperative negotiators believe that their own compromising behaviour will produce similar behaviour in the other negotiator. One could say they are trying to create an atmosphere of 'mutual' compromise—to manipulate their opponent into coming towards them by introducing a moral element of 'fair play' based on joint compromise.

3.5.2 General tactics

Cooperative negotiators will:

(a) show they are trustworthy by opening at a reasonable level, making further unilateral concessions during the negotiation, frequently explaining the basis for the offers on the assumption that this will encourage reciprocal behaviour from the opponent;

(b) be open and honest in the exchange of information, giving information freely and making fair statements of fact, to create trust and produce similar behaviour in the opponent;

(c) take a conciliatory stance, want to trust the opponent, show concern that both parties are satisfied by the settlement, possibly caring more about reaching agreement than what the agreement gives their client. They present as 'reasonable' and courteous, rather than emphatic or forceful, using non-threatening language.

3.5.3 Measuring success

Cooperative negotiators usually measure success by whether or not the negotiation 'feels fair', which may take into account not only the ultimate agreement and what the client gets out of it but whether the process was fair: roughly how much did each side compromise, did the negotiators treat each other 'fairly', was there 'equal treatment' in exchange of information and concession making?

3.6 Collaborative/principled/problem-solving

3.6.1 Introduction

Writing and discussion about the above two strategies, competitive and cooperative, tend to be descriptive rather than prescriptive. People have tried to analyse what people do in negotiations, label the behaviour and categorise it as competitive or cooperative. Some 'How To Do It' guides are also 'prescriptive' in that they recommend the use of the competitive strategy. However, the bulk of the writing merely attempts to assist people to understand what have long been behaviour patterns in negotiations and to see what is and is not effective.

Two main differences require a different approach to this third strategy. First, it encompasses the thinking behind two similar strategies which have formed part of the discussion on strategies, the 'principled' approach, as set out in the book *Getting to Yes: Negotiating Agreement Without Giving In* by Roger Fisher and William Ury, and the 'problem-solving' approach proposed by Carrie Menkel-Meadow of UCLA in her paper about it in 1984 ('Toward Another View of Legal Negotiation: The Structure of Problem Solving' (1984) 31 *UCLA Law Review* 754–842).

Secondly, writing on these approaches tends to be more prescriptive than descriptive. The writing on these two approaches goes beyond describing what people do. Taking on board what negotiation is all about, different behaviours in negotiation, etc, they formulate strategies (ie, prescribe behaviour) which they consider result in better settlements and more effective negotiations. The authors, particularly Fisher and Ury and Menkel-Meadow, argue strongly that their approaches should be used.

3.6.2 Underlying assumptions and ethos

The underlying ethos or approach of both these strategies is that the most effective way to negotiate is to work together (collaborate) to reach settlement. They also share assumptions. They are similar to the cooperative strategy in that they aim to create an open, cooperative atmosphere. However, both take a more reasoned, intellectual approach to negotiation than the fairly basic 'sharing' approach of cooperative negotiation or the 'fighting' approach of competitive negotiation. They share the assumption that taking an open and rational approach is more likely to achieve a settlement which reflects the parties' true needs and interests.

Although the underlying assumptions and ethos are much the same for both these strategies, the specific tactics and ways of measuring success are not the same. The 'principled' approach is much more widely known and discussed and we therefore set out the basic characteristics of this one before the problem-solving approach.

3.6.3 General tactics and measuring success in principled negotiations

This strategy is based on the research and experience of Roger Fisher and William Ury, Directors of the Harvard Negotiation Project at Harvard Law School which runs courses and publishes a substantial amount of material on negotiation, including the *Negotiation Journal*. The work done on negotiation covers a huge range of areas including trade unions, international peace treaties, large commercial transactions and legal negotiations. The strategy is set out in their book *Getting to Yes: Negotiating Agreement Without Giving In* (1991), a small paperback. Below is a brief summary of the main characteristics of the strategy based on the main elements:

(a) separate the people from the problem: ie, concentrate on the substantive issues (what the clients want) rather than the interpersonal relationship (how they feel about each other);

(b) focus on interests not positions: ie, negotiate to achieve a settlement which satisfies the parties' real future interests and needs rather than who was right or wrong;

(c) invent options for mutual gain: ie, analyse items being negotiated to see how they can be broken into parts and converted from 'zero-sum' to 'multiple/integrative' (the classic example given of the two sisters arguing over an orange—they split it in two and only then realise that one wanted the peel and the other the fruit);

(d) insist on objective criteria: ie, replace the subjective will or opinion of the parties with an independent standard against which to judge the settlement;

(e) develop a Best Alternative to a Negotiated Agreement (BATNA): rather than just looking at what your client ought to get out of the negotiation (with the inherent rigid and restrictive strategy of moving along a continuum of 'opening position' to a 'bottom line'), consider what he or she will do if no agreement is reached (which gives you more flexible alternatives against which to measure proposals made in the negotiation).

3.6.4 General tactics and measuring success in problem-solving negotiations

A problem-solving strategy shares much with the principled approach. It emphasises the importance of: identifying the underlying needs and objectives of both the parties; creating solutions which meet the parties' needs; examining closely the shared, compatible and potentially conflicting goals of the clients; and expanding the resources available by looking carefully at all the aspects of distribution: what can be distributed, when, by whom, how, how much, etc.

> In summary, by using substantive strategies such as exploring shared interests, by exploiting value differences in needs, by looking to third parties, by sharing, by aggregating or disaggregating, by neutralizing, by seeking substitute goods, by exploring long- and short-term values, and by using other specific devices, a greater number of solutions may be found [Menkel-Meadow, Carrie, 'Toward Another View of Legal Negotiation: The Structure of Problem Solving' (1984) 31 *UCLA Law Review* 754–842 at p 813].

The strategy also encourages more reasoned interchange in the negotiation, brainstorming for options, sharing information to genuinely assist in solving the problem, and giving reasons when discussing whether or not proposals are acceptable, etc. Thus, like principled negotiation, it encourages an intellectual approach to negotiation. Many of the techniques recommended for principled negotiators are equally relevant to a problem-solving strategy.

The process for the two is also similar in that it encourages full exploration of the two parties' interests before attempting to divide them.

The major difference between the two is that, while a principled strategy involves applying some objective criteria external to the parties, problem-solving seeks fair or just solutions:

> For those who seek the most effective or efficient solutions from a utilitarian perspective, it is enough to settle at a point where no party can gain without hurting the other party [Menkel-Meadow (above) at p 813].

Thus, the test relates more to the actual needs of the clients than some external standard.

3.7 Tactics—an overview

'Tactics' are the different behaviours and specific actions used in the negotiation to achieve the negotiator's desired ends. There is overlap with strategy in that certain tactics are more likely to be used with certain strategies and they include how you use your concessions, the exchange of information, etc. However, when one speaks of tactics, one is referring not to the overall plan and ethos but to particular actions used at specific points in the negotiation to deal with specific situations.

Many associate the word 'tactics' with coercion and manipulation, but they are not confined to use with a competitive strategy. Not all tactics involve tricking the other side. They are skilful devices for dealing with a variety of aspects of negotiation.

Tactics are actions consciously done by negotiators to achieve their ends (as opposed to psychological influences which unconsciously affect a person's behaviour). However, because we have all been negotiating since birth, we may have developed negotiation tactics which we now use almost unconsciously. We may for example have learned as a teenager that we could avoid answering a difficult question put by a parent by deflecting the conversation on to something else. We may use a strategy akin to 'anchoring' in social situations so often that we fail to recognise that we are using it in work situations as well (eg, when 'negotiating' what film to see, wanting a nice 'light' funny one, we 'spontaneously' note the number of new light comedies, focus the conversation on these and, surprise, surprise, the discussion being largely about comedies, that is what is chosen).

Understanding the different tactics which can be used in a negotiation and the purpose for using them enables you to decide whether and how to use them, and to recognise when an opponent is using them and to know how to deal with them. Some tactics are used in specific aspects of a negotiation, eg, information exchange or concessions. We deal with these tactics in the chapters on preparation on those areas (**Chapters 10** and **11** respectively). Other tactics have more general application and we deal with them in **Chapter 14** as one of the final aspects of preparation.

4 Legal negotiations

4.1 Generally

The amount of time spent negotiating and the type of negotiations in which any lawyer tends to get involved will depend on the area of law in which he or she works. Many solicitors spend a large part of their time negotiating. This is particularly true of those who practise in certain areas, for example, commercial or property, where the bulk of their work is negotiating terms of contracts or leases (ie, transaction or deal-making negotiations). Solicitors who specialise in litigation also spend a lot of their time negotiating. Roughly 90 per cent of cases settle and many of these disputes are resolved by negotiations between solicitors.

The concept of dispute resolution is generally applied to civil cases on the basis that civil cases are disputes between the parties. Criminal cases can also be resolved without trial. However, the underlying concept here is different in that, in a criminal case, a person is prosecuted for an offence against the state, with the prosecution almost invariably being brought by the state or a body with delegated powers, such as a local authority. It is not uncommon for the prosecution and defence to negotiate or 'plea bargain' to resolve a criminal case without going to trial. The main issues involved in such a negotiation are the number and seriousness of the charges which will be considered by the court when sentencing, the defence seeking to get the prosecution to drop or reduce the charges, and the prosecution seeking to get guilty pleas on sufficient charges to represent the seriousness of the behaviour for which the defendant is charged. While 'plea bargaining' does take place, the recognition given to it in the system is far from clear and there are very different ethical and strategic considerations from those which apply to civil cases. This manual focuses on negotiation in the context of civil dispute resolutions and does not attempt to deal with the dynamics, ethics and considerations of plea bargaining (see the ***Professional Conduct*** manual).

Most barristers specialise as advocates within the litigation process. Like litigation solicitors, they too will be involved largely in dispute resolution negotiations. Negotiation within the context of civil disputes will take place throughout the various stages of the process from the time the dispute is identified to its ultimate conclusion. Exactly what is involved in the negotiation and how it is conducted will vary depending on the stage reached in the litigation process and the incentives to settle.

4.2 Why cases settle

People who have a civil dispute have some choice in how to resolve it. The principal choices have in the past been litigation or negotiation, but mediation (really a facilitated negotiation), is gaining ground as an alternative to litigation. There has been some work done, both theoretical and empirical, to attempt to understand why some cases settle and others proceed to trial.

An overview of the position is well set out in the following quote from Gary Goodpaster in the introduction to his article 'Lawsuits as Negotiations' (1992) 8 *Negotiation Journal* 222–39:

> Litigating a dispute is both a major alternative to negotiating it and a way to force its negotiation. Litigation arises when the parties to a 'mature' dispute have attempted to negotiate it and failed, or have ignored, or refused, the possibility of negotiating it. If the dispute goes to trial, the parties will, through the cases they present, importantly influence the result. Nevertheless, a judge or jury, rather than the parties will decide the outcome. On the other hand, parties settle most lawsuits rather than try them. Indeed, it is the deadline that a pending trial imposes on the possibilities of a negotiated settlement, the risk of loss at trial, and possibly the added expense of trial that motivates many lawsuit settlements.
>
> Since most lawsuits settle before trial, it is useful to view litigation not solely as a way to reach an adjudicated result, but also as a highly structured negotiation game, a refined and constrained version of competitive bargaining. Litigation is, in effect, a 'branched track' mode of dispute resolution. Although apparently heading for an adjudicated result, the parties can, and usually do, shunt their dispute away from the trial station and onto a negotiation siding. It is therefore important to consider how and why parties progress toward a litigated result while at the same time moving toward settlement, and to understand why the process works as it does.

4.2.1 Why litigate in the first place?

In his article cited above, Goodpaster sets out six principal reasons why people litigate (ie, issue proceedings) rather than negotiate a settlement:

(a) 'Refusal to deal': one party refuses to negotiate and the other party has no power to compel him or her to do so aside from issuing proceedings.

(b) 'Negotiation failures': negotiation between the parties fails for some reason, eg, lack of negotiation skills. One of the parties thinks that litigation will give them leverage or a better result.

(c) 'Zero-sum situations': the parties see the dispute as zero-sum which puts them in a win/lose situation. Litigation will force the other side to do something and bear the costs. The dispute has usually arisen from a one-time past transaction (eg, an accident) and the parties are adversaries, hostile to one another, see no benefit in cooperating and see litigation as offering a better result.

(d) 'The litigator-negotiator's role': lawyers work in a litigation context, may fail to see alternatives and advise litigation as a way to get leverage in any negotiation.

(e) 'Lawyer–client relationships in lawsuits': issuing proceedings transfers much of the power to decide and shape the negotiation away from the client to the lawyer who manages the case within a litigation context which is itself adversarial.

(f) 'The litigator-negotiator's bias': the lawyer is a representative negotiator which increases the competitive element (see **2.2.6**). This effect is strengthened by the requirement in the lawyers' professional code to, in the case of the Bar (para 303), 'promote and protect fearlessly and by all proper and lawful means the lay client's best interests'.

4.2.2 Why cases settle after issue of proceedings

The two principal theories discussed by Goodpaster on what influences people to settle or proceed to trial once they are into the litigation process are the selection theory and the strategic bargaining theory. In addition, he identified a variety of factors which are influential.

4.2.2.1 The selection theory

Developed by George Priest and Benjamin Klein and set out in their paper 'The Selection of Disputes for Litigation' (1984) 13 *Journal of Legal Studies* 1–55, the selection theory argues that trials are most likely to occur in close cases.

The parties' negotiating stances are determined by their assessment of the likely outcome at trial. They know that the court will apply a standard against which it will judge the case (eg, in a negligence case) and then find for one or other party (ie, the decision is all or nothing, in that the defendant will lose regardless of the distance below the standard he or she falls). Both the claimant and defendant assess their case against this standard by considering the likely size of award multiplied by the probability of judgment in their favour. (The formula also deals with costs but, given the different treatment of costs in the US—each party usually bears his or her own regardless of outcome—this is not relevant to UK cases.) Both claimant and defendant base their offers and demands on their assessment of the case on the above analysis. If the case falls close to the standard (eg, of care in a negligence case), the parties are far more likely to have very different assessments of the outcome, much less likely to have offers and demands that meet, and more likely to see trial as giving them more than a negotiated settlement.

Thus, in this theory, predictability of outcome is the determining factor. The closer the case is to the standard which the court will apply (ie, the more uncertain the outcome) the more likely it will go to trial because the parties cannot accurately weigh up what is a fair risk or settlement.

4.2.2.2 The strategic bargaining theory

Developed by Robert Cooter, Stephen Marks and Robert Mnookin and set out in their paper 'Bargaining in the Shadow of the Law: A Testable Model of Strategic Behaviour' (1983) 11 *Journal of Legal Studies* 225–51, the strategic bargaining theory states that the obstacle to agreement is the strategic nature of the bargaining. Trials can occur, even where neither negotiator is optimistic about the outcome, or where outcomes may be relatively easy to predict, because of the uncertainty about the opponent's behaviour and how much he or she is prepared to concede. A variety of factors influence the parties' expectations and both adopt strategies to increase their potential gain. Thus, a negotiator, even with a weak case, may weigh up the opponent as being averse to risk and therefore consider that he or she will concede more if there is a real risk of trial.

4.2.2.3 The variables

From a variety of studies, Goodpaster has identified a number of variables which influence whether or not a case goes to trial, including:

(a) The parties' ability to predict trial outcome. The litigation process enables the parties to assess the law and facts. Cases where the law and facts are contested are more likely to go to trial.

(b) The benefits and costs of settlement now against those of continued litigation.

(c) How the litigation is financed. A party not liable for costs is more likely to run the risk of trial.

(d) Whether the parties are 'repeat' or 'one-off' players. A repeat player is more likely to run the risk of trial in any individual case.

(e) Whether the parties have differential stakes in trial or settlement. The parties may be seeking different things through litigation with 'asymmetrical' stakes in the outcome. Thus a party sued for professional negligence may really want a trial to clear his or her name whereas the party suing just wants to recoup losses suffered. What each wants will affect their strategy and approach to settlement.

4.2.3 The benefits of settling for the client

While some cases clearly merit a full trial, it can often be in the client's best interests to avoid going to court. Settling a dispute can:

(a) Reduce the friction between the parties. This is particularly important where there is an existing relationship or the prospect of an ongoing relationship, either business or personal.

(b) Reduce the costs by obviating the need for steps in the litigation process, the most obvious and expensive one being the trial.

(c) Reduce the delay in resolving the dispute.

(d) Reduce the anxiety and stress for the client caused both by having to live with the uncertainty of the outcome until trial and worrying about the whole trial process, eg, having to give evidence, having to relive a particularly traumatic experience (such as an accident).

(e) Avoid the 'winner take all' outcome, which is inevitable in a trial where the court can only decide in favour of one party, and enable a more flexible compromise.

(f) Increase the range of possible outcomes for the client. The court has limited powers in what it can order which are circumscribed by the case as pleaded by the parties. A negotiated settlement can include elements which are beyond the court's powers to order.

4.2.4 What cases should go to trial?

Although most cases do settle and there are great benefits for the client in settling in almost any case, provided it is done on satisfactory terms, there are some cases where trial may be more appropriate.

(a) A case may be litigated to seek clarification of the law. Only a judgment of the court will give this. Some cases are run as 'test cases' to establish a principle. While part of the purpose of running the case is to 'test the law', the lawyer should never lose sight of the fact that it is being tested on the back of a client. While the lawyer must balance the benefits which can be achieved for a wider group by establishing a principle against the needs of the client whose case is being run, the ultimate decision as to whether to settle or go to trial remains that of the client.

(b) A client may have a real need for his or her 'day in court'. This is an objective and it is the client's right to use the civil justice system to achieve this. While the lawyer's role includes talking through the pros and cons of trial versus settlement with the client and getting the client to see it in perspective, the decision whether or not to settle is that of the client.

4.3 Negotiations by solicitors and barristers

The role of the solicitor and barrister in the conduct of a case differs. The solicitor has the overall conduct of the case, seeing it from beginning to end, and instructs or briefs a barrister for certain aspects of it. (The ***Case Preparation*** manual sets out the stages of a civil case and the differing roles of the solicitor and barrister in more detail.)

Civil disputes cover a broad range of cases including those conducted through tribunals and courts. Whatever the type of adjudication, a case can be divided into the following stages:

- pre-action (initial consideration by the client and lawyers as to whether adjudication is appropriate);
- initiating proceedings (issue and service of relevant documents to start relevant proceedings);
- interim (exchange of documents and information, collection and preparation of the evidence for trial);
- trial;
- appeal;
- enforcement.

A case can be settled at any of these stages.

Although there is nothing to prevent the parties themselves from negotiating a settlement, once lawyers have been instructed, negotiations are usually conducted through the lawyers, with most of this being done by the solicitors (see **4.3.1**). Generally the solicitor prepares the case for trial (or appeal, etc where relevant) in tandem with negotiating a settlement. While settling early in the litigation process does save the costs of these processes, negotiating a settlement is not an excuse for failing to observe time limits in litigation.

A number of factors will influence when negotiations take place, for example, having sufficient information to assess the case properly and strategic considerations of how the various stages in the litigation process affect the case. Certain aspects of the procedure are specifically aimed at exchange of information between the parties (eg, disclosure, whereby the parties are entitled to mutual inspection of relevant documents, mutual exchange of witness statements and expert reports) and this may affect the timing or conduct of any negotiation. There are a number of devices available to the claimant and defendant to put pressure on the other party to settle (eg, a payment into court by the defendant which restricts the claimant's rights to costs if he or she does not obtain more at trial).

At whatever stage a case is settled, relevant procedural requirements must be considered. Settlement before proceedings have begun will be recorded and enforced as a contract. Settlements on behalf of a minor require court approval even if done before a case is issued. Once proceedings have been initiated, any settlement must deal with the existence of the proceedings, eg, by obtaining the appropriate court order or discontinuing the case (see the ***Civil Litigation*** manual).

4.3.1 Solicitors' negotiations

A whole variety of factors give solicitors more flexibility in what they can do in a negotiation than is available to barristers in most cases. Solicitors see their clients through the case, develop relationships with them and get to know them to a degree. They have opportunities to discuss the case with the other side over a period of time through a variety of methods using a combination of exchange of letters, phone calls and/or meetings with the other side. Although less and less true with increasing control of cases by the courts, they are, to a degree, able to control the speed of the litigation, eg, maintaining a slow pace to enable greater time for negotiation or speeding it up to put pressure on the other side to settle. Solicitors are in a position (subject to costs) to obtain whatever information from the client or others they consider to be relevant to the case. They can investigate alternatives to trial, including options which no court could order.

4.3.2 Court-door negotiations

A barrister's involvement in a case is controlled by the solicitor who instructs or briefs counsel as and when the solicitor considers it necessary. Barristers' principal functions are advising on merit, quantum and evidence, drafting court documents, and advocacy at hearings. While they may be instructed to advise on whether or not an offer of settlement is appropriate, their role as negotiators is usually, at least in their first few years, confined mostly to court-door negotiations. Negotiating in this context is much less flexible.

(a) Negotiating at the court door puts terrific time pressure on the negotiators. Frequently they have very little time (maybe 20 to 25 minutes) in which to reach a settlement prior to the case being called on.

(b) Being a referral profession, barristers have limited access to information. Frequently they arrive at the court never having met the client with only the information the solicitor has chosen to include in the papers. Where counsel is involved in an interlocutory hearing (eg, summary judgment) at an early stage of the proceedings (a frequent role for junior counsel), the solicitor will have been conscious of not taking any steps which might cost the client and be wasted because the case did not proceed to trial. Thus the brief may not contain full information (eg, expert reports), all the necessary documentation, or much in the way of evidence (eg, proofs from witnesses).

The circumstances at court mean counsel also has limited opportunity to get more information from the solicitor or client, both because of lack of time and lack of attendance by those with the information. Those attending court may include the solicitor and the lay client. However, often the solicitor will not attend but send an 'outdoor clerk', ie, a file-carrier from the solicitor's office who may be extremely bright and *au fait* with the client and his or her case, or may be a part-timer who has no idea about the case and very little, if any, legal knowledge. In addition, on an interim hearing which relies on written evidence, although it is wise for the client to attend in case something unexpected happens, there is, strictly, no need for the client to attend as he or she will have no role to play (the evidence being that contained in the witness statement). Thus the barrister may have access to fairly comprehensive information where both the solicitor and lay client attend, or may have to rely solely on information from the brief. However, there may be little space to separate the parties or to discuss the matter with the solicitor or client out of earshot of the opponent.

(c) Barristers generally do not have an ongoing relationship with their lay clients. Their involvement with their lay clients is short-lived. Generally, and particularly in cases of small financial value, their contact is limited to discussions immediately before going into court when the clients are focused on what will happen in court. These factors make it more difficult for barristers to ascertain and understand lay clients' underlying concerns and interests.

(d) Barristers have limited opportunities to give proper consideration to a wide range of options. They act in very limited circumstances, ie, at the court door, with limited time. They have two clients, the lay and the professional, and have a duty to both. These two factors put the following limitations on their ability to create options in any negotiation:

  (i) There is a limited range of options which the court can ratify. This need not necessarily always limit counsel to ratifiable solutions. However, the court's power and interest in ratifying the solution will vary from case to case and barristers negotiate with this as a consideration.

  (ii) There is no time or opportunity to investigate the viability, practicality and enforceability of options not already envisaged by the papers and court hearing.

  (iii) There is pressure to find a solution which satisfies the lay and professional client and, in some cases, the court.

  (iv) Going outside the solicitor's instructions raises issues of professional conduct where the barrister is acting on instructions from solicitors who, given the financial value of the case, have sent a 'file-carrier' who knows nothing about the case.

(e) Barristers negotiating at the court door are doing so at least partway into the litigation process if not at the very end (ie, trial) and this will be reflected in the parties' and professional clients' mindsets and views of the case:

  (i) The clients, lay and professional, may have adopted fairly entrenched positions for a variety of reasons, eg, their investment in time, finances and emotion in fighting the case or purely as a matter of strategy.

  (ii) At the door of the court of trial, the bulk of the costs will already have been incurred and the client may consider that settling at this point will make little difference to the costs.

(f) The facilities in which the negotiation takes place are usually very limited (possibly standing in a crowded corridor), and the whole physical environment may have an effect on the behaviour of those negotiating. Finding a sideroom in which to negotiate may alter this behaviour.

(g) Finally, two other factors might influence the conduct of court-door negotiations:

  (i) The type of case. The fact that the case is at the court door may mean that it is one in which there is greater uncertainty as to the outcome at trial and this is why settlement has not been reached before and is more difficult (see **4.2.2.1**).

  (ii) Barristers at this stage may be taking over partway through the negotiation process, the solicitor having gone through much of the process, leaving only part for the barrister to do.

4.3.3 Other contexts

While many of the negotiations which barristers, particularly junior barristers, conduct take place outside the court door, barristers do negotiate in other contexts. For example, negotiations may take place between counsel early in the process some time before the hearing date. Alternatively, a barrister may receive a phone call from counsel for the other side seeking information, eg, about cases that he or she will be relying on at the hearing. The conversation becomes a discussion about resolving the case through negotiation.

Be conscious of the impact that the different modes of communication have on a negotiation. In particular, ensure that you do not attempt to negotiate a case when your mind is not focused on it (for example, if you have just returned from or are just going to court on another case). Do not be afraid to say, 'I'll phone you back', and give yourself the space to consider carefully how you are going to deal with the matter before speaking to the other side.

4.3.4 Other people

Negotiating with the lawyer for the other side (whether barrister or solicitor) is clearly an important aspect of the work of barristers. However, barristers also spend a fair amount of time negotiating with others.

More and more people are undertaking cases themselves without the assistance of lawyers. Litigants in person are more personally involved with the case and generally (but not always) have limited knowledge of the law. Negotiating with them requires a more complex balancing act than negotiating with another lawyer as, although one is still seeking the best for one's client, one must not take unfair advantage of the litigant in person.

The need to 'negotiate' with a judge does arise: for example, it may be necessary to persuade the judge to give counsel more time to negotiate a settlement when the case should have been called on or to persuade the judge to endorse a consent order where he or she has the power to withhold that consent. This form of negotiation clearly shows the overlap between advocacy and negotiation skills.

There are a huge variety of people who become involved in cases with whom barristers 'negotiate' in one form or another, from court officials (from whom additional time is more frequently sought than directly from the judge), through various witnesses who may be experts (eg, social workers or doctors) or lay witnesses (eg, friends or relations of the client).

Finally, barristers negotiate with both their professional and lay clients. The barrister and solicitor may see the case differently and 'negotiate' over whose view or tactics should prevail. The lay client will also have views about the case. Although the client is in the driving seat in that he or she instructs the lawyers to conduct the case and ultimately makes many of the decisions about the case, the lawyers owe the client professional duties to ensure the case is conducted in the best possible way and this gives rise to rather complex considerations.

4.4 The role and influence of the lay client

Legal negotiations in a split profession can involve a complex variety of relationships (ie, between barrister and solicitor, solicitor and client and barrister and client) because of the differing roles and views of the case each player has. Both of the lawyers have professional duties to the client and to each other. This gives rise to different areas of consideration: the different roles of the lay client and the lawyers, and how the different roles of the lawyer and the client influence the negotiation.

4.4.1 It is the client's case

A lawyer is negotiating for the client. It is the client's case. The lawyer is the expert, the professional adviser and representative acting on behalf of the client. This gives rise to four basic factors to remember when so acting.

4.4.1.1 The client's objectives

A lawyer negotiating for a client must ensure that he or she really does understand the client's objectives, interests and needs and pursue these in the negotiation. What the client wants should be fully explored with a wide view taken of the various needs or interests which may be included. The client may have short- and long-term interests. While money may be an objective, there may be other matters such as a need for vindication or an apology. While the client may express the objectives in money terms, it is important also to find out the interests and needs behind the objectives. It may be that what the client is seeking is financial security, which may come from reinstatement in a job rather than a large money settlement.

The lawyer must also understand the client's priorities. What are the relative values placed on the different interests and needs?

4.4.1.2 Act only with authority

A lawyer acts as his or her client's agent in a negotiation and general agency rules apply. The lawyer has actual authority to act only within the client's instructions and should never settle outside this actual authority. However, from the other party's point of view, a lawyer is acting for the client and has the apparent or ostensible authority to settle a case after proceedings have been issued. The extent of this apparent authority can of course be cut down by giving the other side notice of any limit on it. A lawyer who acts outside his or her actual authority but binds the client because the agreement comes within the apparent authority will be liable to the client.

A barrister's brief will normally contain a lot of information which makes it clear what the client will or will not accept, ie, it sets the parameters of the actual authority of counsel in negotiating a settlement. However, there may well be matters of detail on which it is not clear exactly what the client wants. Making it apparent to the other side that any negotiation is subject to the authorisation or approval of the client leaves counsel open to agree detail on condition that the client does approve (ie, giving notice of the limited authority). By setting this parameter, it leaves counsel free to try to tie up the detail in the best way possible without binding the client.

4.4.1.3 The lawyer's professional role

The lawyer's role in any civil case is to deal with matters of law, procedure and evidence. It is the lawyer's professional duty to the client. The lawyer must advise the client both of his or her view of the case and of what, in his or her judgment, the best course of action is. This means ensuring the client understands how the strengths and weaknesses of the case or any procedural or evidential matters affect the chances of achieving the objectives that he or she is seeking. It is the lawyer's job to ensure that, when the client decides whether or not to accept an offer or agree to settle, the decision is a fully informed one. The terms of the settlement must be fully explained as must the effect, in particular that settlement will mean the end of the matter and there will normally be no possibility of reopening it or seeking more.

Failing to advise the client properly or just accepting a decision where the client clearly does not understand his or her legal position or consequences of the decision is a breach of duty to the client. (See the ***Conference Skills*** manual on the subject of advising the client.)

4.4.1.4 The client must decide

Decisions about substantive matters, eg, whether or not to negotiate, what issues are open to negotiation and whether or not an offer should be accepted, must be made by the client. It is the client's case and the lawyer must ensure that any decision about whether to settle or not is that of the client and not of the lawyer. Whether the settlement is acceptable must be measured against the client's objectives, needs and interests. Having advised fully (see above), the lawyer must then accept the client's decision and abide by it. If the client is not prepared to accept a settlement, that is his or her prerogative. The only exception to this may arise if the client is publicly funded and the lawyer has to advise on the merits of pursuing the claim.

4.4.2 Influence of client and lawyer on negotiation

The fact that the lawyer is acting as a representative and not on his or her own behalf can mean that he or she tends to be more competitive (see **2.2.6**). In addition, the lawyer's role in the litigation process and his or her resulting bias may produce a more competitive stance. It may also influence the way the client sees the case, reframing it by the words used and advice given on the possible options so the client alters his or her objectives to reflect the litigation process and what is available within it (see **4.2.1**).

4.4.3 Lawyers as repeat players

Although lawyers may negotiate for clients who are one-off players, they themselves are repeat players (ie, they will probably be negotiating against the same lawyers over time). This is particularly true of a small profession like the Bar. The lawyer owes a duty to the client in any single negotiation to achieve the best for that client. On the other hand, he or she will have to maintain a working relationship with what are, in effect, his or her colleagues. This may produce tensions. For example, taking a very competitive stance in one case may produce the best for that client. However, this may make it more difficult to negotiate for future clients because the previous behaviour may colour later negotiations. Alternatively, there may be a temptation to settle a case because of peer pressure when in fact the offer does not achieve the best for the client. A possible middle ground is to develop a reputation as a firm but fair negotiator.

4.5 'Without prejudice' negotiations

Negotiations with a view to settlement should be conducted 'without prejudice' whether by letter, fax, phone or face-to-face meeting. This basically means that the contents of the negotiation cannot be revealed to the court to assist it to determine the case. While any negotiation with a view to compromise is impliedly without prejudice, the position is also frequently expressly stated, eg, by putting the words 'without prejudice' on a letter.

More detailed guidance on the evidential position of 'without prejudice' communications is contained in the ***Evidence*** manual, in the ***Professional Conduct*** manual and in **Chapter 16** of this manual where it impacts on the conduct of the negotiation.

4.6 Effective legal negotiators

4.6.1 Do we know what is effective?

The reaction of some students to negotiating is immediate enthusiasm. They have always liked debating and arguing and are keen to start winning negotiations. Other students are immediately wary; they do not like arguing and are rather apprehensive of their chances against an aggressive opponent. In fact, both reactions are based on a quite common misconception that people are successful negotiators because they can be aggressive, state their views forcefully and believe wholeheartedly in winning or, the reverse side of the coin, that people who wish to avoid conflict, appear fair and reasonable and reach a good compromise are not good negotiators.

While there is much discussion in the literature about effective negotiation techniques, there is little empirical data about what lawyers do in negotiations. Carrie Menkel-Meadow summarised in her paper 'Lawyer Negotiations: Theories and Realities—What We Learn From Mediation' (1993) 56(3) *Maryland Law Review* 361–79, 'empirical work on negotiation in a variety of legal contexts remains relatively paltry, but is depressingly consistent'. She then reviews several studies which show that lawyers settle quickly, with few exchanges of offers, use conventional patterns of negotiation behaviour and seek standardised solutions.

That there clearly are varying degrees of effectiveness in negotiations between lawyers is demonstrated by an experiment by Gerald Williams, Professor of Law at Brigham Young University, in which he got 40 experienced practising lawyers to prepare and conduct a negotiation to settle the same personal injury case and compare results. The settlements varied from $15,000 to $95,000 (average $47,318), with a number of pairs not settling.

Clearly this shows that different lawyers get very different results with exactly the same case. The fact that some lawyers get far better results than others (eg, obtaining $95,000 for the claimant and $15,000 for the defendant are both well away from the average) leads one to assume that they are more effective negotiators (although they may in fact just be less ineffective than their opponents).

There are few empirical studies of actual legal negotiations in which behaviour is observed and considered to see what is and is not effective. Much of the literature is based on experiments in game theory (ie, people playing highly structured games which require them to decide a strategy against an opponent) or observations of students doing simulated negotiations.

One study which has been discussed in much of the literature was done by Gerald Williams. Using questionnaires, interviews and videotaped performances, lawyers were rated on a huge number of traits to determine whether they were effective, average or ineffective and whether they were competitive or cooperative. He concluded that:

(a) 49 per cent were rated as effective, 38 per cent as average and 12 per cent as ineffective.

(b) 65 per cent of negotiators could be categorised as cooperative and 24 per cent as competitive (11 per cent had insufficiently consistent patterns to be categorised).

(c) Neither approach guaranteed effectiveness. However, 59 per cent of cooperative and only 25 per cent of competitive negotiators were rated as effective and 3 per cent of cooperative and 33 per cent of competitive negotiators were rated as ineffective.

Williams also analysed the traits which people associated with effective, average and ineffective cooperative and competitive negotiators. While there are differences in the characteristics for the two approaches, some of the characteristics which were shared by effective 'cooperatives' and 'competitives' are:

- rational, analytical, intelligent;
- realistic;
- thoroughly prepared on the facts and law, legally astute;
- convincing;
- perceptive, skilful in reading opponent's cues;
- honest, ethical, trustworthy, adhered to customs and courtesies of the Bar;
- creative, versatile, adaptable;
- self-controlled, poised;
- took satisfaction in using legal skills.

Williams' study is not the definitive answer on effectiveness and can be criticised, eg, he does not distinguish between strategy and style (see Condlin, 'Bargaining in the Dark: The Normative Incoherence of Lawyer Dispute Bargaining Role' (1992) 51 *Maryland Law Review* 1–104 at 17–22 in particular). However, his study and results have been used in many discussions about different strategies as they do give some insight into how legal negotiators are perceived and what is and is not seen as effective. It counters the misconception that all lawyers are tough, aggressive, hard-nosed negotiators. It also confirms what a number of writers on negotiation state: that competitive negotiators are not frequently seen as effective. It would appear that it is easier to be an effective cooperative negotiator than an effective competitive one.

There is scope for all students to become effective negotiators by building on many of the skills they already possess, eg, by being rational, analytical, perceptive, creative. Effectiveness also comes from understanding how these skills are used in a negotiation and from being thoroughly prepared.

4.7 Preparing to be an effective legal negotiator

Doing something skilfully generally means that it appears to be done effortlessly. While there is little overt recognition of the skill being exercised, there is an underlying understanding of the component parts of the skill, the overall context in which it is used and how and when to use various techniques. Skilled advocates are more effective partly because they are very familiar with the context in which they work, eg, they know instinctively when they can and cannot interrupt or what they can and cannot say to the judge. This is equally true of negotiation. Understanding the mechanics and subtleties of the negotiation process allows you to see more clearly what is happening and what may be influencing the negotiation. This enables you to control what happens more effectively. Understanding the different strategies, styles and tactics which you can use and which may be used by your opponent enables you to identify and deal with them more effectively. Rarely an express part of the negotiation, all these factors underpin the activity and a real understanding of them will help you to be an effective negotiator.

Proper preparation and planning is essential to ensure effective negotiation. If you are someone who takes naturally to negotiation, you still need the tools to do it well. If you are someone who is nervous about negotiating, having the tools honed will increase your confidence and ability to control your behaviour in the negotiation. Like good advocacy, good negotiation depends on proper preparation.

The remainder of this manual sets out how to prepare and conduct legal negotiations effectively. At each stage it explains the underlying strategies or tactics which may be used and the psychological effects these may have, and gives practical guidance on how to prepare to use both the substance of the case and the strategies and tactics effectively.

5

Preparation and planning—an overview

5.1 The importance of preparation and planning

In **Chapter 1** we set out some of the similarities between negotiation and courtroom advocacy: both involve using argument persuasively and eliciting relevant information from others. Both therefore involve detailed preparation and planning: understanding the context of the case, carrying out detailed analysis of the facts and the law and planning how to present the case most effectively. A good advocate understands the dynamics of trial and focuses his or her preparation on persuading the court to find for his or her client. Similarly, a good negotiator understands the dynamics of a negotiation and focuses his or her preparation on how to conduct the negotiation to get the best possible settlement. The preparation for both involves many similar steps: eg, analysing the law, facts and evidence, and evaluating the strengths and weaknesses of the case, so that your preparation for trial goes a long way towards preparing for a negotiation.

However, just preparing for the courtroom will not suffice to prepare you to negotiate effectively. In **Chapter 1** we also set out some of the differences between a negotiation and a trial. A negotiation moves ahead much more quickly than a trial, has no formal structure and, most importantly, no independent arbitrator. You will therefore have to deal with new information and new views of the case much more quickly than you will normally have to in court. You will have to persuade your opponent who is partisan rather than someone who is independent and, finally, you will also have to make proposals for settlement yourself and make decisions during the negotiation about whether or not to accept proposals made by your opponent.

Only by preparing thoroughly for the negotiation can you ensure that you do negotiate effectively, make sound judgements on proposals and have a proper basis for judging whether you did cover everything and did get the best possible outcome.

In addition, where you are negotiating at the court door, the case may be one in which the outcome at trial is highly uncertain (see **4.2.2**) and this will make it even more important that you have prepared thoroughly and effectively.

5.2 What preparing and planning to negotiate entails

Effective preparation and planning for negotiation involves a number of stages which can be considered within the approach suggested in the ***Case Preparation*** manual: the **CAP** approach of understanding the **context**, then doing the **analysis** and then planning how to **present** effectively. To be effective in the negotiation you must be properly prepared: you have thoroughly understood the client's objectives, have considered the opponent's objectives, have analysed the facts and law of both your own and your opponent's case, have assessed the strengths and weaknesses of your and your opponent's case, and have considered the arguments which may be used by and against you. You also need to have considered what information may be exchanged and how you will seek and make concessions. Finally, you need to plan the strategy you will use, the structure you will propose and your tactics.

5.2.1 Understanding the context

The brief from the solicitor should contain sufficient information to give you an overview of the case. It should enable you to sort out who the parties are, what the case is about, what stage it has reached, who the solicitors and counsel for the other side are (have you any experience of them?), where and when the negotiation is to be held, what issues are involved and what type of negotiation it is. All this helps you to put your role and the negotiation in context. This step is considered in more detail in **Chapter 6**.

5.2.2 Analysis—objectives

Analysing the case to ascertain the parties' objectives means identifying fully and precisely what they want from any settlement. Clearly it is important to be clear what your client wants. It is important that you consider this broadly, thinking beyond the stated legal claims and remedies, and ascertain the client's real interests and needs. There is a huge range of potential objectives from purely financial (eg, just payment of a sum of money), to purely personal (eg, an apology from the alleged wrongdoer). You need to identify the full range of objectives which your client might be seeking. You then need to consider the client's priorities between the objectives, from the most important through to the least important. You also need to ensure that you are clear on the parameters put on the negotiation by the client, ie, what the client must have or what the client will not accept.

It is also important to try to determine what the other side wants from a settlement. In most cases there will have been a fair amount of communication between the parties and their solicitors about the case prior to you being briefed. There will therefore be some information in the brief about the case for the other side from which you can at least get some idea of what he or she might be seeking. Although this information will be less complete than for your client, you should undertake the same exercise in considering the opponent's objectives as you have done for your client.

Once you have identified and attempted to prioritise the objectives of both sides, you should consider whether there are any objectives which both parties want (eg, they both want the business to continue) or whether they actually want different things (eg, on a divorce they want different items of furniture) and plan how you can use this in the negotiation.

This aspect of preparation is considered in **Chapter 7**.

5.2.3 Analysis—the issues, arguments, information and evaluation

The most important skill of any lawyer is the ability to identify the issues in the case, evaluate its strengths and weaknesses and formulate persuasive argument. This aspect of preparing for a negotiation is not dissimilar to preparing to conduct a case in court.

This involves identifying the issues underlying the legal claims by the parties. What are the substantive issues? For example, in a claim for breach of contract, is the dispute about whether or not there was a term in the contract or whether what the defendant did amounted to breach? Having identified the issues, it then involves detailed consideration of the facts, law and evidence.

You must consider the relevant law. What supports or undermines your case and your opponent's case? How does the law apply to the alleged facts to strengthen or weaken the two sides of the case?

You must identify the facts alleged by each side, distinguishing between those which are agreed, disputed or ambiguous. You must also be aware of the factual gaps. What information do you not have which might be important and/or held by the other side?

In any negotiation, the parties involved will have constructed their views on the basis of the facts as they see them with little regard to the evidence which supports their view. Depending on the stage the case has reached, there may be little formal evidence in the papers (eg, there may be no expert's report or witness statements). However, you must analyse the papers to identify what, if any, evidence there is for the allegations made which can be used for or against you.

Negotiating within the litigation process means that there may well be procedural points which must be considered as they could be used for or against you. For example, your client may have obtained judgment in default (of the opponent filing a defence). While the opponent may consider that the chances are very high that the court will set judgment aside, clearly, when discussing any settlement which alters what your client is getting from that contained in the judgment, you must take this procedural point on board.

This analysis should enable you to formulate a variety of arguments on the issues underlying the case, both substantive and procedural. You should also consider what arguments your opponent may use against you. You also need to evaluate the case. What are the strengths and weaknesses on both sides? Which arguments are most persuasive for you and your opponent? How might they be countered?

The role of persuasion, argument and information exchange in negotiations is discussed in **Chapter 8**. Detailed consideration of this part of the preparation is then covered in **Chapters 9** and **10**.

5.2.4 Analysis—planning your concessions

Negotiation is about moving towards agreement, which means both sides have to plan how they are going to move, ie, what concessions they are going to make. A 'concession' is defined by Donald G Gifford in *Legal Negotiations Theory and Application* at p 141 as 'any modification of a negotiator's bargaining proposal making it less advantageous to his or her client'.

Planning concessions includes planning both the concessions that you will seek from the other side and those that you will offer. Planning what you are going to seek or make by way of concessions, and when and how you will do it, is a vital part of the preparation for a negotiation.

In most negotiations it is reasonably easy to identify what the client wants out of the negotiation and the real skill is in planning how to get it. You should aim to obtain the best outcome you can possibly get for your client and avoid getting near or sinking below the lowest outcome that your client would accept. Your overall approach should also reflect the BATNA (the best alternative to a negotiated agreement) because you need to be clear about the precise point when your client would be better off not settling and when you should walk away. Never lose sight of what you think the outcome would be if you went to court. This should be a yardstick—you should not settle for less than you think the client would get in court unless the costs or risks of going to court would be high.

What is conceded in any negotiation must involve both consideration of the client's objectives, including his or her priorities, and the strengths and weaknesses of the case which are apparent from the analysis of the issues. This puts your client's objectives into a realistic context. You need to be clear about both the most the client might possibly achieve and what is the least that the client might accept. One of your client's objectives might be based on such a strong legal and factual foundation that there should on no account be any concession there. Another objective might be so fundamentally undermined by law and/or evidence that it will be very difficult to achieve. Do not get too pessimistic. Your opponent may not be as well prepared and you may be able to persuade him or her to concede more than you anticipate. Your opponent might have information that puts your case in a better light than you think. If your client has asked for something, you should do your best to get it. However, your expectations, and eventually your outcome, should be related to a sound and detailed evaluation.

You should also consider whether there is an imaginative solution to the case or whether you can find some options that are mutually beneficial to the parties.

When and *how* you make the concessions forms part of your negotiation strategy and must also be planned as much as possible.

The concept of concessions, when and how they are used in the different strategies and the planning of them is covered in **Chapter 11**.

5.2.5 Presentation—planning your strategy

As we saw in **Chapter 3**, strategy includes how you intend to deal with information exchange, and the use of concessions and argument which form steps in your preparation to date (see above). However, in addition to considering each of these elements separately, you will need to step back and consider more generally your overall approach or strategy. Taking an overview of the whole of your preparation should give you a fair idea of your overall strategy, ie, whether it is generally competitive or collaborative or whether it is mixed, which is more likely. You then need to be aware of the benefits and risks of adopting any of the particular strategies and the need to be flexible. This is covered in **Chapter 12**.

5.2.6 Presentation—planning the structure of the negotiation

You also need to consider the overall structure you want the negotiation to take. However, planning a negotiation is not like planning in the other interpersonal skills of advocacy and conference skills. Although those skills are also 'interpersonal', in that they involve interacting with others, in those skills you can set a structure which you can then largely follow or adapt because you are in charge. You are conducting it. Although you must take on board the other person(s) involved, this need not alter your fundamental structure. Thus, in making a submission there may be interventions from the judge which alter part of the structure of what you will say; in examining a witness, you may have to rethink some questions because you are not getting the answers you expected or, in interviewing a client, you may find you have to adjust to take on board the concerns which he or she is raising. In planning a conference you can set an agenda, explain this to the client and then conduct the conference according to the agenda.

A negotiation is a much more dynamic, interactive process. Although there are some identifiable phases through which many negotiations pass, no negotiation can be forced into a rigid structure which one or other party controls. Every negotiation is unique and you need to be flexible. Planning the overall structure of a negotiation means considering how you will open and the general order in which you want to deal with things. Are there basic issues you feel need to be resolved before you move on to others? Are there matters which need clarification before there is any discussion of concessions? Are there a lot of items of equal importance, or just a few items that will dominate the negotiation?

Whatever your plan, you must ensure that you have prepared so that you do cover all the relevant issues, claims and objectives of your client. The agreement reached will bind the parties and it is essential that no aspect is left out through inadvertence.

This aspect of preparation is covered in **Chapter 13**.

5.2.7 Presentation—tactics

In addition to those tactics that form the basics of the different strategies (ie, information exchange and concession planning), there are a vast range of tactics used in negotiations. They extend across a range of methods that enable you to influence the focus of the negotiation (eg, ways to set the parameters of what is negotiated) through to some rather dubious tactics (eg, the use of threats). It is important for you to be aware of tactics and understand the basis for them so that you can recognise them and deal with them in a negotiation. These are considered in **Chapter 14**.

5.3 Summary

Proper preparation and planning is essential to ensure effective negotiation. If you are someone who takes naturally to negotiation, you still need the proper tools to do it well. If you are someone who is nervous about negotiating, having the tools honed will increase your confidence and ability to control your behaviour in the negotiation. Like good advocacy, good negotiation depends on proper preparation.

However, having stressed the importance of preparation and planning, you must be careful that this does not lead you into taking too rigid a view of the case. You will almost certainly have to take new facts, figures and views on board as you go along, and your overall planning needs to be flexible enough to take this into account.

More detailed guidance on preparation and planning is given in the following chapters.

5.4 Case studies

At this point we introduce two case studies which we will use to illustrate the different steps in preparing to negotiate. We will use Case Study A to show what would be done at each of the relevant stages of preparation. We have included Case Study B to enable you to practice your own preparation. In both cases we have included only the papers for one side. Case Study A looks at preparation from the point of view of the defence. Case Study B enables you to prepare from the point of view of the claimant. We have included the papers for the other side at the back of the manual so that you can use the papers to conduct a negotiation. However, we would advise you not to look at them until you have worked your way through the manual and done your own preparation using Case Study B.

5.4.1 Case Study A

MEGADELL FOODS LIMITED

and

ANGUS WARLEY (t/a CHOC FOLIE)

INSTRUCTIONS TO COUNSEL FOR THE DEFENDANT

Instructing Solicitors act for Angus Warley who trades as Choc Folie, and is the Defendant in this matter. Counsel is instructed in a hearing in which the Defendant seeks to set aside judgment in default obtained by the Claimant, Megadell Foods Limited, on 11th February 2009.

Counsel will see the claim made against Choc Folie from the enclosed Particulars of Claim. The Defendant's position is set out in the statement of Mr Angus Warley.

Mr Warley is the sole proprietor of Choc Folie. Mr Angus Warley consulted us a short while ago when he was served with judgment in default (which was regularly obtained). Mr Warley says that he had not known of the proceedings as he had been in hospital following a car accident although unfortunately there is no documentary evidence of this as yet.

Mr Warley has made a witness statement in support of setting aside judgment in default which is enclosed. As Counsel will see he is seeking to set judgment aside on the merits.

Judgment in default was entered for the amount claimed plus interest. Counsel will see that the Defendant not only contests the merits of this judgment but is raising a counterclaim. However, Mr Warley is most anxious that this matter be settled if at all possible as he is struggling to keep the business going. He was happy with the original quality of the chocolate supplied and would like to resolve matters with a view to contracting with the Claimant in the future.

We have spoken to Solicitors for the Claimant and have the impression that their client is keen to settle this matter if mutually agreeable terms can be reached. We agreed that it would be profitable for Counsel to discuss possible resolution of the action prior to the hearing although the Claimant is still formally opposing setting the judgment aside. Would Counsel therefore attend in good time to discuss terms with Counsel for the Claimant. If settlement is not reached Counsel should seek to have the judgment set aside.

Our costs to date are £250 plus Counsel's fees of £175.

STATEMENT OF ANGUS WARLEY

1. About four years ago I opened the shop 'Folie de Chocolat' in Bridgwater, Somerset. The shop sells all kinds of chocolate, specialising in high-quality home made chocolates, truffles and other chocolate items. In 2006 I opened two other branches 'Choc Around the Clock' in Minehead and 'Choc Til You Drop' in Taunton. I set up trading as 'Choc Folie' which employs staff. However, I am a sole trader.

2. I obtained chocolate supplies from various wholesalers and I employed a couple of workers to make up chocolate products in the kitchens in Bridgwater. About half of the sales were from made-up products; the other half were bought-in. About three-quarters of the profits came from the made-up products—things like chocolate truffles, animals and Christmas and Easter products.

3. In July 2008 I was introduced to a particularly fine Belgian chocolate by Mr Leon Haalen, a representative of a company called Megadell Foods of Southampton. I was so impressed I invited him to visit our Bridgwater shop in July (2008). At that meeting I explained to Mr Haalen that I would like to contract on a monthly basis although I reassured him I would probably continue to place orders for several months. Mr Haalen said that Megadell would only supply on a yearly contract, as their suppliers in Belgium traded on that basis, but that it was the policy of the company that if the buyer was unhappy with the product at any time then they would do anything in their power to satisfy the customer and he hadn't known a dissatisfied customer yet. He quoted the company's slogan (which I later saw on its delivery vans) 'The finest foods to your order'. He said that any problems with quality would be investigated at once. I stressed that it was essential that I had a constant supply of good quality chocolate as I depended on good quality to make up the products such as animals and truffles etc, which were my real profit makers. I also explained that several times a year I participated in events to promote chocolate sales, particularly at the fancier end of the market, and that one such event was coming up in the late autumn which was particularly important as it was a country-wide fair or 'Chocaganza weekend'. He seemed to take my concerns on board so I signed on the dotted line there and then agreeing that I would be supplied on a monthly basis but with an overall contract for a year's supply.

4. When I signed the contract at that meeting I knew that it was for a year but I believed Mr Haalen when he said quality was assured and I believed that meant I could end the contract if unhappy. There were further terms that Megadell would deliver to our Bridgwater base and be responsible for the product until accepted by us and would investigate any problems with quality immediately on receiving a complaint. Delivery and payment were as in the Claimant's claim. The price per kilogramme was 10p more than that of our usual supplier, but we were happy to pay it as the chocolate was of a better quality.

5. The first delivery was made on 6th September 2008 (together with an invoice for £1,260). The chocolate was of superb quality. We were extremely impressed. However, when the October delivery arrived on 4th October (invoiced as before) we discovered on unpacking that about a half of the delivery had deteriorated so that there was a whitish layer on it. It was not usable. We endeavoured to contact Mr Haalen who had told us that he was the first port of call for any complaints. Between 4th and 8th October several messages were left for him both at the factory number and on his mobile phone which he did not seem to switch on. Because of the problems I decided not to pay for the September chocolate until everything was sorted out. Mr Haalen had been so reassuring that I was sure it would all soon be resolved.

6. By 19th October we were running out of usable chocolate supplies. This was particularly worrying as we had a contract to supply the Chocaganza weekend at the Royal Taunton Hotel on 25th and 26th October. I had specifically set aside the Megadell chocolate for use as it was a better quality than other supplies I already had and now I was running out entirely. I left an urgent message for Mr Haalen at the factory number, sure that he would sort out the matter. However we had heard nothing by 20th October and I therefore sent a fax for the attention of the managing director of the company with my concerns.
7. On 22nd October I spoke to Mr Rupert Bryson of Megadell. I'm afraid my temper frayed when he seemed to know nothing about the problem and was very casual about the whole matter, saying the problem would be investigated when the November delivery was made. I exploded and told him what to do with his chocolate. He then had the cheek to say that we should pay for the September supply immediately. At this I told him there was no way he would get a penny and neither would I pay for anything else delivered, a comment I regretted as soon as I put the phone down, but which felt good at the time.
8. Thereafter I phoned around for other supplies and was re-supplied by my usual supplier on 25th October. We then worked through night and day on the Chocaganza contract to get everything ready but there was simply not enough time to make the more ornate designs ordered. The organisers refused to pay the full fee for supply of the products and I can't say I blame them. We accepted a lesser fee which cut our profit by £2,000. I fear they will not use us next year.
9. During October the three shops' profits were down £1,500 in total compared to the previous year as we did not have enough chocolate items to supply them. I have accounts for the two periods that show this and can produce them if asked. I still have the mouldy chocolate if Megadell care to see it.
10. As far as I was concerned the matter ended in October. I must say I was regretful at losing such a quality supply of chocolate but forgot about the episode being far too preoccupied with keeping the business going and fulfilling contracts with customers. Shortly after this in early November, I began to feel increasingly unwell, always tired and lethargic which I put down to heavy work commitments. Regrettably I let the paperwork slip and have only just come across Megadell's final demand dated 14th November 2008. On the 12th December I was injured in a car crash and was rushed to hospital. I remained in hospital until 20th February. I was dumbstruck to receive the judgment a few weeks ago. It seems very harsh that Megadell are seeking to claim from me for ending the contract. In my view I was totally justified in doing so.
11. I do feel this matter has got totally out of hand. Perhaps if I had known about Megadell's claim earlier I could have sorted this out. I'm aware that I will have to accept some responsibility for letting things get this far. I really need this whole matter sorted out as quickly as possible and at maximum benefit to me.
12. The funny thing is that even after all this hassle I would consider being resupplied by Megadell if I can be clear about the terms. The chocolate that was properly supplied was of a better quality than my original supplier—people buying from the shops actually mentioned it and I haven't found anything else as good. I would be interested in ordering about 500 kilogrammes per month from them. I'd want a personal assurance from their managing director that I would have no more problems and prompt attention if I had any more complaints though.

IN THE TAUNTON COUNTY COURT Claim No. TA501008

BETWEEN

MEGADELL FOODS LIMITED Claimant

and

ANGUS WARLEY (t/a CHOC FOLIE) Defendant

PARTICULARS OF CLAIM

1. At all material times the Claimant was a company engaged in the import and sale of foodstuffs to retail outlets and the Defendant was a sole trader engaged in the manufacture and retail sale of chocolate confectionery to the general public.
2. By a written agreement dated 11th July 2008 between the Claimant and the Defendant, the Claimant agreed to sell to the Defendant 6,000 kilogrammes of premium grade Belgian chocolate. The chocolate was to be delivered in 12 monthly instalments of 500 kilogrammes per instalment at a total price of £15,120.
3. There were express terms of the contract that:
   (i) Deliveries would be in the first half of each month, commencing in September 2008;
   (ii) Payment would be made monthly against invoices drawn by the Claimant;
   (iii) Payment would be made to the Claimant by the Defendant 30 days after delivery of the invoice and interest was payable thereafter at a rate of 12.75% per annum.
4. Pursuant to the contract the Claimant delivered to the Defendant 500 kilogrammes of chocolate on 6th September 2008 and 500 kilogrammes of chocolate on 4th October 2008.
5. The Defendant has failed and refused to pay the sum of £2,520 or any part thereof under invoices drawn by the Claimant for the deliveries.
6. By a telephone conversation on 22nd October 2008 the Defendant purported to terminate the contract. Further by his conduct in failing and/or refusing to pay the sums due as set out in paragraph 5 above the Defendant evinced an intention no longer to be bound by the contract and therefore repudiated the contract.
7. By reason of the matters set out above the Claimant has lost the benefit of the contract and has thereby suffered loss and damage.

PARTICULARS OF LOSS AND DAMAGE

Loss of profit on the sale of 5,000 kilogrammes of chocolate @ £0.82 per kilogramme .... £4,100.

8. The Claimant claims interest under the terms of the contract on the sum claimed in paragraph 5 above from 30 days after the delivery of the invoices at the contractual rate of 12.75% per annum amounting to £47.52 to the date of the issue of the summons in this action and at a daily rate thereafter of £0.88 per day.
9. Further the Claimant claims interest under section 69 of the County Courts Act 1984 on the sums claimed in paragraph 7 above at such rate and for such period as the Court thinks fit.

AND the Claimant claims:

(1) Under paragraph 5 above the sum of £2,520;

(2) Under paragraph 7 above damages for breach of contract;

(3) Under paragraph 8 above contractual interest;

(4) Under paragraph 9 above interest under section 69 of the County Courts Act 1984.

STATEMENT OF TRUTH

DATED 15th December 2008

Made on behalf of the Applicant
Witness: A Warley
1st Statement of Witness
Exhibits: AW1
Dated: 27.2.2009

IN THE TAUNTON COUNTY COURT Claim No TA501008
BETWEEN

MEGADELL FOODS LIMITED Claimant/Respondent

and

ANGUS WARLEY (t/a CHOC FOLIE) Defendant/Applicant

WITNESS STATEMENT OF ANGUS WARLEY
IN SUPPORT OF APPLICATION
TO SET ASIDE JUDGMENT IN DEFAULT

1. I live at 10, The Close, Swainton, Bridgwater, Somerset, and I am the proprietor of an unincorporated business called Choc Folie and make this statement in support of my application to set aside judgment in default which was entered on 11th February 2009. In so far as the content of this statement is within my personal knowledge it is true, and in so far as it is not within my personal knowledge it is true to the best of my knowledge, information or belief.

2. I became aware of the Claimant's claim only on 20th February 2009 when the judgment was served upon me at my business address. Regrettably, on 12th December 2008 I crashed my car sustaining a broken leg and other injuries. I was taken to hospital and remained there until 19th February 2009. In fact from October onwards I had been finding it difficult to keep up with all the demands running your own business entails. I know I overlooked the paperwork; I simply didn't have the energy to cope with administrative matters. In all the circumstances I believe I have a valid reason for not replying to the summons as well as a good defence to the Claimant's claim.

3. I accept there was a contract as stated in the Particulars of Claim and the terms stated in that contract. The contract was in the Claimant's standard terms and was agreed by myself and Mr Haalen, a sales representative on behalf of the Claimant. However, there were further terms of the contract that the Claimant company were responsible for the chocolate until acceptance by the purchaser and that any complaint about quality could be investigated at once. Further, as this was a business contract I am advised by my solicitor and believe there was an implied term as to the chocolate being of satisfactory quality.

4. The chocolate supplied on 4th October was of poor quality in that approximately one half had a whitish residue on the surface and was not usable. Attempts were made to reach Mr Haalen by telephone and messages were left on his mobile telephone and at the Claimant's offices. There was no response to these messages. A fax sent to the Claimant on 20th October 2008 in a last attempt to get the chocolate resupplied is marked exhibit 'AW1'.

5. I spoke to a Mr Bryson of the Claimant company around the end of October who said that the problem would be sorted out when the next delivery was made. This was not sufficient as we were suffering losses due to the non-supply. The accounts for our three

shops show a loss of £1,500 profit when compared to the same month last year. We did not have enough chocolate to make up chocolate items to sell in the three shops. I told Mr Bryson that if we were not resupplied at once then we did not wish to be supplied further. The shops were losing approximately £50 per day, not to mention customers long-term, so I believe this was reasonable. We could not wait another week or two.

6. Because of the supply of defective chocolate we had to obtain further supplies. This could not be arranged until 23rd October 2008. We were due to supply goods for a 'Chocaganza' weekend on 25th to 26th October 2008. In the event the goods could not be completed to the ornate style ordered because of the limited time and the organisers have only paid two-thirds of the contract price, cutting our anticipated profit by £2,000.

7. I did not pay for the September chocolate (which was satisfactory) because I considered that the Claimant should sort out the problems with the October chocolate first.

8. I dispute that I ended the contract either impliedly or expressly. I assert that it was the Claimant who ended the contract by failing to resupply Choc Folie with chocolate of merchantable/satisfactory quality. If I am found to have ended the contract I assert I was entitled to do so because of the Claimant's own breach of contract. In any event I dispute the Claimant's loss of profit as stated; the Claimant should have made good its losses. I further believe we have a claim for the loss of profits caused by the supply of defective chocolate both for loss of sales and loss of profits on the 'Chocaganza' contract.

9. In the circumstances I believe I have a valid defence to the Claimant's claim and am entitled to set off my counterclaim against the claim made by the Claimant, and I ask this Honourable Court to set aside the judgment in default obtained by the Claimant on 11th February 2009.

STATEMENT OF TRUTH

Signed: Angus Warley

Dated etc.

Exhibit AW1

CHOC FOLIE LIMITED

Offices:

17, Lebbell Spring Way, Bridgwater, Somerset,
tel 0446 234883 fax 0446 234881

also at

BRIDGWATER	TAUNTON	MINEHEAD
17, Garnet Way,	134, High Street,	94, Long Street,
Bridgwater	Taunton	Minehead

20th October 2008

TO THE MANAGING DIRECTOR, MEGADELL FOODS LIMITED 15, THE ESTATE, CHEAM HILL, SOUTHAMPTON, SO33 7JM

URGENT

I NEED A RESPONSE. PLEASE CONTACT WITHOUT DELAY. CHOCAGANZA WEEKEND THREATENED. SHOP LOSSES MOUNTING.

ANGUS WARLEY, CHOC FOLIE

Made on behalf of the Applicant
Witness: R. Bryson
1st Statement of Witness
Exhibits: none
Dated: 4.3.2009

IN THE TAUNTON COUNTY COURT
BETWEEN

Claim No TA501008

MEGADELL FOODS LIMITED — Claimant/Respondent

and

ANGUS WARLEY (t/a CHOC FOLIE) — Defendant/Applicant

WITNESS STATEMENT OF RUPERT BRYSON OPPOSING THE APPLICATION TO SET ASIDE JUDGMENT IN DEFAULT

1. I am the managing director of Megadell Foods Limited, the Claimant in this action, and make this statement in response to the Defendant's application to set aside judgment in default obtained on 11th February 2009. In so far as the content of this statement is within my personal knowledge it is true, and in so far as it is not within my personal knowledge it is true to the best of my knowledge, information or belief.
2. I oppose the application on the ground that the Claimant has no real prospect of defending this claim. The price claimed is due as the goods were delivered and the time for payment has long passed. The goods were delivered on 6th September 2008 and 4th October 2008 and payment under the contract was due 30 days after delivery of the invoice. On both deliveries the invoice was delivered with the goods. The Defendant does not deny this.
3. The Defendant's defence that the goods were delivered on 4th October is not sustainable. Although I agree that the company did receive a fax from him, it was on October 20th more than two weeks after the delivery. However, the fax did not say what the problem was. When the fax was received I phoned the Defendant to try to find out what the problem was. I offered to have someone examine the goods on the next delivery that would be on 1st November. The Defendant became abusive, said he was not interested in our product, would not pay for anything else and put the phone down. At no point in this conversation did he state the dates on which he needed the chocolate.
4. The Defendant has repudiated the contract by his actions both in what he said in the telephone conversation and in his failure to pay. Our damages claim flows directly from this repudiation.
5. On the 14th November 2008 the Claimant sent a final demand to the Defendant stating clearly that if payment was not made within 14 days court action would be commenced. The Claimant had no response to this letter.
6. The Defendant has little if any prospect of successfully defending this claim. I would respectfully ask this court not to set aside judgment.

STATEMENT OF TRUTH

Signed: Rupert Bryson

Dated: 4th March 2009

5.4.2 Case Study B

PRISTINE CONSERVATORIES AND SUMMER HOUSES LIMITED

and

THE HARROGATE ENCHANTED CONSERVATORY LIMITED

INSTRUCTIONS TO COUNSEL ON BEHALF OF PROPOSED CLAIMANT

Counsel has herewith:

(1) Statement of Patrick Batchelor.

(2) Memo dated 14th March 2009.

Instructing Solicitors act for Mr Patrick Batchelor, owner of Pristine Conservatories and Summer Houses Limited. Mr Batchelor has been advised by ourselves to commence legal proceedings to recover £30,000 owed to him under a building contract dated 10 March 2008. The contract, which Instructing Solicitors approved, was for the erection of a novel retail sales unit comprising six linked conservatories with 'themed' areas for the sale of exotic plants. The work was finished on time and to the specifications stipulated.

The dispute between the parties, whose owners are related by marriage, concerns two areas.

First, Ms Parker, of the Defendant company, alleges breach of clause 15.1.5 of the contract which specifies the fitting of a teak floor to the Japanese Conservatory area. Mr Batchelor states that although a birch wood floor was fitted this was due to an agreed oral variation of the contract.

The second area of dispute concerns the door 'air lock' system which was installed to ensure that the various temperature and humidity levels required by the different areas remained stable. Ms Parker has informed our client in several rather fraught telephone conversations that the system does not work. Mr Batchelor feels that he could rectify any defects if Ms Parker would allow him to visit the site.

Mr Batchelor would rather not commence formal legal proceedings because of the family connection and possible bad publicity, however he will do so if no solution can be found.

Instructing Solicitors have agreed with solicitors for the other side to see whether settlement is possible. Counsel is accordingly instructed.

ASSUME YOUR INSTRUCTIONS ARE RECEIVED IN THE 2ND WEEK OF JUNE 2009

AND THAT EASTER WAS 12TH APRIL 2009

Your fee is £70.

STATEMENT OF PATRICK BATCHELOR

Patrick Batchelor of Golden Towers, Burn Bridge, Harrogate will say:

I am the owner of a successful conservatory and summer house manufacturing and installation business called Pristine Conservatories and Summer Houses Ltd. Business is fairly slow at the moment which is why I may be forced to commence formal legal proceedings against The Harrogate Enchanted Conservatory Ltd, even though it is owned by my sister-in-law.

My company built the premises to house a retail exotic flower shop. It's based on a highly unusual concept which my wife's sister, Felicity Parker, came to me with in late 2007. She told me that she wanted a unit which would feature six themed conservatories of slightly larger than domestic proportions. The conservatories were to be filled with plants based around a particular theme—for example a desert theme using cacti and the like. The areas were to be linked by doors which worked on an air lock principle. She said it was important that the micro-climate in each area be maintained because the plants were very sensitive. One of the conservatories was to be set out in the Japanese style with teak flooring and maple screens.

I agreed to do the job for not much more than cost—£180,000—because of the family relationship. Payment was to be in six instalments.

Work went ahead as planned until early March 2009. We were under pressure to finish the set-up by early April so that she could stock it with plants and open over the Easter weekend (April 12th). Unfortunately our teak supply was disrupted and I could not get the materials for the Japanese floor. I told Felicity about the problem and suggested that we should put a birch wood floor in instead. I got a telephone message that she agreed so I went ahead. When she saw the floor she went mad. She screamed and yelled and said it would have to come out. I told her to get lost since I'd done a damn good job. I don't know why she was so bothered.

Our relationship just got worse in the weeks leading up to Whitsun. I stopped returning her calls because she just got hysterical. She said the air lock system didn't work but she wouldn't let me in to have a look at it. For all I know the customers might have interfered with the system.

Felicity withheld the last £30,000 due to me under the contract. I really do need the money to keep my business alive until the economy picks up. I accept that there might be a problem with the air lock but I can't do anything about it if she won't let me in.

This business is putting a strain on my marriage. My wife, Tamsin, has stopped speaking to Felicity and family relationships are poor. I'm worried that publicity about the dispute might land me with the label 'cowboy'—the local rag would have a field day.

I will sue if I have to though, since my business depends upon it.

MEMO

14.3.09

While You Were Out

Paddy,

Felicity called. She says go ahead with the birch floor.

Anne.

6 Understanding the context

6.1 Putting the negotiation into context

The first step after familiarising yourself with the basics (who your client is, what the case is about, etc) is to ensure that you are clear about the context in which you are going to negotiate. This includes ascertaining from the brief the context of the case (deal-making or dispute resolution), the stage the case has reached (in a dispute resolution, where in the litigation process is it), where the negotiation will take place and what you are being asked to negotiate. All of these aspects can affect the negotiation and therefore need to be taken into account in your preparation and planning.

6.1.1 The stage the case has reached

6.1.1.1 Deal-making negotiation

There is no set pattern for the progress of a deal-making negotiation (eg, agreeing a new commercial contract or partnership agreement). The larger and more complex the deal and the contract, the more negotiations may be spread over time. Your solicitors may have done a fair amount of negotiation already and you may be instructed only for particular aspects in the final stages. This may influence both what is possible and how you approach it.

6.1.1.2 Dispute resolution negotiation

Dispute resolution negotiations are generally heading for court or already being litigated. Check whether a claim has been issued or not. If so, is it still in the early stages (eg, you have been asked to seek an interim injunction just after issue) or is it nearing the end of the process (eg, you are instructed to represent the client at trial)? Whatever stage a case has reached, it is important to consider what procedural possibilities there are for getting information from, or putting pressure on, your opponent and how these procedural possibilities may be used in the negotiation by you or by your opponent.

Before issue

In most cases, solicitors will attempt to negotiate a settlement before any claim has been commenced in an attempt to avoid going to court. It is rare for solicitors to instruct counsel to negotiate at this stage, although it is sometimes done where the solicitor feels that a counsel-to-counsel meeting might be more effective in reaching settlement.

Generally there will be little information and few documents included in a brief prior to issue. There will be no statements of case to define the issues so it may not be very clear precisely what they are. However, you should be able to glean what they are likely to be from the brief or correspondence. There is unlikely to be any evidence (eg, expert reports or evidence of witnesses) as the solicitors will be reluctant to obtain evidence before it is needed as this may add to the client's costs unnecessarily (eg, if the case settles).

An advantage is that your opponent is very unlikely to have seen the evidence provided to you by your client. However, the disadvantage is that, because the lawyers are likely to have been told conflicting versions of events by their clients, your opponent is more likely to be able to surprise you with the evidence available to him or her. In addition, procedural issues will be of less importance, although a pre-action protocol may apply which may raise procedural points. In addition, the possibility of issuing proceedings can be used as a tactic.

Post issue

If a claim has been issued, you need to check precisely where in the process the case is. Have all the statements of case (particulars of claim, defence, counterclaim and defence to counterclaim) been exchanged? Clearly, prior to filing of the defence, only the claimant's case will be set out and the position will be less clear. If all statements of case have been served, you will have a much clearer idea of the issues and the allegations of fact by both sides to be determined by the court. What has or has not been alleged?

Have directions been given as to the exchange of evidence? If not, the information and evidence available will still be limited (eg, there are unlikely to be any documents from the other side, expert reports or witness statements—unless a pre-action protocol applies which requires earlier disclosure). If directions have been given, have both sides complied with them (eg, given disclosure and inspection of all relevant documents, exchanged witness statements, etc)? Could you make use of any appropriate procedural step, for example, to get further evidence?

The further through the litigation process the case has progressed the clearer the issues and evidence available to both sides will be. Although this gives you the advantage of a clearer picture of your opponent's case, the disadvantage is that your opponent will also know more about your case.

Procedural matters become more important and will need to be considered. First, what will happen to the claim will become an item to be negotiated. Secondly, the client may have the option of claiming interim relief such as an interim injunction or interim payment, which can be used as a bargaining tool. Thirdly, either party can take advantage of CPR, Part 36 and make a Part 36 payment (defendant) or a Part 36 offer to settle. This puts pressure on the other side to settle as there are costs consequences of failing to accept the payment/offer.

Court door

A negotiation at the door of the court just before a hearing has particular characteristics (see **4.3.2**). There may be particular pressure to try to settle. If the hearing is an interim one (eg, to seek an interim injunction), there may be reasons why one or both of the parties wish to avoid the hearing or the court making an order. If the hearing is the trial of the case, it is the last stage at which the parties will have control of the outcome rather than leaving it to the judge. The parties may also focus their minds at the last moment on trying to avoid the stress and costs of a full trial. At the door of the court there will also be particular considerations, such as trying to avoid keeping the judge waiting for too long and recording any agreement reached in a consent order.

6.1.2 The circumstances in which the negotiation will take place

Your preparation for the negotiation must take into account both the time which will be available for the negotiation and the circumstances in which it will be conducted. You will prepare differently for a negotiation that will take place in the comfort of chambers and can take as long as is necessary than for a negotiation that will take place outside court with at most, 20 to 30 minutes before you are called into court.

6.1.2.1 Not negotiating at the court door

You may be instructed to conduct a negotiation where there is no immediate court hearing. Thus for example you may be asked to conduct a negotiation in respect of a merger between two companies or a dispute before proceedings are issued. Generally this will mean that you have both time and resources for research, etc to prepare in a more leisurely fashion than where you are instructed to negotiate at the court door. However, it also means that you will need to decide in conjunction with your instructing solicitor the method of negotiation, when it shall happen, who will be there, the time limits on the discussion, etc.

The method

Negotiations may be conducted wholly or partly face-to-face, by exchange of letters or by telephone. You will need to consider the relative pros and cons of each method given the stage of the case, what the client wants, etc. If exchange of letters is inappropriate, should the negotiation take place by phone or in person? It may be that a phone conversation between you and your opposing counsel would be the most efficient way to deal with a relatively straightforward case. However, a more complex case may require a meeting.

Venue for a meeting

If you decide that a meeting is required, decisions will have to be made as to the location (in your or your opponent's chambers or at the offices of the solicitors). If you have any choice about the location of the negotiation, you should make the best you can of it. Is it tactically better to try to hold the negotiation in your chambers where you have everything to hand and you have control over who has coffee, when, etc? Is it better to meet in your opponent's chambers so that you do not have to bother with things like making coffee and it is easier to leave if necessary?

Who will be at the meeting?

You will also need to consider who should attend the meeting. For example, should it be both counsel and solicitors or just counsel-to-counsel? Should the client attend or not? There are no set rules for who should be present at a negotiation, so you should consider what is most appropriate for the case. The barristers appearing for both sides may simply be briefed to meet together. Having solicitors present will be more expensive, but may be useful if, for example, there is a lot of documentation to deal with. It may occasionally be useful to have an expert such as an accountant present for at least part of the negotiation.

Sometimes the clients themselves will wish to be present. This can make it easier for the barrister to take instructions. However, it may also be undesirable because clients may quite unwittingly undermine the strategy or tactics being used with oral interjections or body language. It may be better for clients to be available in (separate!) rooms nearby so that they can be asked for instructions or be briefed on what is happening privately as and when appropriate. If the client is present, the role of the client in the negotiation should be clearly agreed beforehand.

Arrangements for seating and papers

A negotiation can be facilitated or frustrated by simple things like comfortable chairs, adequate table space for papers, etc. To the extent that you have control over matters like this, you can support your strategy and tactics for the case by offering your opponent good provision or inadequate provision in these areas. Do you want to show a competitive start by taking all the space available for your papers, or do you want to make a facilitative start by arranging the chairs more comfortably round the table? If you want to make any point about existing arrangements at the start of a negotiation, you should see this tactically as part of the negotiation itself.

6.1.2.2 Court-door negotiations

Frequently you will have no choice on the above matters as you will be instructed to appear at court on an interim application or for the full hearing and any negotiation will take place at the court door. This will mean that you will have both limited time and few resources available during the negotiation. You may have to work very quickly and with full awareness of the time factor. This requires thorough preparation to ensure you use the time in the negotiation efficiently and effectively.

6.1.2.3 Special circumstances

Are there special circumstances about this case, for example, is the case one such as a settlement in respect of child where, even if it is pre-issue, court approval of the settlement is required to make it binding?

6.1.3 What are you being asked to negotiate?

Chapter 2 (see **2.2**) set out different types of negotiation and how this can influence the negotiation. Your preparation for the negotiation should take into account the practical realities of why the dispute has arisen and the particular circumstances of the parties. Thus the dispute may be purely about what happened in the past (eg, a personal injury claim for damages) or it may include the regulation of future behaviour (eg, a claim for damages for breach of contract and how future deliveries will be made). Clearly you will need to take into account in the latter case that the parties will need to be able to continue in a working relationship and this will affect how you prepare to negotiate. The case may be one which is highly personal (eg, a divorce) or less personal (eg, a claim for repayment of the price of a defective washing machine). Again your preparation needs to take into account any potential emotive issues there may be between the parties.

In addition, you need to be very clear what you are being asked to negotiate. You may be instructed to appear on an application for an interim injunction immediately after issue of proceedings. The claimant may be seeking both an injunction and damages against a defendant who is counterclaiming for damages as well. You must understand precisely what you are authorised to negotiate. Does the client just want you to reach agreement on the matters contained in the injunction (ie, is prepared to accept an undertaking by the defendant provided it is in appropriate terms)? Or does he or she wish to try to resolve the whole case (ie, agree both what will happen on the injunction and the two damages claims)?

6.2 Check you have complete instructions

Your brief should contain clear instructions from your professional client on the context of the case, the stage the case has reached and precisely what you are being asked to do for the lay client (see above). If any of these is not clear, you will need to check with the solicitor.

Where you are briefed to appear in court, the brief may not explicitly also instruct you to negotiate a settlement on behalf of the client. Although generally a barrister has the apparent authority to negotiate in these circumstances you must ensure that you have the actual authority to do so. If it is not clear whether you are actually authorised to negotiate or the extent of your authority is uncertain, check this with your solicitor. You may also consider whether there is anything to be achieved by waiting to negotiate until a slightly later stage in the case. You must discuss this with your solicitor. In addition, you may, for example, wish to check with the solicitor:

- to clarify aspects of your instructions which are unclear (eg, have there been any proposals from the other side for settlement?);
- to ask the solicitor to get some further information from the client (eg, to clarify what the client is not prepared to accept by way of settlement).

In addition, you need to check that you have all the relevant papers and information necessary for you to carry out your instructions. As explained above, the amount of information contained in your brief will depend on the stage it has reached in the litigation process. Taking this into account, you may still wish to ask the solicitor to:

- supply documents that should be available at the stage the case has reached;
- obtain further evidence that is likely to be crucial to a negotiation at this stage rather than just generally relevant to the case.

Your solicitor will not thank you for bothering him or her unnecessarily or asking for things which will increase the costs. You must therefore ensure that any further discussion, request for information or documentation is crucial to carrying out your current instructions.

6.3 Application to Case Study A

The basics

County court claim for debt and damages from our client (the defendant) arising from a breach of commercial contract to supply him with goods; breach alleged is failure to pay price of two instalments and damages for loss of profit due to alleged repudiation by our client. Our client alleges the claimant was in breach and repudiated and that he has a counterclaim for damages.

Stage reached/circumstances of negotiation

Dispute resolution case. Judgment in default entered because our client failed to file a defence in time. Negotiation to take place at court door of client's application to set aside judgment.

Asked to negotiate

A settlement of the whole case. Other side ostensibly opposing application to set aside but also keen to settle.

Papers/instructions

Have particulars of claim and defendant's witness statement to support application to set aside and claimant's witness statement opposing this. Additional statement from client with copy of fax.

6.4 Application to Case Study B

Do the same exercise for Case Study B.

7 Analysis—objectives

7.1 Objectives of the negotiation—strategies compared

A good settlement should reflect what the client wants, the circumstances of the dispute and the parties (eg, whether it is an impersonal commercial dispute or a divorce case), and the underlying legal case (eg, where in the process it is and the relative strengths of the parties' cases on the merits).

As we saw earlier (in **Chapter 3**) the different strategies generally adopted in a negotiation have different objectives and different ways of measuring success, ie, whether or not the objectives have been achieved. The objective of a competitive negotiator is to win, almost at all costs. He or she wants victory! The objective of the cooperative negotiator is to reach a settlement, also almost at all costs. He or she wants agreement! The objective of the collaborative negotiator is more complex. It is to achieve a settlement that is fair and reflects both parties' real needs or interests with the lowest transaction costs relative to desirability of the result (problem-solving negotiator) or a settlement which is objectively fair by some external authoritative norm (principled negotiator).

The more sophisticated approach of the collaborative negotiator (ie, working together to reach a settlement which is fair objectively or when compared with the transaction costs) is more likely to take into account all the relevant factors in a legal negotiation and produce a better settlement than either a straightforward competitive or cooperative approach.

7.2 Useful collaborative techniques

At this point it is useful to set out three of the techniques used by collaborative negotiators (developed by Harvard Law School) to think more deeply and creatively about what the parties want from a settlement before we move on to the practical steps of detailed consideration of objectives.

7.2.1 Separate the people from the problem

Negotiations can centre on the interpersonal relationship rather than the substantive issues which require settlement. This is inefficient, reduces the effectiveness of the negotiators and can result in a less good settlement for the parties. To avoid emotion and personalities interfering in the negotiation, separate people's feelings from the substance being negotiated. 'People' problems may stem from different perceptions: the different parties will almost invariably have different perceptions of the problem. Thus in preparing:

(a) Try to see it from the other side's point of view.

(b) You need not agree with it but try to understand their point of view.

(c) Do not assume they intend to do what you fear.

(d) Do not blame them for your problem.

(e) Consider the perceptions held by each side.

(f) Allow the other side to save face wherever possible. People often hold out because they do not want to be seen to be backing down. So make your proposals as consistent with their principles, past words and deeds as possible.

7.2.2 Focus on interests not positions

Negotiations can focus on the negotiators' statements of their positions rather than on the real interests or needs of the parties. The example given is of two people working in a library. One wants the window open to get fresh air; the other does not want to sit in a draft and wants it closed. Each states their position on whether the window should be open or closed. They limit the negotiation to simply arguing about how much it should be open: a quarter, half, two-thirds, etc, none of which satisfies either of them. Focusing on interests (ie, a solution which provides fresh air without a draft) may produce more alternatives to consider which may in the end satisfy both of them (for example, opening a window in an adjoining room which brings in fresh air without a draft).

Negotiators must differentiate between:

(a) Issues: the matters on which the parties disagree, for example, in a personal injury case, there are the issues of liability, possible contributory negligence and quantum.

(b) Positions: stances or proposals put forward on the issues, for example, the defendant is liable, there is no contributory negligence and the claimant will accept nothing less than £x.

(c) Interests/needs: the real wants or concerns of the parties which underlie the positions, for example, the claimant has suffered substantial injuries, has had to pay substantial medical expenses, has had to take a less taxing job with less income, has had social and recreational activities curtailed because of the injuries, etc, feels very aggrieved about what has happened, feels a loss of self-image because of reduced mobility and job status, etc.

Positional bargaining occurs where negotiators lock themselves into exchanging stances or proposals without finding out what the underlying interests are. Using the principled approach, negotiators try to identify and explore the underlying interests on the basis that there may be some which are shared (ie, both want the same thing, such as a continuing relationship) or, if not shared, compatible (as in the window example above), as well as those which conflict. The techniques suggested for focusing on interests are:

(a) Identify them:

  (i) Seek an understanding of the needs, fears and desires which underlie their position.

  (ii) Try to analyse why an opponent may not agree to what you want; what would be the effect for him or her?

(iii) Be conscious that both sides are likely to have a variety of interests that motivate them.

(iv) Do not overlook the most powerful interests (basic human needs—security, economic well-being, etc).

(v) Write down the interests to help you to remember them and possibly stimulate ideas about how to meet them.

(b) Be prepared to discuss them:

(i) Consider how you can describe your client's interests as clearly as possible. Be specific; make the interests 'come alive'.

(ii) Consider how to acknowledge that his or her interests are part of the problem. Be sympathetic where appropriate.

(iii) Consider telling the other side what your client's interests and needs are first and then tell them your proposals for how those needs can be met (ie, put your reasons before your proposals so they hear the reasons).

(iv) Look forward for solutions, not back to where the problem came from.

(v) Identify your options but be flexible in your approach to each option.

(vi) Be hard in your approach to the problem but soft on the people.

7.2.3 Invent options for mutual gain

Many negotiations are seen as single issue, ie, existing along a single dimension such as the sale of a piece of land where the single issue appears to be the price. If the price is viewed as the single issue, one party's gain is the other party's loss. The more the seller is forced to compromise on price, the more the buyer gains. By inventing options for mutual gain this part of the strategy seeks to avoid the win/lose dynamic by inventing options that can bring gains to both sides. For this reason some writers refer to this part of the principled strategy as 'expanding the pie'.

Central to the concept is the ability to reconsider the issues in the negotiation and view them not as single issue and zero-sum, but multiple issue and integrative. The concept is best illustrated by the often used example of two sisters arguing over an orange. Having finally agreed to split the orange into two, one sister took off all the peel and ate the fruit, whilst the other discarded the fruit and saved the peel for a cake she was making. Neither had stopped to consider the other's underlying reasons for wanting the orange so they missed the opportunity for both to have more of what they wanted.

Consider the following example as an illustration of pie-expanding:

EXAMPLE

An owner of a vineyard and exclusive resort property is in financial difficulty. A local financier is looking to invest capital. A few of the options available are:

Sale

Sale of the resort property and the vineyard.
Sale of the vineyard whilst retaining the resort property.
Sale of the resort property whilst retaining the vineyard.

Lease

Lease the resort property and vineyard and seller continues to manage both.
Lease the resort for a lower price and the seller receives financial assistance in maintaining the vineyard.

Joint venture

Sell 49 per cent of the resort property and vineyard and retain 51 per cent, the seller to continue to manage the resort and vineyard.

One reason that mutually beneficial options are overlooked is the time and commitment they take to generate. The above example has only looked at some of the possibilities and then only in outline. Given the time it takes to create ideas and mutually beneficial options, it is tempting to take what appears to be the short cut of splitting the difference.

Another obstacle to creating mutual options is the assumption of the fixed pie. There is an assumption that the negotiation can only ever be about a single issue and therefore the negotiators do not bother to invent options. Negotiators cannot see the negotiation as being anything other than linear, with winning and losing at opposite ends. In this climate, it is difficult to see the other options that could solve the problem.

Another obstacle is the firmly held belief of many negotiators that how the other side will get what they want is their problem. However, if the other side's interests are not satisfied, you will not reach an agreement. Their problem therefore really is your problem as well.

In order to invent options, you will need to allocate part of your preparation time to this activity. When negotiating in a team, this can make team members uncomfortable. They may be tempted to see option-creating as a process that 'clouds the issue' rather than a process that can in the long run save time and money. You will need to spend time uncritically gathering ideas that could help you solve the problem. Do not attempt to evaluate any of the ideas as you think of them as it is important that you keep the process of inventing and evaluation separate. Inevitably, if you are critical of new ideas, you will stifle their creation. You may collect some outlandish ideas but, if necessary, these can be weeded out at the evaluation stage.

Once you have assimilated the options then you can evaluate them. At the evaluation stage you will be looking to determine how practical, workable and enforceable each solution is and measuring the extent to which it is capable of meeting the interests of both sides of the negotiation. Try to select criteria for evaluating the options. Do not forget the other side's interests at this stage. Try to select options that really are mutually acceptable.

7.3 Using these techniques in your preparation

7.3.1 Separate the people from the problem

In your preparation try to ascertain why the dispute arose, what might have prevented the parties resolving this matter themselves without recourse to litigation and how this might be influencing what they say they want out of any settlement. It is important to try to understand what both sides want from the negotiation and their motivation for that. The context of the case may be important, eg, it may be a family dispute and therefore highly charged emotionally, with both parties actually unclear about precisely what they do want to get out of the negotiation. What may appear to be a very impersonal commercial dispute may in fact contain some personal issues, eg, a contested claim for breach of a supply contract may involve two parties who are also friends or have built up their businesses together in a small town. In both cases emotions may be interfering

with sound judgement. In such case it may be down to you to seek to persuade them to consider what realistically can be achieved by a settlement and to 'separate the people from the problem'.

7.3.2 Distinguishing legal positions from needs and interests

It is important to identify what your client wants from the negotiation and to distinguish this from their legal position, particularly in a case involving a past dispute. The parties in a legal dispute will almost invariably want a practical solution to the dispute. While they may feel very strongly about the case and say they want to 'win', when it is all boiled down, the 'win' is generally translated into practical outcomes such as a payment of money, an apology, a new contract.

In a very rare case a person in dispute may have as an objective the defeat of his or her opponent in court or have a genuine reason for wanting the case to proceed to trial (see **4.2.4**). For some people it is their 'day in court' and an opportunity to 'be heard' which is of utmost importance. Where a client takes the position that his or her prime goal is to win against their opponent, you need to check that he or she understands what this means in practical terms and that this is genuinely what he or she wants. If you are certain that this really is what the client wants at the expense of all else, there is clearly little point in attempting to negotiate with the other side.

In the overwhelming majority of cases, clients want a practical outcome from the litigation (eg, payment of money) and you need to separate the merits of the case (eg, the client's position that he or she has a very strong case and should win) from these practical objectives (the client's needs and interests). The practical objectives are the matters to be negotiated; the merits of the case can be used to argue and persuade your opponent to give your client all or much of the practical outcomes he or she is seeking. Thus, in planning your objectives of the negotiation, you should focus on what practically your client wants from it, which we deal with in this chapter. The merits of the case are used to formulate the arguments or reasons which will support what you propose to do by way of settlement in the negotiation—these are dealt with in **Chapters 8** and **9** (persuasion and argument)—and to assist you to judge whether or not any proposal is reasonable.

7.3.3 Inventing options for mutual gain

When considering what your client wants, it is important to think laterally, to consider both what your client wants and what the opponent might want in order to see whether there is any way to 'expand the pie'. Thus, for example, the claimant may be most concerned about the amount of money he or she can get from the negotiation and the defendant concerned about having time to pay. A mutually beneficial arrangement may be that the defendant will pay more provided he or she can delay payment or pay by instalment. Alternatively you may find that there are shared objectives. The dispute may be about a restraint of trade clause in a contract of supply of goods: the buyer alleging that the seller must supply to him exclusively and the seller alleging that there is no such clause. Both wish to continue trading if the current problem is resolved. Identifying what both parties really want and looking at ways in which that could be avoided in the future (eg, by an appropriate term in the contract) may assist to resolve how to deal with the current problem. Thus you may find that the buyer only needs exclusivity in his town and the seller wants to expand nationally. An exclusivity clause which reflects this may suit both parties.

7.4 What your client wants from a settlement

The solicitor may have summarised in the brief what the client is seeking. The client's statement should contain not only information about what happened but also information about what he or she wants. However, this is unlikely to be set out in a precise list of items. Other documents, eg, correspondence between solicitors, may also give you information about the client's objectives.

You will have to read through the instructions, any correspondence, etc, to determine, based on both the basis of what is expressly stated and common sense, the full range of potential objectives of the client. Many people think of legal negotiations as being strictly about how much money will change hands. While many negotiations do have a financial element, some do not and most will include non-financial objectives as well. Even where the claim is for money (ie, damages), it is important to try to see behind stated objectives to the client's needs or interests (eg, in a road accident claim, the client may be seeking damages to cover a variety of needs including loss of wages, other benefits lost from being laid off at work as a result of the accident, medical expenses, the cost of repairing the car, etc). Get the full list of items.

You will also need to check whether there are any limits or specific instructions on what the client will or will not accept. The instructions may merely state that you should get the 'most possible' or that the client is 'very reluctant' to pay anything on the claim. Alternatively, the instructions may state very clearly that the client will not pay more than £x or accept less than £y. Finally you must determine, if possible, what the client's priorities are. What does he or she want most from a settlement and what things are less valued and could be forgone?

If you are not clear about the full range of the client's objectives, the client's priorities and any general or specific limitations of the client, not only do you risk acting outside your instructions (a professional conduct issue) but you are also more likely to reach a settlement which the client will not approve. This will of course mean that time and costs will be wasted. If in doubt, ask.

In considering both what the client's interests are and the priorities given to them, you need to be conscious that the interests identified and the priorities given are those which accord with the client's values, needs and interests and not your own. A client from a different cultural or ethnic background or of a different sex may well have very different views from you as to what he or she wishes to achieve in the case. Your knowledge of the norms, expectations, etc of that particular culture may be very limited. Your lack of experience or knowledge of that culture may mean you are working on stereotypes and wrong preconceptions. In addition, just because someone is of the same sex, ethnic and class background as you, you should not assume they view the case in the same way you do. Try to be conscious of your expectations and how these may be influencing your view of your client's objectives.

7.4.1 Get the whole list as precisely as possible

It is important that you consider carefully the full range of potential objectives of the client. Read your instructions carefully with the context of the case in mind. Look beyond the stated goals at the underlying reasons and factors that might influence those goals. A client will often not state everything that he or she hopes to achieve with the case. Consider both why the problem which forms the subject of the dispute arose and what, if any, future relationship the client may wish or be compelled to have with the opponent. Consider all your client's needs and interests. For example, if your client is seeking damages for personal injury, what needs does he or she have, both immediately (eg, medical expenses) and in the future (payment of a housekeeper to undertake work he or she can no longer do). Are there alternatives to a money payment which might better satisfy your client's objectives or be an equally viable alternative?

You should try to think as broadly as possible about your client's possible objectives, considering the full range of potential objectives that may include any or all of the following.

7.4.1.1 Money payments

Most civil cases involve some claim for money. Be clear precisely what the money claim is about and what precisely the client wants or needs the money for (see the above example of a personal injury claim for damages). In a claim for damage/loss of property, ascertain whether it is in respect of one item or several items, the amount claimed in respect of each item and how the amounts are calculated. Thus, for example, if there is a claim for loss of profit, how has this been calculated? If the claim is for damage to an item, is the claim for the cost of replacing it and, if so, has it already been replaced or is this just an estimate of what it will cost? Alternatively, if the cost is to fix the item, is it an estimate or the actual cost already incurred by the client? Consider whether the money claim may be satisfied by other means (eg, replacement of the item damaged).

Do not forget associated matters. What is the total sum claimed? When should it be paid? Should it be paid as a lump sum or in instalments? Is there a claim for interest? If so, what is the rate of interest and over what period has it been calculated? What are the tax implications of payment of a sum? These can be equally important and give you room for manoeuvre in the negotiation (see **Chapter 11**).

7.4.1.2 Legal rights

The client may be claiming a legal right or want a legal right to be confirmed. How might this be achieved? Is a declaration of the court needed or would written confirmation by the other party suffice? Is there any way of establishing the right apart from a declaration (eg, a charge on the register against the land)? Thus there may be a dispute over a right of way and the client seeks a legally binding confirmation that it exists (or does not exist). How might this be done?

7.4.1.3 Terms of any future relationship with the opponent

The parties may be in dispute but still wish to continue a relationship in the future. Thus, for example, there may be a dispute about a commercial contract for the supply of goods that the parties wish to resolve, but your client also wishes to continue trading. Does the dispute have an impact on the terms on which they will continue to trade? If so, which terms and what does the client want in respect of those terms? Alternatively, the circumstances may be such that the parties, whether they wish to or not, are compelled to continue some form of relationship in the future. Thus, for example, they may be neighbours. Are there any matters which need to be resolved about future dealings which could or should form part of the negotiation?

7.4.1.4 Personal objectives

The client may wish to achieve something quite personal, for example, an apology from the opponent.

7.4.1.5 Time limits

There may be time limits which you need to consider. Thus, the client may need to have something done by a specified date. Alternatively, the client may not be able to pay any money before a certain date. In addition, once issued, the case itself will have built in time limits, ie, procedural steps which must be taken within times set by the court, which may be open to negotiation.

7.4.1.6 Costs of the litigation

Once lawyers are instructed, every step taken in the case costs money. Who pays the costs is always something you should consider. The costs include not only those of the particular event at which you are instructed to negotiate (whether this is a free-standing negotiation or one which you are doing immediately prior to a court hearing) but also all other costs to date. Check that you know what these are. Although you may not have specific figures, you should at least have a rough idea of the overall costs.

Costs are a consideration even if the case is being run on a conditional fee basis. First, the client will still have to pay for all disbursements (ie, non-lawyer expenses). In fact a barrister's fee may be a disbursement if he or she is not also acting on a conditional fee arrangement with the solicitor. Secondly, just because the client is not paying the lawyers up front and may not pay if he or she loses, the lawyers are still expending time and time is money! Most conditional fee agreements contain terms for what happens in the case of settlement and you need to be clear what this is.

7.4.1.7 Form of the agreement

Consider what form any agreement should take. Is an oral agreement through counsel sufficient? Should there be an exchange of letters? Is more formality required? Should a detailed contract be drawn up by solicitors on the basis of the heads of agreement specified as a result of the negotiation settlement? Does the agreement need to be in a particular form to be enforceable, eg, an agreement in respect of land? Alternatively, is a court order needed or desirable?

7.4.1.8 The court hearing/the case as a whole

Barristers generally negotiate cases at the court door, either of an interim hearing (eg, for an interim injunction) or the final trial of the case. It is important not to forget that, in addition to reaching a settlement on the above matters, you need to consider what you will suggest on these in the negotiation.

Where there is an interim hearing, you will need to consider what will happen if you reach settlement. What would be most appropriate for your client, given his or her objectives? Undertakings from one or both of the parties? A consent order? Dismissal of the application?

Clearly, where you negotiate a settlement outside the door of the court immediately before trial, you will have to consider the best option for your client in respect of the case. Again this may be undertakings, a consent order or a discontinuation of the case. Where you are instructed to appear on an interim hearing, consideration of the case as a whole may or may not be within your instructions (see **Chapter 6**). If it is, you will need to plan what you will suggest on this. A stay on proceedings? Discontinuation of the case?

7.4.2 Limitation on what the client will accept

Sometimes instructions will be very general, and the barrister is simply asked to get as close as possible to the client's objectives, with any settlement being subject to client approval. However, there may be some specific instructions in the case. For example, the client may specify the least that he or she is prepared to accept, or may make it clear that in no circumstance does he or she wish to go to court. Check whether there are any:

(a) Specific parameters: the client will not accept any settlement in which he or she does not get a particular item or term, eg, the client must have the right of way confirmed by some enforceable legal method.

(b) General parameters: the client specifies a maximum and/or minimum limit for a particular issue but is otherwise flexible, eg, the client will not pay more than £x to the opponent.

7.4.3 Establish the client's priorities

Even in a simple case, a client will often have several objectives. Having identified all the client's objectives, you need to prioritise them. The criterion for prioritisation is the importance to the client. Thus a client who has been wrongfully dismissed may put obtaining an apology from the employer high on the list of objectives. You must be aware of this and give it its proper weight in the negotiation. Although financial objectives will frequently be important, do not always assume they are exclusively sought or the most important objective.

The client's priorities may have particular implications for a whole case. You may need to give more attention in preparation and more time in the negotiating process to the issue that is most important to the client. For example, the future relationship may be more important than recouping past losses and you may therefore spend much more time on this in the negotiation.

7.4.4 Make a clear, detailed note of the client's objectives

Having done the appropriate analysis so that you have identified all of the client's potential objectives, any limitations on any of them and the client's priorities, write them down so that you can bear them in mind while negotiating and so that you can check that any agreement you finally reach is within your client's instructions.

7.5 What the opponent may want from a settlement

In most cases there will have been a fair amount of communication between the parties and their solicitors about the case prior to you being briefed. There will therefore be some information in the brief about the case for the other side from which you can at least get some idea of what he or she might be seeking. Although this information will be less complete than for your client, you should undertake the same exercise in considering the opponent's objectives as you have done for your client.

Consider carefully what the other side is likely to want to obtain from the negotiation. Within the framework of the legal case, look at what factors might be motivating them to settle and what their interests and underlying needs might be. Their objectives are likely to be as wide-ranging as your client's. Read the brief and documents carefully and consider comments from the client and solicitor and any previous correspondence or dealings with the opponent to ascertain what information you do have about the opponent and his or her likely objectives. Using this information, your knowledge of the potential range of objectives (eg, see the times set out above at **7.4.1**) and common sense, consider precisely what they are likely to want from a settlement, what their priorities might be and any limitations they might have on what they are prepared to consider by way of settlement.

7.6 Shared and opposing objectives

Once you have identified and attempted to prioritise the objectives of both sides, you should consider whether there are any which are shared (ie, that both parties want), compatible (ie, where the parties value things differently), or whether they genuinely conflict. This assists in a variety of ways. It enables you to see exactly what is genuinely in dispute (ie, what really needs to be negotiated as opposed to merely agreed) and enables you to formulate possible offers which are almost certain to appeal to the other side while also achieving your client's objectives.

One example of a shared objective is where both parties want a continuing relationship, either personal or business. Thus, for example, two parties may have fallen out over a past business deal but both have good reasons for wishing to trade with each other in future. They may not agree fully on the terms for this future dealing which have to be negotiated but a strong common factor is the desire to continue the relationship.

7.7 Application to Case Study A

What does our client want from a settlement?

(a) Judgment set aside.

(b) Would like to continue trading with Megadell:

   (i) good quality product; better than other suppliers; comments from customers;

   (ii) would order 500 kilos a month;

   (iii) wants a personal assurance from managing director that there would be no more problems and prompt attention to complaints.

(c) Pay the claimant as little as possible on its claims which include:

   (i) the price of the two instalments:

   - £1,260 for 1st instalment;
   - £1,260 for 2nd instalment;
   - contractual interest;

   (ii) the lost profit on the remainder of the contract: £ 4,100 plus interest.

(d) Get as much as possible on his own claims:

   (i) £2,000 for Chocaganza weekend;

   (ii) £1,500 for loss of profit in shops.

(e) Have his costs to date paid by the claimant:

   (i) £175 for hearing;

   (ii) £250 generally.

(f) Not pay the claimant's costs—£?

(g) Have the whole case dropped/not pay any further legal fees:

(i) claimant drop his claim;

(ii) defendant not have to continue his counterclaim.

Are there any limits on what he will accept?

500 kilo limit on any future supply from claimant(?)

What are his priorities?

Clearly getting judgment set aside is of prime concern.
Getting something on the money claims/pay as little as possible:

- Claimant's total is £6,620 plus interest.
- Defendant's total is £3,500 plus interest.

Future trading—appears to be less important than the money.
Costs—get some of his costs paid/resist paying claimant's costs.
Case dropped including his counterclaim (provided above are satisfactory).

What does the other side want?

On money—the reverse of the above.
Query do they want to continue trading?

7.8 Application to Case Study B

Do the same exercise for Case Study B.

8

Persuasion—the role of argument

In this chapter we consider the different methods of persuading an opponent to make compromises used in the various strategies. We then consider the role of argument in being persuasive. Finally we have a brief look at evaluating the case—an essential step in determining how to use argument persuasively. In the next chapter we will consider how to prepare to use argument most effectively in a negotiation.

8.1 The role of persuasion in negotiation

Chapter 2 set out various definitions of negotiation which include 'confer (with another) with a view to securing compromise' and 'a basic means of getting what you want from others'. It is 'back-and-forth communication designed to reach an agreement when you and the other side have some interests that are shared and others that are opposed' and 'a process in which two or more participants attempt to reach a joint decision on matters of common concern in situations where they are in actual or potential disagreement or conflict'.

Common to all the definitions is mutual need for an agreement. Whether or not the parties are in actual or potential conflict, have shared interests or equal bargaining strength or not, both sides need something from one another and have come to the negotiating table in order to get it via a negotiated settlement. A very large part of the skill of negotiation therefore lies in persuading the other side to give you what you want.

To persuade means to cause somebody to believe or to do something. There are a variety of techniques that can be used to persuade: from extremely brutal methods (eg, threats of physical harm), through to subtle methods that work on the subconscious (eg, subliminal advertising). There are numerous books covering the subject; many of them are based on successful sales techniques such as how salespeople get you to buy things you do not want. Some books are based on empirical research of what actually happens in negotiations. What is clear from the literature is that, while negotiators do not generally use the two extreme ends of the range, they do use a wide variety of techniques that vary from behaviour bordering on bullying to the use of reasoning and rational explanation.

8.2 Persuasive techniques of the three strategies

The three strategies—competitive, cooperative and collaborative—take very different approaches to negotiating and these approaches depend on different methods of persuading the other side to compromise. We consider each one in turn.

8.2.1 Competitive negotiators

8.2.1.1 Taking a strong stance, being tough!

Competitive negotiators seek to persuade by adopting a strong stance, hoping to be seen as tough, determined and unyielding in order to intimidate the opponent and push him or her to move significantly towards the competitive negotiator because he or she believes this is the only way to reach a compromise. This strong stance is underlined by being on the offensive, single-minded, out to win and not bothered by doubts or indecision that may produce a more reconciling approach. Competitive negotiators will seek to control the negotiation and will therefore generally take the initiative at the start, the aim being to gain the upper hand. They will maintain pressure throughout by stressing the sense of urgency, the need for rapid progress, to 'deal with this issue now'. This often leaves the opponent little space to exert pressure back. The competitive negotiator may use additional tactics to increase this pressure, eg, using 'the deadline' (real or fictitious) and the 'walkout' (see **Chapter 14**).

Competitive negotiators seek to take every advantage and concentrate on achieving their objectives. The objectives of the opponent have little or no relevance to them. They are slow to express sympathy for or even acknowledge the opponent's position. They are not interested in any rational or fair analysis of the case. Their discussion about the two sides will be done in an attempt to exaggerate the strength of their case and stress the weakness of the opponent's case.

Competitive negotiators will also use a variety of techniques to confuse or divert the opponent away from obtaining information or discussing issues they find difficult (eg, because it exposes a weakness in their case). They may stick to one point tenaciously, refusing to discuss any other issue. Alternatively, they may jump to another issue when discussion on the current one gets too difficult.

Competitive negotiators generally distrust their opponent and assume all effective negotiators are competitive. They see cooperative negotiators as weak, naïve and deserving of exploitation. They interpret cooperative behaviour as a sign of weakness and seek to exploit it.

8.2.1.2 Using an argumentative style

A negotiator using a competitive strategy may also use a competitive style which tends to be argumentative rather than conciliatory, using emphatic language, tone of voice, etc to appear tough and uncompromising. A competitive negotiator presents from the basic standpoint that he or she is always right and/or superior and the opponent wrong and/or inferior. A competitive negotiator may also use blame as a tool in creating the impression that the problems are caused by the opponent or his or her client. While not always intended to be so by the competitive negotiator, many of the aspects of the competitive style are perceived by the recipient as aggression towards him or her. Some competitive negotiators positively seek to cause discomfort to the opponent, for example by being sarcastic, using ridicule, making accusations and threats (within ethical limits), and by using intimidation in an attempt to wear down the opponent on the basis that some people have real trouble with coping with aggression and will adopt avoiding behaviour to stop it.

Few people using a competitive strategy with a competitive style will use all the stylistic techniques described above as this would result in belligerent and obvious behaviour. They are more likely to use different aspects of the style at different times throughout the negotiation. A person with a competitive strategy may, however, not adopt a competitive style. Competitive negotiators are as able to be charming and friendly as cooperative ones.

8.2.2 Cooperative negotiators

8.2.2.1 Taking a conciliatory stance, producing trust and reciprocal behaviour

Cooperative negotiators generally act on the belief that by being overtly reasonable themselves they can persuade their opponent to be reasonable and make compromises. They take a conciliatory stance, and want to be seen as trustworthy, open, honest, ethical and fair to engender trust in their opponent. They will seek to be seen as concerned about both their own client and the other side and reaching a fair agreement. They possibly concentrate more on reaching agreement than on what the agreement actually gives the client and appear to be concerned more with maintaining the relationship than getting the best result.

Cooperative negotiators focus on building and maintaining an open, honest and trusting environment and avoiding the generation of conflict. They do not want to be seen as taking advantage or using questionable tactics to achieve their ends or as being aggressive. They want to trust the other side and have the other side trust them. They hope that this will persuade their opponent to act in the same 'spirit of cooperation' to reach agreement.

8.2.2.2 Using a pleasant and friendly manner

Cooperative negotiators generally match their style with their strategy. They are courteous and pleasant. They seek to deal with the opponent on an equal footing—they do not try to undermine or intimidate. They use non-threatening language and present in a manner which is 'reasonable' rather than emphatic or forceful.

8.2.3 Collaborative negotiators

8.2.3.1 A rational stance—working together to solve the problem

Collaborative negotiators seek to work together to further both parties' interests and aims, to maximise the gain for both, in order to achieve a 'win/win' settlement. They assume that negotiation is not simply about each side stating their position, that it is more complex than each side simply determining the best they can get, the worst they will accept (the bottom line) and then doing an information exchange and 'concession dance' to meet somewhere between the two opposing sides' bottom lines. This behaviour (ie, that used in both competitive and cooperative negotiation) is known as 'positional'. The principled and problem-solving approaches have specific techniques to enable both parties to look more closely at the substance of the negotiation and the standard against which the settlement will be judged and to do this jointly. Collaborative negotiators assume that few negotiations are about a single issue or zero-sum. Basically they seek to persuade by reducing the competitive element of the negotiation and emphasising the rational and objective aspects. We considered some of the techniques used by collaborative negotiators in **Chapter 7** when considering the parties' objectives: separating the people from the problem (**7.3.1**) and focusing on interests not positions (**7.3.2**).

It is useful here to consider two additional techniques used by those who developed the principled approach. Both techniques influence the persuasiveness of negotiators where collaborative techniques are used because they assist the negotiators to gauge whether or not to agree to proposals for a settlement.

Developing a BATNA

'BATNA' stands for Best Alternative to a Negotiated Settlement and is the principled negotiator's equivalent to the 'bottom line' used by a competitive or cooperative negotiator.

The purpose of a 'bottom line' in a competitive or cooperative strategy is to ensure that the negotiator resists pressure exerted in the negotiation and does not succumb to temptation and give away more than is good for the client. However, determining when to walk away from a negotiation on the basis of a single 'bottom line' is a rigid approach and can be very restrictive. It assumes that negotiation is just about trading concessions and moving along a continuum to a single point beyond which that party will not go. It does not take into account information received or alternatives proposed in the negotiation, options which may be considered and which, although they technically do not meet the bottom line, may in fact satisfy the client's real interests.

Planning the BATNA is an important part of preparation. Rather than looking at what the client ought to get out of the negotiation, an analysis is made of the client's underlying interests to determine the options available which best satisfy those needs. It is then possible to identify the alternatives against which to compare proposals made in the negotiation.

It is also necessary to consider the BATNA for the other party to assess what proposals they may or may not accept.

The strength of the negotiating position depends on the attractiveness of both your and your opponent's BATNAs. The better the BATNA, the stronger the position. It is therefore important to consider and develop the BATNA by making a list of possibilities if no agreement is reached. These can be converted into practical options to identify which is the best. The stronger the BATNA, the more useful it is to disclose it to the other side.

Developing objective criteria

The main difference between a negotiation and an adjudication is the lack of an independent third party to determine the outcome. The negotiators themselves have to decide whether to accept a proposed outcome/settlement. Principled negotiators attempt to bring an objective element into a negotiation by the use of objective criteria. This means that the settlement is based on an objective standard and not on the will or opinion of one or other of the parties (ie, on principle not pressure).

- Develop objective criteria by use of precedent and independent standards, eg, an expert where appropriate.
- Frame issues as a joint search for objective criteria.
- Use reason not positional statements to determine the standard to apply.
- Be open to reason but closed to pressure.

Settlement standards

The persuasive aspect of both the use of a BATNA and objective criteria is that they assist negotiators in developing a more flexible and rational 'settlement standard' against which to judge proposals than a simple bottom line.

8.2.3.2 A reasonable but firm manner

Collaborative negotiators are likely to adopt a manner which falls somewhere between that used by the competitive and the cooperative negotiator. Unlikely to be overtly aggressive or argumentative, they will nevertheless be firm and emphatic when necessary. While acknowledging the emotional aspects of a negotiation or a party's needs, they are unlikely to use emotive language as a tactic. The language and tone used is more likely to be objective and professional, demonstrably not personal or emotive.

8.2.4 Summary

None of these strategies recognise explicitly the role of argument in their persuasive techniques and many negotiators would deny that they placed any reliance on the use of argument. However, all of these strategies rely on argument to some degree. Lawyers who negotiate use argument in one form or another even if they are not consciously aware of it. Yet lack of understanding of the role of argument can lead to mistakes and disappointing results. Negotiators who understand the use of argument in persuasion, can distinguish different types of argument and know how and when to use it have significant advantages over those who do not. This is true whether the negotiation is dispute-resolving (ie, that which seeks to settle conflicts about historical events) or deal-making (ie, that which seeks to regulate future conduct), whether it concerns one issue or several, or whether it is distributive or integrative. We therefore now turn to considering what argument is and how it can be used.

8.3 The use of argument to persuade

8.3.1 Argument—what does it mean?

Argument can be used to mean a reason advanced (for or against a proposition or course of action); hence 'it is arguable that X'. Alternatively, it can be used to mean a heated exchange or discussion. Using argument in the first sense, ie, using methodical reasoning to persuade, must be distinguished from its use in the second sense, ie, being argumentative, becoming heated in discussion. Many negotiations founder because the negotiators fail to make this distinction. Because they equate argument with being argumentative, they spend little time or energy considering the arguments used, distinguishing between different types of argument and their possible impact. A lawyer working in the adversarial system of dispute resolution can easily fall into an argumentative approach because of the emphasis on winners and losers. However, a good advocate who uses argument well in court can use argument equally well in a negotiation.

The ability to use reasoned argument persuasively is a skill necessary to be an effective lawyer whether acting as an advocate or a negotiator. Argument should always be used with a specific purpose in mind. To use argument persuasively as an advocate or negotiator, you need to identify the purpose of your arguments and the type of arguments used and to judge accurately whether your arguments are fulfilling their purpose. In court, merit-based arguments (ie, those based on the merits of the case) are used to persuade the judge to find in your client's favour. A negotiator uses argument to persuade the other side to move towards him or her in the negotiation.

There are cases in which argument does not play a role, eg, where both sides discover they have compatible interests and desire the same outcome (see the example, above, of the sisters who both wanted the orange but one wanted the peel for baking, the other the fruit to eat—**7.2.3**). Simple exchange of information and requests will enable both negotiators to get what they want for their clients. Not surprisingly, such cases are extremely rare. In most negotiations the parties want different outcomes (eg, they both want half the rind and fruit of the orange) and this requires a reconciliation of views as to what compromises should be made and what a reasonable settlement is. Argument can be used on both counts, first, to justify compromise and, secondly, to persuade the other side as to what a reasonable settlement standard is.

8.3.2 Argument and settlement standards

As noted above, a settlement standard may be developed by using a combination of the two collaborative techniques of developing BATNAs and using objective criteria to assess the alternatives available to the client. This may be purchasing an item under negotiation from another source. This may give an objective criteria against which to gauge an offer (ie, what is the usual price for such an item).

In the case of a litigated dispute, the potential solutions may have been narrowed by the process. The only alternative to settlement may be going to trial. The likely outcome could be seen as an objective standard against which to gauge offers. Thus in negotiations concerning disputes which are or are likely to be litigated, the settlement standard against which to gauge offers is likely to be the outcome of the case. The merits of the case will therefore matter and arguments based on the merits are likely to be very persuasive.

8.3.3 Types of argument

Argument in a legal negotiation can take many forms, eg, factual, legal, practical, personal, moral, social, normative, etc. When considering how to persuade an opponent, it pays to be able to make the distinction between different types of argument as, depending on the context, some types of argument are likely to be more effective than others. We now consider those forms of argument which can be used.

8.3.3.1 Merit-based argument—using the law and the facts

As noted above, arguments based on the lawyer's view of the facts and relevant legal principles form the basis of arguments used in the court room. These arguments are equally useful, if not essential, in a negotiation, particularly in respect of a settlement to resolve a litigated dispute. As settlement positions are closely related to the legal principles and relevant facts, legal and factual argument can be a useful part of a negotiator's persuasion arsenal. The lawyers relate what they seek by way of settlement to the likely outcome in court. For example, the claimant's lawyer in a personal injury case may suggest a figure acceptable to his or her client based on a finding of liability on the basis that the facts do not support contributory negligence. Conversely, his or her opponent may suggest a lower figure which takes into consideration contributory negligence on the basis that the facts do support such a finding.

Legal argument can be defined as argument concerning the interpretation of legal rules and principles from whatever source they may be derived, be it statute or common law, whether concerned with substance or procedure (including the rules on evidence). So, for example, a dispute may arise concerning whether a client has received the appropriate notification of events. For the notification to be valid, it is a statutory requirement that the client must receive written notice at his or her 'principal place of abode'. The meaning of the words 'principal place of abode' and what they are intended to cover will form the basis of the argument.

Factual argument focuses on disputes over what has happened, is happening or is likely to happen and how this will affect the legal principles relevant to the dispute. So, for example, in a dispute-resolving negotiation concerning a contract for the sale of goods, factual argument may be concerned with whether or not the goods were delivered on the date specified in the contract (that term not being in dispute).

In legal negotiation the most common form of argument is probably factual, as most disputes requiring negotiation are concerned with the application of settled law to controversial facts. For example, in a contract for the sale of goods it is clear that the law requires the goods to be of satisfactory quality, but there could be considerable debate over whether or not the goods delivered met this standard.

It is not at all uncommon for legal negotiation to require both factual and legal argument where, for example, the applicable legal principle is ambiguous and the facts relating to the rule are also controversial. To use the example above, legal argument may be concerned with interpreting the meaning of 'principal place of abode' and whether the defendant's country home falls into this category. Factual argument may be based on how many days out of the last year the defendant actually spent at the country home.

8.3.3.2 Practical arguments—the parties' circumstances

By practical arguments, we mean those arguments which relate to the practicalities of achieving a possible compromise. Practical arguments depend very much on the circumstances of the individual case. They may relate to the personal circumstances of the parties, for example, a case in which the parties are in a commercial relationship but have fallen out over some past dealing you may be negotiating. The opponent may be an up-and-coming business which is trying to establish a reputation in the area. Your client may be a well-established business with a voice in the local business community. Pointing out the benefits of trading with your client would be a practical argument.

Alternatively, practical arguments may relate to consideration of alternatives available if the party to the negotiation does not get what he or she is seeking. For example, you may be negotiating a case in which the opponent is seeking payment of £5,000 immediately from your client but your client does not have all the money at present. However, your client will have more money in two weeks' time. The opponent could press for the money immediately by seeking judgment but is unlikely to get any more even using the available methods of enforcement. In any event, obtaining judgment will take more than two weeks. Thus, in practical terms, it may well take the opponent a lot longer through the courts than two weeks.

8.3.3.3 Norm/fairness-based arguments—moral, normative, 'fairness' arguments

Moral arguments are based on concepts of right and wrong which may not be universally accepted; they may be culturally or religiously specific. An example of a moral argument which may be viewed differently depending on one's culture and religion is that sex outside a formally recognised monogamous marriage is wrong. Normative arguments are based on the 'norm' or usual custom, practice or understanding in particular circumstances, areas, cultures, etc. An example of a normative argument in Western culture (although not as persuasive as it used to be) is that a very young child is better off with its mother. Fairness arguments are to an extent based on both perceptions of morality and norms. An example of a fairness argument that is possibly universally held is that, on the break-up of a partnership, each party should receive a share of the assets which reflects his or her original contribution when setting up the firm.

All of these arguments can be and frequently are used in negotiations. However, you should be aware that the basis of your argument may not be shared by your opponent or indeed by your client. As stated above, many of these arguments are based on a view of the world that is not universal. The argument may therefore not be seen as persuasive by your opponent.

The most frequently used of these arguments is the 'fairness' argument. Although one may simply argue that 'it is fair to...' if the concept of fairness is invoked, the meaning needs to be clarified. Fair to whom? Is one speaking of equity (to each according to the contribution made) or equality (split down the middle)?

8.3.4 Use of argument in the three strategies

We noted above that the three strategies used argument as part of their persuasive tool kit, albeit without explicitly labelling it. Having considered the three main types of argument used in legal negotiations, it is now useful to look again at those strategies to identify how they use argument. In the same way that negotiators will rarely use a purely competitive, cooperative or collaborative bargaining strategy, most negotiators do not use argument in a purely competitive, cooperative or collaborative way. Most negotiators use a mixture of bargaining strategies. It is no less true for the use of argument. However, it is useful to consider each in turn and to consider the most common type of argument associated with each strategy and how it is used.

8.3.4.1 Competitive strategy

As we saw above, competitive negotiators persuade by adopting a strong stance and being inflexible (eg, making few concessions, giving little information). They are out to win and are preoccupied with the position of their client and generally uninterested in that of their opponent. Truly competitive negotiators seek to exploit the fears and insecurities of the opponent. Their strategy is to use argument (and concessions and information exchange) to coerce rather than persuade, to manipulate and not to promote understanding.

Competitive negotiators are more likely to use argument in the sense of 'heated exchange' rather than in the sense of 'reasoned argument'. Although they may use merit-based, practical, moral, normative or fairness arguments, the 'argument' is more likely to be simply stating their client's position (he or she has a strong case, cannot do something, is right, etc) and stating it repeatedly, possibly in an aggressive, confrontational manner such as speaking more loudly and increasing their demands. They are unlikely to go behind the positional statement, eg, to explain why they consider their client has a strong case or cannot do something. They are also unlikely to listen to any response or enter into a constructive exchange of views, eg, on the merits or practicalities. The point of the argument is to wear the opponent down and seek capitulation rather than to persuade rationally of the validity of what they are saying.

8.3.4.2 Cooperative strategy

In contrast, cooperative negotiators are characterised by concern with fairness and being reasonable to both parties to the dispute. They are likely to open with moderate statements and make offers that are not an exaggerated view of what their client is seeking; they look for cooperation and a mutual solution. Cooperative negotiators are more likely to rely on arguments relating to norms, morals and fairness to foster understanding of the way the case is viewed and tolerance of requests made. Cooperative argument is characterised by rationality based on a desire to be 'fair' in the circumstances. It seeks to justify the client's case on the merits only insofar as this can help both negotiators to reach a 'fair' agreement somewhere between the stated positions of the parties.

8.3.4.3 Collaborative strategy

Collaborative negotiators are concerned to satisfy the underlying needs and interests of both parties. Collaborative negotiators, be they principled or problem-solving, are primarily negotiating with a view to mutual gain and a win/win solution. They seek to persuade the other side to reach a settlement which satisfies the clients' interests and needs. They therefore use practical arguments to enable the other side to understand the interests and needs of the parties. The merits of the case may or may not be discussed. They worry that argument is 'playing the adversarial game' and may avoid discussing the merits of the case beyond where they can be comfortably agreed. Thus, most of the arguments are directed towards the clients' interests and needs. While the merits of the case may be discussed, this will not be a prime focus and the settlement may or may not reflect the merits.

8.3.4.4 Summary

The lack of recognition of the type or use of argument in all three strategies risks the unadulterated use of these approaches to argument. The risk of using the competitive approach is that the discussion becomes sterile and repetitive. Neither party gets any better feel for the case or for what might be a reasonable settlement standard for their client. The risk of the cooperative approach of concentrating on fairness is that both merit-based and practical arguments are very likely to be overlooked so the settlement may reflect neither the merits of the case nor the practical circumstances of the clients. The risk of the collaborative approach of focusing on the practicalities of the parties' needs is that the settlement reached will fail to reflect the merits of the case which completely ignores that the settlement is about a matter with some legal substance where legal rights may be of importance to the clients.

8.4 Using merit-based argument in legal negotiations

When parties negotiate, they decide whether to accept what is offered, depending on whether they can better that offer elsewhere. If a person is proposing to buy a car, he or she judges the price offered by one garage against the alternatives and presumably accepts the vehicle that represents the best buy, often the car of greatest quality, costing the least money. If a person is proposing to settle a case at the door of the court, he or she will judge any offers against the chances of winning/losing at trial and what is likely to be won or lost. We now consider the use of argument in these two types of legal negotiations: dispute resolution and deal-making.

8.4.1 Dispute resolution negotiation

In dispute resolution negotiations, the alternative to accepting settlement via negotiation is to go to court. Lawyers therefore judge what is an appropriate overall settlement primarily according to their view of the merits of their client's case. In other words, lawyers will settle if they think that what is offered is worth equal to or more than what they could realistically get if the matter went to court, bearing in mind the risks and expenses involved in litigation. So, for example, if, in a personal injury case as the claimant's lawyer, you consider it highly likely that there will be a finding of contributory negligence of at least 15 per cent, you will no doubt be prepared to accept a figure of settlement that takes such a probable finding into account.

Although the merits are of primary importance in determining settlement levels, it should also be recognised that in some cases there may be other factors that dictate what are acceptable settlement terms. An example would be where a client has pressing financial reasons for wanting an early settlement to litigation. This may motivate an acceptance of terms of settlement that do not reflect the full strengths of the client's legal case. However, it remains true that, in most cases, the merits dictate the settlement positions adopted and what terms are acceptable and therefore the merits of the case are highly significant.

Obviously, making a comparison between settlement terms offered and what is considered to be the most likely court outcome, given the strengths and weaknesses of a particular case, is by no means an exact science. It can be extremely difficult at times to know whether it is better to accept what is on the table in the negotiation or go to court. Such decisions are primarily based on a careful consideration of the merits of the client's case. When evaluating the merits of the case and the competing claims involved, negotiators are faced with two considerable difficulties. First, the uncertainties inherent in the litigation process and, secondly, informational uncertainty.

Generally speaking, litigation is risky, given the focus on finding a winner and a loser. Courts rarely impose a compromise, particularly at the trial stage. Uncertainties in the litigation process can take many different forms. Thus, for example, the way the witnesses give evidence and their perceived credibility will influence the outcome of the case and will therefore be of great concern.

The second factor causing difficulty in evaluating the merits of competing claims is informational uncertainty. The view of the merits is not static but changes constantly. Each time a new piece of information is added, its impact on the merits of the negotiation must be evaluated. Information received on discovery, exchange of experts' reports and witness statements can have a huge impact on the view of the merits of the case.

Both process and informational uncertainty mean that negotiators cannot be certain that their view of the merits is entirely accurate and will not need revising in the negotiation. The problem is particularly acute if new information and evidence is put forward by the opponent whilst negotiations are in process. Such uncertainty gives considerable scope for arguments concerning the merits of the competing claims to have a persuasive effect. Consider the following illustration that shows how process and informational uncertainty gives scope for factual argument to be used to persuade an opponent to move from a stated settlement position.

SCENARIO—PROCESS UNCERTAINTY

Your client is a company defending a personal injury negligence suit brought by one of its employees. The employee is suing for damages as a result of injuries sustained when she slipped on a wet floor. Liability is in dispute with your client alleging that the company is not responsible as the claimant was running at the time she slipped (in an area where running was clearly prohibited) and, therefore, is the author of her own misfortune.

EXAMPLE 1

As the lawyer acting for the defendant, you intend to call a witness at trial who will give evidence that he saw the claimant running just before she fell. In the negotiation you may argue that this witness was:

- standing nearby where the claimant fell and had an unobstructed view of the entire incident;
- the safety officer for the floor where the accident happened and was therefore likely to be paying particular attention to careless and dangerous behaviour.

These two factual arguments strengthen the direct evidence you have that suggests that the claimant was running before she fell. They also use litigation process uncertainty about the credibility of the witnesses.

EXAMPLE 2—INFORMATIONAL UNCERTAINTY

You have recently obtained evidence that shows that the claimant had already received two verbal warnings for being late back from tea break. You may argue that:

- the claimant was returning from the tea break when the accident occurred;
- the tea break had officially ended 10 minutes prior to the claimant returning to her workstation;
- therefore the claimant was worried about being late back to her workstation and was running when she fell.

In this example you are using factual argument based on circumstantial evidence. As your knowledge of the existence of such evidence is revealed for the first time in the negotiation, you are exploiting informational uncertainty.

By using various types of factual argument that relate to the evidence, and both process and informational uncertainty, you can cast doubt on the settlement position of the opponent where it is based upon the merits of the case.

You should remember that using argument rarely culminates in your opponent's express acceptance of your points. Rather, the purpose of using argument is to cast doubt on the basis of the opponent's settlement position, so that the position is moved in a direction or in a manner favourable to you.

Just as legal and factual arguments can be used to move an opponent from a predetermined settlement level, so they can be used by negotiators to justify settlement positions. In many negotiations, opponents want to know why you will not move from a particular stance or position, or on what basis you seek to justify the requests you have made. If you can make a compelling legal or factual argument, you may find you get what you want, or at least more of what you want. Your argument provides justification for the opponent. This is important, especially as most settlements require the approval of the client. By justifying your stance or request with a persuasive factual or legal argument, you give your opponent a reason to take back to his or her client that may help him or her to accept the terms negotiated.

In this sense legal and factual arguments have a dual purpose. They seek to change an opponent's view of appropriate positions whilst justifying your own.

8.4.2 Deal-making negotiations

In deal-making negotiations, legal and factual argument can also play a persuasive role. The factors that shape the settlement positions of the parties will be more diverse and heavily dependent on the context of the particular negotiation. The following example shows how factual and legal argument can be used in the deal-making context.

Two parties are negotiating the potential lease of a property where the parties are in dispute over two issues. The landlord wants a rent of £12,000 per annum and a covenant against subletting, and the prospective tenant is unhappy about both of these issues.

The prospective tenant might propose an alternative settlement position as follows: £9,000 per annum and a covenant against subletting without the landlord's consent, such consent not to be unreasonably withheld. Any or all of the following arguments could be used to undermine the landlord's settlement position and move it closer to the settlement position of the tenant.

In the matter of the rent: £12,000 is well in excess of the rental sums for equivalent properties in the vicinity; £9,000 is based upon what the tenant is paying in his current accommodation, which is similar.

In the matter of the subletting clause: the landlord is protected because he can refuse to allow subletting provided the refusal is not unreasonable and recent Court of Appeal authority indicates marked reluctance to find landlords' lack of consent unreasonable.

In this example the tenant's lawyer has relied upon factual arguments relating to similar property prices in the area and what the prospective tenant is currently paying. Of course, how persuasive this argument will be, to an extent, depends on the evidence he or she has to substantiate it. Similarly, with the legal argument concerning the subletting clause, the opponent may need to see a transcript of the authorities in question.

8.5 Summary of persuasion and argument

We have considered the role of persuasion in negotiation and emphasised the use of argument to persuade. If argument is going to persuade, it must be relevant, comprehensive and intelligible, and appropriate to the context. Argument that is irrelevant, incomplete and unintelligible, and inappropriate to the context, can have a negative effect on negotiation. It can do much to confuse and alienate your opponent, make the negotiation inefficient and in extreme cases lead to deadlock. In short, argument, if handled badly, can be dangerous for a number of reasons.

One of the cardinal rules regarding the use of argument is never to argue for the sake of it. Argument has two principal uses in a negotiation. First, it assists you in establishing a settlement standard—an objective basis against which to gauge what your client should get from the negotiation. Secondly, it assists with the concession-making and seeking aspect of the negotiation. Argument can be used to explain or justify what is being sought or offered by way of concessions. We deal with this in **Chapter 11**. In the next chapter we give guidance on how to prepare to argue effectively in legal negotiations.

9

Analysis—formulating arguments

9.1 Introduction

In the last chapter we considered the crucial role of argument in a negotiation. In this chapter we look at how to prepare effectively, and how you should analyse and evaluate your case prior to the negotiation to ensure that you use and respond to argument to get the best for your client. In all cases, the only way to ensure that your arguments will be relevant, comprehensive and persuasive is to have analysed the case papers properly and thoroughly. We look briefly first at the difference between the focus of your preparation for deal-making and dispute resolution negotiations. We then consider in some detail how to prepare for a dispute resolution negotiation.

9.1.1 Deal-making negotiations

In legal deal-making negotiations, preparatory steps are diverse and depend on the context. This is because, as has been seen in **8.4.2**, settlement positions are shaped by factors more diverse than in dispute-resolving negotiation where it is mainly the merits of the case which will be fought in court which matter.

The main preparatory steps in a deal-making negotiation relate to researching the bases for your possible settlement positions and evaluating the factual and legal arguments that support them. From here you can compare your arguments for their relative strengths. A common settlement standard on price will be comparators (ie, the price charged for a similar item) and arguments will focus on the extent of the similarity or difference from the subject matter of the negotiation and how this should affect the price. Thus in the example given at **8.4.2** of a tenant and landlord negotiating the rent of a property about to be leased, the comparator proposed by the tenant of £9,000 is based on the rent currently being paid for similar accommodation. The arguments will focus on any differences or similarities in size, location, terms of the lease, etc. The landlord may, of course, propose a different comparator and, again, both sides will need to consider how they argue this as the settlement standard as opposed to the £9,000.

9.1.2 Dispute resolution negotiations

As pointed out in the last chapter, both parties are conscious that the resolution of a litigated dispute without settlement is the outcome promulgated by the court. This may be the standard against which the parties themselves gauge proposals for settlement. In the circumstances, this is appropriate. As a lawyer acting for a client in such circumstances, you should be aware, even if your client is not, that in a litigated dispute the likely court outcome must be a significant factor in determining the settlement standard and that the merits of the case do matter. Of course, any settlement may also need to reflect other relevant aspects as well, eg, the practicalities of the settlement. However, your preparation must include analysis of the merits and how they could affect the settlement standard.

Your preparation in respect of argument on the merits of the case is no different from that required for any other activity at the Bar when involved in a litigated case, be it writing an opinion, preparing for a client conference, or preparing for court. In particular, this aspect of preparing to negotiate overlaps considerably with preparation to represent someone at trial. The main aim is identification of the issues in the case and evaluation of the strengths and weaknesses of both sides.

Thus, you prepare for court by determining what you are seeking from the court and identifying and understanding the law which underpins your case; the legal framework here will be the cause of action and its elements. So, for example, in a claim for damages for breach of contract, the main elements would be existence of a contract, breach and damage. In a more complicated case, you may need to do legal research to determine precisely what the elements are of the cause of action underpinning the case. The next step is to identify which elements are agreed and which are in dispute. So, for example, there may be no dispute over the existence of the contract or its terms but considerable dispute over whether its non-controversial terms have been breached. You then identify the allegations of fact by either party relevant to the legal issues (ie, those in dispute). From this analysis you can then decide how you will question the witnesses and what documents you wish to include in the bundle. You should then consider the case from the view of the opponent on exactly the same matters to see what evidence your opponent is likely to include and seek from the witnesses. From this analysis you can formulate arguments with which to persuade the court to find for you and identify what arguments your opponent may use to persuade the court to find for him or her. You also need to decide how you will respond to the arguments that your opponent may use. Finally, you need to evaluate the evidence and arguments for both sides and decide how you will use the evidence and which arguments are persuasive and which are not. From this preparation you can put together as persuasive a submission or speech as possible using the strongest arguments and countering as best you can the arguments likely to be raised by your opponent.

Similarly with a negotiation, to be successful you need to prepare your own case fully and anticipate your opponent's case as far as you can. Much of the above preparation is useful for the negotiation. Thus the arguments which you plan to use in court can equally be used in the negotiation and your analysis of the information which may be produced in evidence may assist you in considering the information to be exchanged in the negotiation. Your evaluation of the case can also be used to assist you in deciding a reasonable settlement standard against which to gauge proposals for settlement.

In addition to adapting your preparation for the courtroom, you will also have to consider practical arguments which may or may not have been relevant to preparing for the trial. Those arguments will depend on the particular circumstances of the case and in that way will be similar to arguments in deal-making negotiations.

9.2 Analysis to formulate argument

We look now in some detail at how to undertake the steps outlined above to assist you in preparing to argue the case. Careful preparation will ensure that you formulate soundly-based arguments to use in the negotiation and that you are prepared to deal effectively with the arguments which may be used against you.

9.2.1 The legal framework

Your brief may set out the legal framework. However, it is unlikely, particularly where proceedings have not been issued, to cover all the potential issues arising, eg, that remoteness of damage or particular procedural details are in issue. It is part of the barrister's job to look for and develop such points where appropriate. The first step in your analysis in a litigated case is therefore to identify and understand the underlying substantive and procedural law.

9.2.1.1 The substantive legal framework

The substantive legal framework includes considering the cause(s) of action, the remedies sought and any potential defences.

Cause(s) of action

You need to be clear as to the causes of action on which the parties rely, all the elements of each cause of action which must be proved to succeed, and on whom the burden of proof lies for each element. You will also need to ensure that you understand precisely what each element involves and to check where the issues lie in the case. Thus, for example, in a claim for breach of contract, are the parties disputing some or all of the following: the existence of the contract, a term or terms, that a term or terms were breached, or the standard required to prove breach?

Remedies

You need to be clear precisely what remedies are being sought and the law which underpins their availability. For example, if damages are claimed, the issues of causation, remoteness, foreseeability, mitigation, etc may be relevant. Again, you need to be clear about the law on each of these elements and which elements are likely to be disputed.

Defences

Finally, what defences are available in respect of each cause or causes of action, eg, limitation, contributory negligence, etc, in addition to the principal defence of disputing that the elements of the cause of action have been made out? You need to ensure that you understand both the defence and how it relates to the particular cause of action. Thus, for example, what is the limitation period and when does it start to run for this particular cause of action? Is contributory negligence available as a defence to this particular claim? Which defences are therefore possible?

Thorough analysis

In respect of all of the above, you need to consider the whole of the case. Is there just one claim, eg, in contract for damages, or several claims, eg, in contract and negligence for an injunction and damages? Are several heads of damage claimed which relate to different issues? For example, is the case about both delivery of poor quality goods and a failure to make further deliveries giving rise to two claims for damages (the cost of the goods delivered and the losses suffered from the non-delivery)? The dispute underlying the loss for poor quality goods may relate to the terms of the contract, whereas the dispute for the non-delivery may relate to whether the contract has been repudiated and, if so, by whom. Is there a counterclaim by the defendant? Is the defendant alleging that a third party is liable wholly or partially? The more complex the case, the more likely it is that there will be a number of issues in the case which are in dispute. You need to identify and understand the whole of the substantive legal framework of the case and all the elements which are likely to be disputed.

Prior to issue, it may be more difficult to determine precisely what the issues are as there will be no statements of case to define them, although correspondence and your instructions should give you information from which this can be determined. Where you do have the statements of case, the issues should be defined by them. However, bear in mind that the statements of case may be amended so do not assume that what is pleaded is necessarily definitive.

9.2.1.2 The procedural legal framework

You also need to consider how procedural law affects the case. You may be negotiating at the court door of a particular application, eg, to set aside default judgment or to obtain summary judgment, an interim injunction or an interim payment stage. You must be aware of the effect success or failure of the application will have on the case, eg, if the court refuses to set aside judgment or grants summary judgment, the person with judgment will have won and will be able to enforce the judgment. The test to be applied by the court in determining the application will raise issues relevant to the merits of the case and these may be argued in the negotiation. Thus, for example, if the claim is for an interim injunction, the court will consider whether there is a serious issue to be tried, whether damages would be an adequate remedy and where the balance of convenience lies. Ensure you know the order in which the court applies the elements of the test and how the elements are interpreted.

You may also be instructed to appear on an application relating to procedural matters, for example, an application for an unless order or strike out on the basis that one party has failed to take a procedural step as required by the court directions. Again, it is important to understand the orders the court can make and the tests which are likely to be applied as these, too, may affect what the parties can expect from the court at this stage and may therefore be the subject of argument in the negotiation.

9.2.1.3 Necessary legal research

In preparing a case it can be tempting to do a considerable amount of legal research, simply because you do not know how your opponent will argue the case. However, unfocused research can both waste time and obscure the issues. Resist the temptation to leap into detailed legal research after a cursory reading of the papers (eg, having identified that the claim is about nuisance and negligence, do not immediately leap to research the whole law on nuisance and negligence). To ensure that your research is focused and helping rather than hindering you, read the papers and identify the underlying legal framework and the aspects which are likely to be disputed. Where you are unclear on a particular aspect, eg, the elements of a particular cause of action, look it up. Where a particular aspect is likely to be heavily argued, such as whether a particular head of damage (eg, injured feelings) is recoverable, do more thorough research to ensure that you know the cases, areas of certainty and uncertainty in the law, etc.

Consider how to summarise your research so that it is useful and can be referred to readily and easily both in your preparation and in the negotiation. Writing a summary of the law is one way to check whether you really understand it. If you have difficulty summarising a particular principle, you probably do not understand it. In addition to making your own notes, consider whether having a copy of the full judgment of the case, the headnote or a particular aspect of the judgment would be useful for preparation or for use in the negotiation.

9.2.1.4 Identifying the issues from the legal framework

Once you have identified and understood the legal framework and the aspects which are likely to be in dispute, you need to consider the basis on which these aspects will be disputed. Any one case will usually involve a number of aspects which are disputed. You should consider each aspect separately to determine whether the dispute is about the law or the facts or both.

We looked briefly at the different types of argument based on the merits—legal, factual and mixed in **Chapter 8** (see **8.3.3**). Is the dispute purely about the law, ie, there is no dispute about the facts, but there are different interpretations of the law which are relevant because they favour one or other side in the case? Is the dispute purely about the facts, ie, the facts are disputed and to determine the case the court will have to determine only which party's version of the facts it finds most credible, both the legal principles and how the facts relate to them being clear? Does an issue involve both legal and factual disputes, ie, will the court have to determine not only whose version of events is the most credible but also the legal principle to which the facts relate before making a finding on the issue?

Most cases, particularly in your early years, will involve factual argument/dispute as the law will be relatively straightforward. We therefore consider the formulation of legal argument only briefly before moving on to consider in some detail the analysis of the facts.

9.2.2 Legal argument

Legal argument is used where there is dispute about the interpretation of the law, statute or case law, whether substantive, procedural or evidential. Where a case involves legal argument, it generally does so because the legal principle is not well established, although it could be that, although well established, it now has to be reinterpreted in light of recent changes, for example the implementation of the Human Rights Act 1998.

A case involving argument on the interpretation of the law will generally require you to do more extensive legal research than one in which the legal principles are well established (unless the case is in an area with which you are unfamiliar when you may also have to do a fair amount of legal research). Legal research purely because you are unfamiliar with an area is, however, likely to be different from researching an area of unsettled law. In getting up to speed on an unfamiliar area you can generally rely on standard practitioner texts such as *Chitty on Contract*. Researching the law where the principle is uncertain will generally require more than this. The practitioner texts may simply state that this is an area in which the law is unclear and set out the author's view of the law. You will need to look up relevant cases and determine which cases support your position, as well as the facts on which the decision relies, the level of court which made the decision, whether the case has been subsequently considered by the courts and, if so, was it approved, distinguished, overruled, etc.

You will then need to consider all the cases on the point, which are most relevant and assist you, how you will argue that they should be followed in your case and how they support a finding for your client. You will also have to consider which are likely to be used by your opponent, how he or she may argue they should be followed and how they support his or her client's case.

9.2.3 Analysis of the factual disputes

In order to understand fully what the factual disputes and potential arguments are on either side, you must be clear about your client's version of the facts, how it differs from the other side's version, and any potential gaps in your and your opponent's information (ie, what might you know that he or she does not and vice versa and what information might neither of you have). You also need to consider how the allegations of fact will be proved (ie, consider the evidence available, its relevance, admissibility and weight). In this section we consider the analysis of the allegations of fact. In the next section we will consider the analysis of the evidence.

Analysing the factual allegations involves identifying the allegations of fact made by each side, determining which allegations are agreed and which disputed, identifying which allegations are known to both sides and from this determining any gaps or ambiguities about which either side may be able to supply information. Finally, you need to ensure that you are familiar with the facts so that you can present them accurately, absorb new information from your opponent and make necessary adjustments to your view of them during the negotiation. This includes being aware of the figures and being able to use them effectively in the negotiation.

9.2.3.1 Factual allegations by both sides

It is likely that your client has given a one-sided view of events. While you must accept what your client tells you in presenting the case, be wary of assuming that your client has told you the whole truth in an objective way. His or her version of events is based on his or her allegations of what happened. The two parties are likely to have viewed the events leading to the litigation very differently, will remember it differently, and will have had to mentally reconstruct what happened and have done so very differently.

Until your client's version is proved (ie, the court finds the facts happened as your client alleges), what he or she says is merely allegation. However, you must be clear precisely what he or she is alleging on each of the issues which form the basis of the dispute. For example, if the case is a claim for breach of contract, what does your client allege the term to be and does he or she allege it was an express or implied term; if express, does he or she allege it was agreed orally or in writing or a bit of both; what does he or she allege the other side did which amounted to a breach of that term?

Where statements of case have been exchanged, you should be able to determine the main allegations of fact by both parties as the Civil Procedure Rules require parties to include those on which they rely. In addition, witness statements, correspondence and your instructions will add to and amplify the statements of case. Identifying the factual allegations where proceedings have not yet been issued may be more difficult as you will not have court documents such as statements of case, witness statements, etc.

9.2.3.2 Which facts are agreed and which are disputed?

Although both parties may have different versions of what happened, is happening or is likely to happen, there will be some facts which are not in dispute. Thus, for example, although there is an issue about the term of the contract, both parties agree that there was a relevant term and that it was agreed orally. The dispute is about the precise wording of the term. You need to go through the case and determine which allegations of fact are disputed and which are not.

In cases pre-issue, it may be more difficult to ascertain precisely what is and is not disputed. Once proceedings have been issued, the further along in the litigation process the case is, the easier it becomes to determine the factual disputes because the exchange of court documents makes each party's case clearer. The statements of case should indicate the main areas of dispute through the defence responses to the allegations of fact in the particulars of claim (or counterclaim). Where expert reports and witness statements have also been exchanged, you will gain a clearer understanding of the allegations which are agreed or disputed.

9.2.3.3 Which facts are held in common and which are not?

Identify which factual information in your brief is likely to be available to the other side as well as to you. Again, the further through the litigation process the case is, the more shared information there will be. All allegations in the court documents which have been exchanged will clearly be available to both sides. This will include statements of case, witness statements, exhibits to those statements, the bundle of documents to be put before the court, etc. In addition, information contained in correspondence between the parties and solicitors will be shared. However, information in a client's proof of evidence (not yet in the form of an exchanged witness statement), or in documents which the client has simply given to his or her solicitor, will not necessarily be known by both sides.

9.2.3.4 What are the gaps or ambiguities?

Looking largely at the allegations of fact in dispute, you need to consider which gaps or ambiguities may impact on the merits of the case. For example, your client may allege that he was driving at a reasonable speed but not state his speed or the speed limit. Alternatively, the other side may allege that he was driving too fast but again give no details of the facts to support this statement.

At this point you need to remind yourself that your client's version is unlikely to be an objective statement and you need to approach the matter with some scepticism. Thus, for example, although your client says (and believes) that he was driving at a reasonable speed, he generally drives quite quickly, does not consider speed limits important, etc. Where you do have information about the allegations made by the other side, consider how the versions differ. Given the disparity between the two versions of events, which seems more likely? Why do you consider it more likely? What gaps are you having to fill in reaching this conclusion? Are these gaps on which your client may be able to help and/or might your opponent have information on them? Is the information which your opponent may have likely to be beneficial or harmful to your client's case?

Where you have little information about the allegations put forward by the other side (which is likely to be the case if the negotiation takes place before the case has commenced), be aware that your opponent may have been given a rather different version of the facts. He or she may have information that is a surprise to you, and/or contradicts what you have been told by your client. Look at your client's case with a critical eye to try to identify any gaps or ambiguities which may mean that the picture is not as positive as it has been painted.

9.2.3.5 Being on top of the facts and figures/able to use them

The facts

Your analysis of the facts should include consideration of how best to ensure that you are clear about them and able to use them effectively in the negotiation. This means having a method of remembering or recording the allegations of fact by both sides so that you can state them accurately and do not need to check them during the negotiation. Misstating facts may impact on how the negotiation proceeds and what is eventually agreed. It can result in deadlock or a vague compromise which does not satisfy your client. If you mislead your opponent, it may also be an issue of professional conduct (see **Chapter 16**). Having to constantly check facts wastes time and may annoy your opponent. This is not something you should do unless used as a clear tactic with a purpose. In any event, being uncertain about the facts is far more likely to give your opponent the opportunity to take control of the negotiation or use your confusion to push you into a concession you should not be making. You also need to be familiar with your version of the case to be able to put additional or amended material into context quickly.

The figures

Most cases involve money as part of the claim, even if this is not the only claim or the most essential one for your client. It is important to be prepared to deal with this aspect of the case as it is all too easy for confusion over the figures to cloud the issue in the heat of a negotiation. The starting point is to understand how the figures are calculated, check that figures are added accurately and know the total amount of the overall claim.

In many cases your opponent will see the figures differently. He or she may argue that they should be calculated in a different way. This may be obvious from the papers. Thus, for example, it may be clear from the statements of case or witness statements that the opponent is arguing that a claim for loss of profit should be calculated on a different basis or for a different period. Alternatively, the case may be before issue, and it is unclear whether the method of calculating the profit is disputed, but you should know how your client calculates it. In either instance, prepare your figures in a flexible way so that you can quickly adapt them if necessary. This means understanding how the figures are calculated and breaking them down into component parts. It also means setting out the figures in a way that enables you to alter one or two figures and make a new calculation easily.

If you are not prepared to deal with the figures in a detailed way, you may easily be led into making concessions you do not wish to make, or get confused and waste time or lose any initiative you previously had.

9.2.4 Consideration of the evidence

Although you do not have to formally prove anything in a negotiation, your arguments on the merits of the case will be based on the chances of the parties in court. The court's finding on the issues which determine the case will depend on the relevant allegations of fact either being admitted or, where disputed, proved to the required standard. As pointed out above, all facts stated by the parties which are not admitted by the other side are merely allegations until the court rules by making a finding on the facts. Therefore a case which looks strong because there are a number of relevant allegations of fact which tend to support one side may nevertheless appear weak in court because few of the allegations can be proved. It is therefore necessary to consider both how the parties will seek to persuade the court that their version of events is true and how the burden of proof affects their ability to persuade the court.

9.2.4.1 How will the allegations of fact be proved?

For each of the allegations of fact on matters in dispute, you need to consider how it is likely to be proved and the strength of the evidence that may be used to prove it.

The oral evidence of the parties themselves is subjective and the court's finding on the facts is likely to rest on the credibility of witnesses. One party's version of the facts may be inherently more plausible than the other's or one witness may come across in the witness box much more persuasively than another. If there is documentary evidence, you need to check whether or not the parties agree that the document was exchanged and relevant to the issue and the different interpretations which could be put on the words in the document. On the basis of this analysis you should determine how likely it is that the evidence is weighted for or against your client.

You also need to consider whether the evidence relied on is admissible (if in doubt, check). You should check whether any of the rules of evidence could affect the weight which the court is likely to give to it (eg, although hearsay is admissible, the weight given to it by the court is likely to be minimal). Can you use admissibility or weight as arguments against your opponent? Is he or she likely to use them against you?

The closer the case to trial when you negotiate, the more evidence will have been collected and exchanged. However, even where a case has yet to be issued, there will be some information in the brief which indicates how matters are likely to be proved. Thus, for example, it may be clear that proof of the terms of an oral contract agreed between the parties depends solely on their oral evidence, or your papers may indicate that there was someone else present at the time (ie, an additional witness). Alternatively, there may be correspondence which refers to one of the terms either directly or obliquely.

On issues where there is little information about the evidence to support the allegations, you need to be ready to challenge your opponent on the allegations of fact by his or her client. Be ready to ask what evidence there is to support the allegation and how his or her client is going to prove it. Conversely, you need to be ready to deal with similar challenges by your opponent on the allegations of fact by your client. How will you respond to questions as to the evidence to support the allegation, or how it will be proved? You need to think logically and laterally. Given the allegation, how is it likely to be proved and how can you use this to respond in the most positive way? If the evidence is determinate of the case as a whole and uncertain, is it feasible, given the stage of the case and the time before the negotiation, to check with the solicitor whether or not evidence is available?

9.2.4.2 Where does the burden of proof lie?

An equally important matter to consider is on whom does the burden of proving each allegation lie? The general rule in civil cases is 'he who alleges must prove'. However, this is not always the case and, if in doubt, do the necessary legal research. The general standard of proof is on the balance of probabilities. In order to win the person on whom the burden lies must prove that his version is 'more probable than not'. If the probabilities are equal, ie, the evidence equally supports both parties, the person with the burden loses. This can be an important factor in court and in a negotiation, particularly where the balance of the evidence is unclear or the evidence consists solely of one party's word against the other.

9.2.4.3 Whose allegations of fact are likely to be proved?

Having considered how the various allegations of fact may be proved, the weight of the evidence and the burden of proof, you should be able to gauge how likely it is that the court will accept your client's version of events rather than your opponent's. Where the information about the evidence is minimal, any conclusion will be more speculative and uncertain. You need to consider how you can use this in the negotiation.

9.3 Formulating persuasive arguments

Argument as we generally use the term means reasons advanced for or against a proposition or course of action. As we saw in **Chapter 8**, there are different types of argument (eg, merit-based, practical, etc). The use of merit-based argument is one of the principal tools of a lawyer, whether acting as an advocate or a negotiator.

How to formulate and present merit-based argument persuasively is covered in some detail in the ***Case Preparation*** manual and its detailed consideration is not repeated here. Basically, merit-based argument means putting the analysis together in a way which will show your opponent that there are cogent reasons for believing what you say or doing what you ask. For your reasoning to be cogent, it must be soundly based on the law, facts and evidence available to you. In addition, when formulating your argument, you should be conscious of any inference or generalisation on which you rely to make the argument cohesive and plausible. Finally, you must ensure that the arguments on each individual aspect do not conflict and that they form a cohesive whole, the themes fitting together to make a plausible and persuasive theory of the case.

9.3.1 The purpose of argument in a negotiation

The purpose of argument in a negotiation is to persuade the other side to move towards you in compromising. It is also used to test the other side to enable you to gauge how far they are likely to move and what you can reasonably expect to achieve for your client by way of settlement (ie, inform your settlement standard). Thus you will use it to persuade the other side that your proposals for settlement are justified. You will also use it to test your opponent, requiring him or her to give the reasons why proposals should be accepted by your client: to justify the proposals by argument. You need to be prepared both to use argument and press your opponent for his or her arguments and to gauge how these arguments affect the settlement standard and the proposals being made. In addition to considering how to use argument to strengthen your own position, you should consider how you can use it to marginalise and undermine the arguments and position of the opponent.

9.3.2 Relating arguments to the relevant issue

Arguments are persuasive only if they are properly focused to achieve the intended purpose. You need to consider again the different issues in the case and determine which arguments relate to which issues. It may be that there are two claims for damages, each one dependent on a different issue (eg, one on whether a particular term exists and another on whether an agreed term was breached). Alternatively, there may be a number of claims (eg, claims for general and special damages and for an injunction), all of which are based to some extent on one issue (whether actions of one party amount to nuisance). You need to relate your arguments to the relevant issue so that they are focused and persuasive. You also need to identify the arguments which may be used against you on this issue. This may have an impact on how you decide to structure the negotiation. At this point you just need to be clear which arguments relate to which issue. We deal in **Chapter 14** with how to structure the negotiation to make the most persuasive use of arguments.

9.3.3 Gaps in information

Your analysis will have thrown up gaps and ambiguities in the information, both in respect of facts alleged and evidence to prove the allegations. When formulating your argument you need to be aware of where and what those gaps are and how they affect the persuasiveness of the argument. Consider what information you need before you attempt to use an argument. Look at the arguments which your opponent may use against you. What gaps are there? Do you have information which may strengthen or weaken the opponent's arguments? We deal in the next chapter with information exchange, the risks and benefits of it and how to deal with information exchange which may affect the arguments used.

9.4 Evaluating the arguments

An important part of preparing to negotiate lies in evaluating the arguments, those which may be used by or against you. Effectively, this means considering all the arguments carefully to assess how strong they are. Is the argument based simply on an allegation of fact? Can it be challenged on the evidence? Who bears the burden of proof? How does this affect the relative strengths of the arguments for and against you? Is the credibility of witnesses an issue which goes for or against you? Can you use interpretation of the law to assist? How can you present your weaker arguments in as strong a light as possible? How can you attack your opponent's arguments? Think laterally about the different aspects of each argument and how they may be undermined.

Having done this, you should be able to determine which arguments are strong and which are weak. Where do your strengths lie and where do your opponent's strengths lie? On which issues is the court likely to find in your favour and on which to find for your opponent?

9.5 Be ready to respond to your opponent's arguments

The analysis above includes consideration of both the arguments which you may use and the arguments which your opponent may use against you. It is crucial that you are aware of and understand the arguments which are likely to be used to test you or justify proposals from the other side. Only then can you be ready to respond to them. Your evaluation of your opponent's arguments should give you a clear idea of which are weak and which are strong. It should also assist in identifying how you can reduce the impact of his or her arguments, even some of those which appear strong on first glance. This will assist you not only in responding when your opponent raises an argument, it will also help you to be proactive rather than merely reactive, ie, to reduce the impact of any argument which may be raised before your opponent uses it.

9.6 Summary

Formulation and evaluation of argument likely to be used in the negotiation is done principally to determine your settlement standard and to prepare to use argument to persuade your opponent to make concessions or justify the proposals you plan. Before looking at how to do this, we first consider information exchange, an equally vital aspect of the negotiation in respect of concessions. In **Chapter 11** we then deal with concession planning and, amongst other aspects which affect your preparation, look at how you use argument to plan concessions.

9.7 Application to Case Study A

Relevant law

NOTE: These notes set out the various legal principles relevant to the case. The notes below may well be in much more detail than you would set out. The extent of your legal research and need to make notes will be dependent on your general knowledge of the law.

Setting judgment aside—CPR, r 13.2

Apply by notice of application and witness statement.

- If wrongly entered: varied as of right.
- Otherwise: only if D has real prospect of successfully defending the claim/some other reason; court also takes into account D's explanation for allowing judgment to be entered/delay in applying to have set aside.
- May set aside on terms: D pay sum into court.
- Costs incurred usually awarded against D.

Contract for supply of goods

Sale of Goods Act 1979 and Sale and Supply of Goods Act 1994 (contracts *made* after 3.1.95). NOTE: no exclusion clause pleaded. Non-consumer contract.

Instalment contract (test: where instalments delivered and paid for separately > severable (instalment) contract). For delivery and acceptance each instalment regarded as a separate contract which can be sued on (*Jackson v Rotax Cycle Co* [1910] 2 KB 937, CA).

Failure to pay—seller sue for price

- Section 27 B duty to accept/pay.
- *B 'accept':* Section 35 if intimate to S; B does act inconsistent with S's ownership; B retain without intimate to S that rejected; not deemed until B has reasonable opportunity to examine goods.
- *B right to reject:*
  - failure to comply with implied terms (breach of condition);
  - implied condition includes s 14(2) of satisfactory quality: s 14(2A) ie: meet standard reasonable person regard as such taking account of description, price, relevant circumstances; s 14(2B) state and condition (including fitness for purpose, appearance and finish, freedom from minor defects, safety, durability); s 15A if breach so slight to be unreasonable to reject > breach of warranty (not condition but burden on S to show);
  - right to reject can be lost by deemed acceptance (see above s 35) > breach of condition become breach of warranty;
  - if reject, B no duty to return (s 36) but must make available for collection at place of examination;
  - lawful reject > property revest in S; B sue for non-delivery *but* no lien.
- *S sue for price:*
  - s 49(1) if property passed to B and B wrongfully rejected or refused to pay;
  - Section 49(2) even if property not passed to B: where date fixed for payment irrespective of delivery and wrongful failure to pay;

- property passes (specific v unascertained goods, s 61—here unascertained become ascertained when separated and irrevocably attached to contract; s 18, rule 5: property passes when unconditionally appropriated to contract by S with consent of B or by B with assent of S).

Set off?

- Section 53(1)(a) B may set off counterclaim for breach of warrants or where B elects/compelled to treat breach of condition as breach of warranty against S claim for price.
- Breach of warranty: normal *Hadley v Baxendale* measures (directly and naturally resulting *and* unusual in contemplation of parties) (s 53(2)).
- Section 51 (damage for non-delivery) goods rejected where there is a market: *prima facie* measure difference between contract and market price.
- Loss of profit recoverable where at time of contract S knew/ought to have known the use to which goods were to be put and that B intended to produce a profit and breach likely to reduce/extinguish that profit.
- Damages may also be available for loss of repeat orders from customers (*GKN Centrax Gears Ltd v Matbro Ltd* [1976] 2 Lloyd's Rep 555).

Repudiation?

Sale of goods s 31(2): instalment contract for sale of goods, where S makes defective delivery/B fail to pay for 1/more instalments > terms of contract and circumstances of case > whether breach = repudiation of whole contract or severable breach of one instalment.

- Failure to perform must go to root of contract (*Mersey Steel and Iron Co v Naylor Benson & Co* (1884) 9 CA 434).
- Main tests are:
  - the quantitative ratio of the faulty instalment to the whole contract;
  - the degree of probability that breach will be repeated (*Maple Flock Co Ltd v Universal Furniture Products (Wembley) Ltd* [1934] 1 KB 148, CA).
- The further the parties have proceeded with performance of the contract the less likely it is that one party entitled to claim contract repudiated by one breach (*Cornwall v Henson* [1900] 2 Ch 298).

General Contract By renunciation: where one party evinces unconditional intention not to perform or be bound by contract or essential term (*Freeth v Burr* (1874) LR 9 CP 208).

Anticipatory breach: where party renounces before time to perform > innocent party may elect to accept repudiation and sue OR wait for time for performance.

Seller's claim for damages

Section 50 B refuse to accept/pay > S can sue for damages for non-acceptance.

- Section 50(2) measure is estimated loss directly and naturally resulting in the ordinary course of events from B's breach.
- Section 50(3) available market > difference between contract and market price at time ought to have been accepted (*prima facie* rule which may be displaced if unjust/inappropriate (*WL Thompson Ltd v Robinson (Gunmakers) Ltd* [1955] Ch 177).

- Section 50(3) no available market (eg, unique, manufactured to B specification) > usually contract price and price at which sold (*Gebruder Metelmann GmbH & Co KG v NBR (London) Ltd* [1984] 1 Lloyd's Rep 614).
- 'Lost volume' S can recover loss of profit (eg, B throw back onto S's hands goods of same type as in stock, difficulty shifting because supply exceed demand > prevented opportunity to sell to same B the S's remaining stock. Profit on 2nd sale recoverable, presumed to be same as profit on sale to B (*WL Thompson* above).

The analysis—formulating and evaluating arguments

NOTE: the following telescopes the various stages because setting them out in detail would probably not be helpful as it would be very lengthy. Much of the analysis will be done in your head or by marking your papers. What you want to end up with is a useful note of the issues and the arguments for and against you. We therefore only set out some of the main steps: identifying the issues; identifying whether there are any purely legal disputes; and the arguments for and against on the relevant issues.

The issues

- Judgment in default—does D have a real prospect of success?—(dependent on issues below).
- C's claim for the price—does D have a defence?
  - 1st instalment
  - 2nd instalment.
- C's claim for loss of profits—who repudiated?
  - proof of loss
  - mitigation.
- D's claim for losses:
  - causation
  - remoteness
  - mitigation
  - proof of loss.
- Costs—who pays?

Disputes on the law

Probably none, fairly clear.

The issues and arguments

NOTE: Whether or not judgment will be set aside is dependent on the substantive issues in the case and is therefore not set out separately. All reference to section numbers are to the Sale of Goods Act 1979.

C's claim for the price

Different arguments arise on each instalment so deal with them separately.

Instalment 1–£1,260 + interest (c£30)

Arguments for D: no merit-based argument; practical argument that if judgment set aside C will have to wait for payment.

Arguments for C: D accepted and used, said was 'satisfactory'; payment 30 days of invoice; no dispute invoice delivered; price legally due.

Evaluation: D virtually no legal argument. C very strong.

Instalment 2–£1,260 + interest (c£20)

Law: C liable until D accept; D not accept until chance to inspect (s 35(2)); D right to reject if not satisfactory quality s 14(2).

Arguments for D:

- Poor quality; 1/2 whitish residue on surface; not usable; try to contact Mr H by phone; messages left on mobile and at office (para 4 ws) see para 7 statement that 'mouldy'—argue for show so both look and taste are important.
- Representation by Mr H re quality and immediate action by company (para 3 ws; para 3 statement) and D reliance on statements (para 4 statement).
- Unpacked same day and attempts to contact Mr H; Mr H 'first port of call'; messages left (para 5 statement).
- Appears to have used good part of chocolate (query exactly how much bad—says 'approximately half' in para 4 ws and 'about half' in para 5 statement (assume must pay for this—if half £630).
- Still has the 'mouldy' chocolate; no duty to return to C, s 36; C no attempt to inspect to date (para 7 statement—no request).

Possible arguments by C:

- D did accept—no notice or contact until 20.10.08 (para 7 statement). Delay too great for period of inspection (perishable goods).
- D no evidence that chocolate faulty—not offer on 20.10.08 to allow to inspect; not state what was wrong (see para 7 statement—no details of conversation and D puts phone down).
- Inspection of chocolate now not suffice (deteriorated).
- Cannot use chocolate now as too old?

Evaluation: On law and evidence (assuming has chocolate) D has strong argument to resist paying 1/2 the price on this instalment.

Lost benefit of remainder of contract

(5,000 Kilo @ 82p per Kilo £4,100)

Law: s 31(2) whether defective delivery/failure to pay amount to repudiation depends on terms of contract and circumstances of breach; look at quantitative—ratio of fault to whole contract and likelihood breach be repeated (*Maple Flock v Universal*); further in to contract > less likely repudiation (*Cornwall v Henson*). Common law—where one party evinces an unconditional intention not to perform or be bound by contract/essential term.

Arguments for D:

- Repudiation by C by faulty 2nd instalment; breach of condition of satisfactory quality s 14(2); only 2nd instalment in 12 instalment contract; reaction by C (Mr RB para 5 ws and para 7 statement).
- C just not deliver further instalments. C's decision *not* D's decision so D not liable for C's decisions (weak).

- C must prove loss: s 50(3) *prima facie* measure; no loss if resold to another; no loss if sell now to us (*but* can argue specialist goods etc, see below) *but* C must still *prove* his loss.
- Query C mitigate?

Arguments for C:

- Particulars of claim para 6 fail/refuse to pay sums due = repudiation (see above para 7 statement); use *Maple Flock* etc—reverse of D's argument above—ratio—only 1 instalment; other perfectly good; *not* sufficient for repudiation.
- Particulars of claim para 6 D terminate contract: in phone call 22.10.08; para 5 ws 'told Mr B that if not resupplied not wish to be supplied further'; para 7 statement 'exploded, told not get a penny/not pay for anything else delivered'.
- Section 50 measure: no available market (specialist goods); lost sale (*Centrax* case). Ditto argument if sell to us.

Evaluation: On repudiation: C's arguments are stronger; on C's losses: D's arguments are stronger.

D's loss of profit on Chocaganza weekend

(£2,000)

Law: dependent on finding on arguments on item 2 (ie, was the chocolate faulty). Additional relevant law: causation, foreseeability, proof of loss and mitigation.
Arguments for D:

- Loss clearly flows from breach by C (delivery of faulty goods on 4.10.08).
- Clearly in contemplation of C when contract made: C did have notice on making contract (para 3 statement) and on breach (phone call; fax etc).
- Took all reasonable steps to mitigate loss (reasonable attempts to get supply from C, phone call 22.10.08 only three days before event and D offer clearly not suffice particularly in light of fax (investigate on Nov delivery—ie, *after* event) then purchase from usual suppliers.
- As claim is for loss of profit and not related to price of substitute goods: not double recovery if get this and reduced price for 2nd instalment.

Arguments for C:

- Consequential loss: s 53(2), this loss of profit claim not in contemplation of parties; what said to Mr H not sufficient so not liable.
- Notice on fax and phone call end of Oct not sufficient. (Content of phone call?)
- D did not give C opportunity to rectify (t/c 22.10.08).

Evaluation: If succeed on arguments re: defective goods (see above); D's case on remoteness is not strong; stronger on mitigation, very strong on proof of loss.

D's loss of profit on shops

£1,500
Law: as above for C loss on Chocaganza weekend.
Arguments for D:

- Loss flows naturally from breach by C; s 53(2) (delivery of faulty goods on 4.10.08 and failure to replace once notified that faulty).

- Can prove loss of profit by comparing accounts for the two months.
- Did all necessary to mitigate loss (see above—but delay in obtaining goods and the quality was not as good).

Arguments for C:
As above except no argument on foreseeability.

Evaluation: If succeed on arguments re: defective goods, D has strong arguments on these losses.

Costs

D's to date £250 and £175 for today £425. Query C's costs?

For C to prove good service of summons (presumably via court); C's action precipitous given C knew of complaint re: 2nd delivery.

Usual order: for D pay to have set aside but in hospital so query ordered.

Resist any request to pay C's costs/probably can't argue that C pay D's costs.

Evaluation: D's arguments stand a moderate chance of success in defeating order for costs against him.

9.8 Application to Case Study B

Do the same exercise with Case Study B and set out the issues with your arguments.

10

Information exchange

10.1 The role in negotiation

Negotiation is as much about exchanging information as argument or making and seeking concessions. No negotiation can proceed without some information exchange. The amount of information negotiators seek and are prepared to disclose will have a real impact on the negotiation process and outcome. How the information is conveyed and assimilated will also have an impact on the negotiation. The transmission of information invariably includes distortion both in the stating and the hearing of it. There is considerable research on how people's expectations and preconceptions influence the way in which they present information and the way it is assimilated. Much has been written about information exchange as used in the different negotiating strategies. It is therefore important to recognise that some negotiators use information exchange as a tool in their strategy, eg, to exploit in a competitive strategy. Some also use the whole negotiation process as a means of finding out about the opponent's case (a fishing expedition).

It is therefore important not to underrate this element of a negotiation. Be aware of the potential distortions, think carefully about the information being exchanged and the purpose of it and check whether the other side is exploiting it. We consider factors which may distort information, then how information exchange is used in the three strategies and some tactics used in information exchange, before turning to how to prepare to deal with these aspects in the negotiation process.

10.2 Factors which may distort information

Whenever we approach any negotiation, we have expectations about what will happen and why. These expectations will influence our view of the information we have and how we receive and assimilate information from our opponent.

10.2.1 Expectations and preconceptions

We all have views of the world based on our own experience. These views will inform what we expect from a given situation. We are likely to approach most situations, including negotiations, with some preconception of what is likely to happen. Such expectations or preconceptions assist us in making decisions both before and during the negotiation. Some of these expectations have a positive effect on the negotiation, eg, if our expectation is to win, it can provide us with a determination that may make winning more likely. But expectations can also have a negative effect. This is particularly so where expectations are based on limited and unreliable information, as this increases the scope for our own personal biases, preconceptions and misconceived expectations to shape our view of things, the decisions we take and the way we behave. Thus, for example, the more limited information we have about what the other side wants or their motivation, the more we rely on our own expectations and preconceptions about how they are likely to act.

We also have expectations about our own case and what we want to achieve from the negotiation. It is important to remember that, at whatever stage of the litigation process a negotiation takes place, there will almost invariably be gaps in the information available to you and your opponent. There may not yet have been exchange of documents, witness statements or expert reports. Even at the court door, you may find that documents which should have been disclosed were not. Even where witness statements and expert reports have been exchanged, there remains the important factor of how well the witnesses will present in court. In particular, where there is a dispute of fact, the credibility of the witnesses will be crucial. You may not have encountered your opponent before and therefore his characteristics and negotiating abilities are unknown. You are unlikely to know his view of the case, including the concessions that may be sought or his view of when settlement becomes less attractive for his client than facing the court hearing. The greater the gaps in our information, the greater the scope for our expectations and perceptions to play a role in the decisions we take during the negotiation. This is true whether the gaps relate to the subject matter of the dispute or the personalities involved in the negotiation.

It may be that your perceptions and expectations are correct, but in all negotiations it pays to consider what expectations and perceptions we have, and why, and question the underlying basis for such expectations and perceptions. From such an analysis you can consider whether those expectations should be informing your decisions.

10.2.2 Cross-cultural negotiations

Cross-cultural negotiations are open to misunderstanding because ignorance and lack of experience of another culture can lead to expectations of behaviour based on stereotypes. These stereotypes are often based on generalised and inaccurate information. Expectations based on them can influence the negotiation by dictating, or to some extent influencing, our behaviour. As we saw in **Chapter 7**, when considering a party's objectives it is advisable to remember that their objectives may be very different from yours. Similarly, you cannot assume that the other side wants the same result as you from the negotiation. Particularly where the opponent is from a different culture, be aware that your lack of experience or knowledge of that culture may mean you are working on stereotypes and incorrect preconceptions.

10.2.3 Selective filtering of information

Information exchange involves assimilation of new information. One of the difficulties negotiators experience is trying to listen, analyse and evaluate the relevance of the information received. In order to deal with the information, and process it, it is inevitably simplified and categorised. Selective filtering tends to occur as part of this process. Both in your preparation and in the conduct of the negotiation, you should consider the impact this has on information exchange.

All too often we are unaware of how our preconceptions and expectations influence our perceptions and how we receive information. Having analysed the facts, law, etc, we take a view of the case. We make a generalised decision about the strength of the case based on the information we have. This may include information from a conference with the client and our response to him or her as a person. Our view will also be coloured by experience of past cases of this type or with this sort of client. Our initial view may be an over- or underestimate of its strength. This view can then be confirmed through a process of selective perception that rejects material contrary to our expectations, leaving only information that confirms them.

Selective filtering can explain a negotiator's over-confidence about the merit of his or her client's position. If, during the preparatory stages, a negotiator has evaluated the strengths and weaknesses of his or her client's case and concluded that, on issue X, the client has a virtually unassailable claim, the negotiator will often selectively filter the information received from the other side during the negotiation. That which is contrary to the previously held view is not digested. The negotiator listens and hears only information that confirms his or her initial views. In such a scenario, it is possible that a selective filtering process will assist the negotiator in securing a better deal for the client than he or she would otherwise obtain, provided the opponent is a weak opponent. However, the danger is that, by rejecting information concerning the weaknesses in the claim, the negotiator holds out for too much and the negotiation founders when the opponent is unwilling to concede.

Equally, a negotiator may have underestimated the strength of the case and believe as a result that he or she is unlikely to be able to persuade the opponent to move very far towards him or her in the negotiation. In this case the negotiator may not hear that the opponent's arguments are weak and that concessions are being made well beyond those expected.

10.2.4 Fear of revealing information

Most negotiators, even non-competitive ones, are reticent about revealing information to the other side. As Condlin in his article 'Cases on Both Sides: Patterns of Argument in Legal Dispute Resolution' (1985) 44 *Maryland Law Review* 64 at 75 says:

> Negotiators are likely to approach one another circumspectly, revealing as little as possible until discovering what state of affairs obtains. This is only prudent. One does not expose one's neck until it is clear the head will not be chopped off.

The amount of information revealed by a negotiator will depend to some degree on the strategy adopted. Most negotiators are more willing to reveal information favourable to their case than to the opponent's. The opponent may then make assumptions about the relative strengths of the case. The result of this phenomenon is that information exchange can be difficult and it pays to remember that the information you receive will be presented in the most favourable light for your opponent.

10.3 Information exchange in the three strategies

As would be expected, the three strategies use information exchange very differently. This use of information exchange will also impact on the conduct of the negotiator. You need therefore to be aware of this, both to enable you to consider how to deal with information exchange and to recognise the techniques used by your opponent.

10.3.1 Competitive negotiators

Competitive negotiators proceed on the basis that both parties want the same thing. What one party gets, the other party loses. The negotiation is about staying as close as possible to the negotiator's opening position by forcing the other party down as close as possible to their bottom line. Exchanging information gives negotiators insight into each other's position. What really is the opponent's 'bottom line'? What are the real strengths and weaknesses of the opponent's case? The competitive negotiator uses information exchange as a tool to win. The competitive negotiator's strategy is to press the opponent for information but disclose as little as possible by:

(a) revealing as little information as possible;

(b) being selective in the information disclosed;

(c) possibly giving inaccurate information (which raises an ethical issue on exactly what the information is and how inaccurate it is) (see also **10.4.1** below);

(d) using a variety of techniques to confuse or divert the opponent away from obtaining information (eg, because it exposes a weakness in his or her case) (see **10.4.2** below).

10.3.2 Cooperative negotiators

Cooperative negotiators share information freely. Seeking to build trust, they do not exaggerate or make false statements but make fair statements of fact. In the same way that competitive negotiators use the exchange of information as a technique to achieve their goal (victory), cooperative negotiators use exchange of information to achieve their goal (agreement). They may assume that the other side will automatically give information freely or that, by being open and honest themselves, making fair statements, etc, they can create a trusting atmosphere which will produce open and honest behaviour in the other side who will be equally forthcoming.

Cooperative negotiators are genuinely interested in exchanging information to assist them in assessing what is a fair settlement. They give information and listen to what the other side has to say. They explain their position and give reasons for their proposals.

10.3.3 Collaborative negotiators

It is probably true to say that collaborative negotiators have no particular strategy about how much information to exchange. Rather, their strategy revolves around the type of information which is exchanged. In **Chapter 7** we considered some of the techniques by which collaborative negotiators approach their case and identify and achieve their client's objectives (separate the people from the problem, focus on interests not positions, invent options for mutual gain—see **7.2**). These techniques involve exchanging information in the negotiation to enable them to see the problem from the other side's point of view, to understand the other side's needs, fears and motivations and to look for options which may bring gains to both sides and produce a good settlement.

Like cooperative negotiators, collaborative negotiators are willing to share information. However, to an extent they share information for a different purpose and as a result are probably more selective in the information they reveal (and possibly seek). Cooperative negotiators share information largely to build trust. They focus on the behavioural response to the sharing, not the content of the information shared. Collaborative negotiators share information to assist them in reaching an informed settlement which reflects their client's needs. Thus they focus on the content of the information shared and not the behavioural effect. Principled and problem-solving strategies focus heavily on information exchange both in determining parties' real needs and interests and looking for increased options.

10.3.4 Impact of these strategies on information exchange

The competitive strategy of seeking but not giving information is part and parcel of the overall strategy of adopting a strong stance, having the upper hand and seeking an all out win. As a technique, separate from the context of the other aspects of the strategy, refusing to give information while demanding it of others can be obstructive and lead to deadlock. The cooperative strategy of seeking to use the act of giving information as a way of persuading the other side to reciprocate depends heavily on the other side being so persuaded, which is unlikely with either a competitive or collaborative opponent. It is therefore a risky strategy to adopt.

Information exchange as used by collaborative negotiators can assist the negotiators in reaching a good settlement, as it involves getting and giving information which means that both negotiators have more information about what the parties want. This may enable them to make more informed decisions about how settlement may be reached, which in turn may affect their response to an offer or request for a concession. Similarly, if negotiators give and receive information about the merits of the case, eg, the negotiators' interpretations of the law, the facts alleged by the parties and the evidence to support the allegations, both negotiators will have better information about the likely chances of the parties in court. This may enable them to determine a fair settlement standard which may affect their response to an offer or request for a concession. Thus, for example, the claimant may be seeking damages for breach of contract and the evidence on whether there was a breach appears to be evenly balanced. The settlement standard should reflect this. As the claimant bears the burden of proof, a defendant's offer of 50 per cent of the claim would be an exceedingly generous offer. The risk in full exchange of information on the merits of the case is that weaknesses in your case may be revealed which may have serious implications both for the negotiation and future conduct of the case.

10.4 Tactics on information exchange

There are a variety of tactics which negotiators can use in the fundamental aspect of information exchange which can affect (increase or decrease) the accuracy and/or flow of the information exchanged. To a degree, some of them are based on the recognition of the psychological factors noted above which can influence how information is conveyed and received.

10.4.1 Accuracy of information

Any interchange between two people will almost invariably involve some distortion in the information passed between them. Competitive negotiators are more likely to consciously attempt to distort information to meet their own ends, although cooperative, principled and problem-solving negotiators may do this less consciously. The level of distortion, the deliberateness or consciousness of it and how it is done introduce ethical considerations.

(a) Communication can be distorted because people (consciously or unconsciously) present or hear statements as factual statements when they are not. In discussing the clients' claims, assertions of what happened, etc, a negotiator may present as statements of fact matters which are allegations only (for which there may not be proof). Both negotiators may then treat these allegations as statements of fact. A negotiator may put his or her opinion of the value of something as a statement of fact. The opinion is then accepted as fact (ie, this is the value).

(b) Bluffing is consciously masking one's position by creating an impression of greater strength (usually) or weakness (rarely) than is in fact the case. This can be done by making statements which, although true, create a false impression, or by merely allowing an opponent to form a particular impression. It is contrary to the ethos of all but competitive strategies.

(c) Finally there are statements which are untrue and calculated to mislead, which is always unethical.

Be aware of the possibility of distortion of information, listen carefully to what is said and check the basis of the statements. Do not be swayed by overconfidence in an opponent. What is the evidence to support the statement? Is it in fact untrue? Label misleading behaviour and insist on accuracy.

10.4.2 Flow of information

There is no rule that negotiators must reveal information. As we saw above, most negotiators are wary of revealing information. They are more inclined to reveal information that supports their case. This may lead the opponent to assume the case is stronger than it is. To guard against this, think carefully about what is being revealed. Do not make assumptions. Ask for further information. Seek evidence to support allegations or reasons for proposals.

Some negotiators fail to provide information even when specifically requested to do so and disguise this failure with a variety of devices.

(a) Diverting attention: the negotiator may divert attention and fail to provide the information requested by simply changing the topic to another issue, asking a question rather than providing an answer or focusing on an approaching deadline (real or fictitious). If the information requested is important, do not be diverted.

(b) Apparently answering: the negotiator may respond (like a politician) with information which only partially answers the question or which, although related to the question, does not in fact answer it and is very long and confused. The negotiator relies on the questioner not pressing for clarification because he or she feels responsible for any misunderstanding either because of the way in which the question was worded or because he or she simply fails to understand the answer. Press. If you do not understand, ask for clarification.

Some negotiators may refuse to give the information. Alternatively, they may agree to provide the information only in exchange for information or a concession. Think carefully about the importance of the information requested, about how crucial it is to the negotiation and whether you can continue without it. Think also about any price requested. It may be fine and increase the flow of information. Or it may be a concession which you are not prepared to make.

On the other side of the coin, some negotiators are very good at getting information from the opponent. They have learned to use the fact that most people prefer talking to listening. By asking questions and speaking little themselves, they obtain a great deal of information from the other side. They are careful not to ask questions which put the opponent on the defensive. Guard against being exploited by this tactic and providing too much information to someone who may misuse it. Think carefully about the question asked. What is the purpose of it? Consider whether the information requested really does need to be provided. Do not get carried away by the desire to do most of the talking.

10.5 Preparing to exchange information

10.5.1 What it involves

Your analysis of the case to date should have identified the gaps in your information which include: details of what your opponent's client wants from the negotiation; what he or she is prepared to give to your client; your opponent's interpretation of the law and the cases which support this; details of allegations of fact by his or her client; his or her client's response to an allegation of fact by your client; and evidence to support allegations of fact. Once you have identified these potential areas of information exchange, you need to consider carefully: what information you want to get from your opponent; how you are going to respond to requests from him or her; and how you are going to deal with joint gaps in the information (ie, where neither you nor your opponent has the relevant information). Whatever strategy or tactics you adopt in the negotiation, your preparation should be thorough. Thus, even if you intend to adopt a competitive strategy, revealing little, you need to be aware of the information your opponent may seek from you. Your strategy may not work (you may not be able to keep up the competitive stance) or it may make you look weak (as though you do not know your case).

10.5.2 Seeking information from your opponent

Your preparation should include considering what information you want or need to get from your opponent on the full range of matters likely to be discussed in the negotiation: objectives, law, facts, evidence. There are both practical and tactical considerations in deciding what information to seek from your opponent. Remember that your opponent is far more likely to reveal information which supports his or her case than that which does not.

Getting information about what your opponent's client wants from the negotiation is useful as it gives an idea of the matters on which settlement may be easy or difficult. However, you need to be aware that asking for this information, aside from simply getting a list of those matters on which he wants settlement, is in effect asking your opponent to state his opening position. This is getting into the realms of concessions which we deal with in **Chapter 11**. Seeking information about the underlying needs and interests of the other side may also assist you in understanding why he or she is concerned about an issue. Your opponent may be more willing to share this either because he or she feels it bolsters the client's position on what is being sought or because your opponent is taking a more collaborative approach to the negotiation. This could be useful because it may give more information to enable you to 'expand the pie', ie, create alternatives for settlement which had not previously been considered.

Seeking information about your opponent's interpretation of the law may also be useful as it gives a further insight into how the case will be argued in court and may affect your view of the likely outcome and, therefore, give a clearer idea of a reasonable settlement standard. If you have done your legal research properly, you should not get a nasty surprise from your opponent. It may be, however, that you discover he or she is weak on the law and you can then use this in the negotiation.

Seeking information about the allegations of fact and evidence requires more careful consideration as this can be a double-edged sword. If your opponent has the information, it is a cheap and quick way to get it. Asking for detailed information on important issues can show how well prepared you are. If your opponent does not have the information, it may be interpreted as a weakness in his or her case (lack of preparation on his or her part or lack of full instructions from his or her client). On the other hand, asking for information, particularly on fairly basic matters, could be seen as a weakness on your part. Asking for information also makes you more vulnerable as it exposes to your opponent the fact that you do not have this information and because your opponent is not bound to answer your questions.

Your decisions on what information to seek must take into account both what it is important for you to know and whether the request is a genuine challenge to your opponent. As pointed out above, getting information about what your opponent's client wants is important. Asking your opponent for the evidence to support their allegations, particularly in cases before or just after issue, is a challenge and in most cases worth the risk. First, he or she may not have this information, so their client's statement of fact is pure allegation. Secondly, even if he or she does have some information to support his or her case, it gives you a better basis on which to view your client's case. In any event, his or her evaluation is likely to have taken this into account and revealing the information to you is unlikely to change his or her view on concessions.

When planning information exchange, bear in mind that, where the case is in the early stages of litigation, neither you nor your opponent is likely to have full information. This could affect the tactics because it alters the expectation of both sides as to which information it is reasonable to have at this point.

10.5.3 Responding to requests from your opponent

Your opponent will be planning what information to seek from you with precisely the same considerations in mind. You should be prepared to respond to the requests in the most effective way. More care needs to be given to your responses to requests for information than to your requests for information. Many of the considerations set out above also apply. In particular, like your opponent, you should be circumspect about revealing information and clear what information is favourable to your case.

Giving information about what your client wants from the negotiation and is prepared to give to the other side beyond the list of items to negotiate is giving away your opening position and this must be properly planned. We deal with how to do this in **Chapter 11**. Sharing information about your client's underlying needs and interests can assist in the same way as set out above but be wary of giving information which may reveal to your opponent something which puts you in a weaker position. For example, your client may be claiming damages and there is a dispute as to how much this should be. Revealing early on that your client has a cash-flow problem will give your opponent information which he or she can then use to reduce the amount offered. Although you may already have considered making a concession on the amount claimed if your opponent were to pay immediately, by revealing your client's position you have lost the initiative. The reduction in the sum may therefore be greater due to the early payment than would be the case had the information not been revealed.

Giving information which relates to the merits of the case, ie, your view of the law, and the facts and the evidence, also needs careful consideration, distinguishing clearly between information which assists your case and that which does not. Giving information about your view of the law and the basis for it can be helpful where your view (based on thorough legal research) is that the law is heavily weighted on your side. Similarly, when dealing with requests for information about the facts and evidence, be clear about the potential gaps and ambiguities that your opponent may use against you. Reveal information in a way that is more likely to make it credible and persuasive to your opponent. If you do not want to reveal information, consider what tactic you could use to avoid doing so. Could you respond with information which partially answers the question or diverts attention?

10.5.4 Gaps which neither party can fill

There may be gaps in the information which neither party can fill, and you will need to plan how to deal with this in the negotiation. It is likely that during the course of a negotiation you will find that some pieces of information relevant to the negotiation are known by neither you nor your opponent. For example, in respect of an allegation that an accident was caused because one of the parties was drunk, there may be no indication of how much he or she had drunk, over what period, etc. One side may have a witness to an accident who states that the defendant was driving too fast but, when pressed for further information, it becomes clear that there is no indication of the speed or how close the witness was to the car. Even where the outcome of a case is determined, the decision is invariably made on less than complete information because witnesses cannot remember the details or are unclear, etc. You need to take this into account when negotiating.

The further along in the litigation process, the fewer gaps there should be. Early on, there may be large gaps in the evidence. You will be expected to reach a settlement without filling these gaps unless the information is essential to reaching a proper settlement. Collecting evidence is expensive and one of the main reasons for reaching an early settlement is to avoid this cost. Where the gap in the information is not essential, you should proceed as best you can without it. If you have incomplete factual information, you should proceed on the basis of what you do have and what the court is likely to find in the absence of full information, taking into account who would bear the burden of proof. There is also likely to be other evidence and arguments on which the merits of the case rest.

Where there is a crucial gap, eg, in a dispute over the ownership of an antique item for which neither party knows the value, you will need to be prepared to deal with it. Consider not only how to get the information but also whether the cost of getting it outweighs the benefit of having it. Who should obtain the information? How long might it take? What will it cost? Who will pay the cost? Are the costs likely to be disproportionate to the value of the item? You also need to think whether to reach agreement given that this information is still needed. This could involve agreeing a formula settlement, eg, X will keep the item and pay Y an amount equal to half the valuation plus the costs of the valuation within seven days of receipt of the valuation. A less satisfactory solution, but one which may be necessary where a case is more complicated, is to finalise the settlement of the issue by telephone when the information is available.

10.6 Summary

You need to ensure that you can use your analysis of your preparation on information exchange so that it is effective in the negotiation. Making a note of the areas on which information may be exchanged is useful. You need to consider how and when you will exchange information in the negotiation. We look at this aspect in the chapter on planning your structure (see **Chapter 13**). In the negotiation you will also need to be aware of the strategy and tactics the opponent may use in response to your requests. We look again at this aspect in the chapter on the conduct of the negotiation (see **Chapter 16**).

10.7 Application to Case Study A

NOTE: because this case is still in the early stages of the litigation process it may well be that neither party will have information beyond that given in the witness statements. Both parties are likely to have some information but this is more likely to be further allegations of fact rather than evidence. The use of information exchange in this case is likely to be to a large extent to challenge the other side, to show that many of the allegations of fact are just that at this stage.

Information to seek from opponent

C's knowledge of calls made prior to 22.10.08.
Records kept by Mr H re contract/later dealings?
Mr H's record at the company—why has he left?
Company record keeping system.
C's recollection of phone call of 22.10.08 (what precisely was said?).
Where to get chocolate from? Any previous difficulties?
Does C still have any of the chocolate left?

- What state is it in?
- How much?
- What efforts to sell?
- What is the market (Belgian chocolates)?
- How calculate profit?
- On what terms sell to us?

Information which may be sought from us

Our record keeping system—specifically records of:

- Mr H's representations.
- Phone calls to Mr H.
- Phone calls to C.

What wrong with chocolate?

- How much did D use?
- Why not use?

- Still have it? Where keep it? How keep it? (ie, got worse)
- Why not return it?
- Why not tell C in phone call?

Chocaganza weekend:

- How prove loss due to lack of 'ornate style'?
- How prove this down to late start (not lack of skill)?
- How calculate loss of profit?

Loss on shops:

- How prove loss due to chocolate?

Information which may be sought from third party

Independent view on the chocolate (query whether useful given the delay; also regard must be given to cost of doing this).

10.8 Application to Case Study B

Do the same exercise for Case Study B.

11 Preparation—concessions

11.1 Introduction

Negotiation is about moving towards agreement. Each side must know what moves (concessions) they will offer to their opponent and what moves (concessions) they will seek. Seeking and making concessions is one of the main ingredients of reaching settlement and will be one of the principal activities in a negotiation. It is perhaps the most difficult aspect of negotiating. It is therefore important for you to understand why many people find this difficult and how the different strategies can use these difficulties and turn them to an advantage. Proper preparation on concessions will assist you to overcome these difficulties and negotiate effectively.

In this chapter, we look first at the psychological influences on negotiators when making concessions, then how concessions are used in the three different strategies (competitive, cooperative and collaborative) and a variety of specific tactics used in the concession-making aspect of conventional negotiations. We then look more closely at legal negotiations and distinguish matters which legitimately form the basis of concessions and those which do not. With this context in mind, we then turn to a more detailed consideration of planning concessions in dispute-resolution negotiations.

11.2 Psychological influences of concessions

11.2.1 Opening—its impact

Research has shown that the level of settlement achieved is often related to the [illegible] demand. Where the ball starts rolling in this process will influence the outcome. Thus, the higher the demand, provided it is not outlandish, the more one gets. Judging exactly where to pitch the demand can be difficult. An unrealistic demand has little chance of success unless the opponent is very weak. If it is not believable (ie, has no rational basis and does not take into account the strengths and weaknesses of the case from both sides), it reduces the negotiator's credibility. If it is too far above what any reasonable opponent would agree to, it may require a climb down (ie, many and/or large concessions) which will also reduce the negotiator's credibility.

Starting too low can severely limit room for manoeuvre. First, the demand may be so close to the least the negotiator is prepared to accept that it leaves no room for further concessions. Secondly, it may increase the expectations of the other side who may assume that it is a far greater distance from what the negotiator is genuinely prepared to settle for than it is in fact. The other side may therefore maintain pressure to reduce it.

11.2.2 Losing credibility

All negotiations involve compromise and compromise requires both parties to move from their initially stated position to something less favourable. However, making concessions can, and frequently does, have psychological influences on both the person making the concessions and the person receiving them. First, the person making a concession may fear that it is too much (ie, a smaller concession would have been accepted by the opponent). Secondly, making a concession can be seen both by the maker and receiver as a sign of weakness, a loss of credibility by the negotiator who made the concession. It can also be interpreted as an indication that the maker will move further, may not be able to resist an opponent and therefore may be open to being pushed to give away more than he or she has planned. Conversely, refusing to make concessions may be seen as a sign of strength, an indication that the negotiator will not move from his or her stated position and will therefore win. Thus, making a concession may result in the maker losing credibility. Fear of this loss of credibility can influence whether concessions are made.

The psychological influences surrounding concession-making are used in many of the strategies and tactics in negotiations. To an extent, their use relies on the opponent being distracted by emotions, expectations and the dynamics of the situation and, as a result, failing to negotiate on the basis of reasoned analysis of the case, ie, what the parties want and the merits of the case. Thus concern over loss of credibility and determination not to back down can mask the realities of the situation. Negotiators may hold firm to their position on an issue that is relatively minor compared with others on the table for negotiation. The fear that any movement from the stated position is an invitation for exploitation produces deadlock, when a rational approach could move the negotiation forward. Understanding this and using your analysis of the case, reviewing what both parties are seeking and the merits of the claims, where there is room for compromise, can all assist you to deal with the psychological impact of the particular strategy or tactic.

One risk of being overly influenced by the psychological impact is that, despite pressure to settle given the costs and stress of court, both sides have such a fear of losing credibility that neither side is prepared to make concessions. The longer neither side is prepared to move, the more is at stake and the more parties become trapped in their positions and likely to reach deadlock. However, the dynamic of the negotiation may be changed by either party and this could break the deadlock, eg, by moving to a different issue or by acknowledging the problem and looking for alternative ways to overcome it.

Exactly how you react to concession-seeking and making will depend to some degree on your psychological make-up. Being well prepared will assist you in dealing with concessions on a rational rather than psychological basis. In any event, understanding how the strategies and tactics use the psychological influences will help you to use them effectively and combat their negative effects when used against you.

11.3 Use of concessions in the three strategies

11.3.1 Traditional assumptions—I win/you lose

As we saw in **Chapter 3**, traditional bargaining strategies (eg, competitive and cooperative strategies) proceed on the assumption that all parties want the same thing. Therefore, concessions are seen as gains and losses; what one party concedes (loses) the other party gains (wins). Their concession planning is based on this assumption and they see this as part of the negotiating process as the parties move along a single line between their opening demands and their bottom line. Their concession-making strategy reflects their assumptions and planning.

11.3.2 Competitive strategy

Competitive negotiators are out to win and this means staying as close to their opening position as possible (ie, as far as possible from the bottom line). They attempt to use the psychological influences set out above to their advantage by maintaining their own credibility and trying to force the other side to concede and lose credibility.

11.3.2.1 Opening/demands

An integral part of a competitive strategy is to open high (ie, to open at the most extreme position maintainable), stay high and sometimes increase demands. Throughout the negotiation the demands will remain near to the best possible outcome. The demands made may be inflated, ie, above what the negotiator actually considers to be the best possible outcome.

11.3.2.2 Concessions/offers

Another integral part of a competitive strategy is to make as few concessions as possible while obtaining as many as possible from the opponent. Thus a competitive negotiator:

- makes few concessions;
- makes small concessions;
- makes unimportant concessions;
- makes false concessions (ie, suggests a particular point is important and makes a concession on it when in fact it is of little importance);
- is slow to make concessions (ie, does not make them early in the negotiation).

The competitive negotiator demands concessions from his or her opponent and:

- may impose them as a condition of the relationship;
- focuses on concessions from the opponent;
- may require a concession from his or her opponent before considering making one himself or herself.

11.3.3 Cooperative strategy

Cooperative negotiators seek settlement and use concessions to encourage reciprocal behaviour by their opponent. They attempt to use the psychological influences to their advantage by showing there is nothing to fear by making concessions, that it need not be seen as a weakness. Cooperative negotiators hope that making concessions will be seen as building trust and confidence. Once this has been achieved, the opponent will be less anxious about making concessions and the negotiators can reach agreement by mutual concession.

To a lesser degree, this strategy is also probably based on another psychological phenomenon, that of 'mirroring behaviour' which we will consider in more detail when we look at communicating effectively in **Chapter 15**. This phenomenon occurs when two

people are in discussion. In addition to speaking, people also communicate using physical gestures (ie, body language). Our physical gestures (eg, how we sit, hold our heads, etc) can convey information about our attitude towards the other person (eg, that we are friendly, want to agree or are unapproachable, feel superior). Two people in discussion will often unconsciously 'mirror' each other's behaviour. This can influence the content of the discussion. Cooperative negotiators may be using this either consciously or unconsciously themselves. Their 'friendly/approachable' manner induces similar behaviour in their opponent which in turn affects how their opponent reacts.

11.3.3.1 Opening/demands

Cooperative negotiators open in a way which shows them to be trustworthy and willing to view the negotiation as a compromise. Their opening proposals will be reasonable and they will make fair suggestions, frequently explaining the basis for what they are seeking.

11.3.3.2 Concessions/offers

Cooperative negotiators make unilateral concessions based on the assumption that this will encourage the other side to reciprocate. On the basis that both parties want to reach agreement, they assume this means movement by both sides. They focus on this aspect of the negotiation (ie, an equal amount of movement by both sides). They make concessions on the assumption that the other side also sees the negotiation as mutual movement towards agreement or that they can encourage the other negotiator to view it in this way. The cooperative negotiator hopes that the other side will 'follow their example' and reciprocate to make the negotiation 'fair'.

11.3.4 Collaborative strategy

Collaborative negotiators do not make the traditional assumption that in a negotiation one party wins and the other loses. They adopt a win/win approach (ie, both parties getting a fair deal from the settlement) and see the negotiation as a joint exercise in solving the problem by reaching an objectively justified settlement. They seek to collaborate in looking for ways to expand the resources or opportunities, taking into account the needs and interests of both parties. They seek to reach a settlement which reflects both parties' needs with low transaction costs (problem-solving) or which is objectively fair (principled).

In **Chapter 7** we looked at some of the techniques used in considering the parties' objectives (separate the people from the problem, focus on interests not positions, find options for mutual gain). In **Chapter 8**, we looked at the way in which principled negotiators develop a BATNA (Best Alternative to a Negotiated Agreement) which is generally more flexible than a bottom line and how they seek to develop an objective standard against which to gauge settlement. These strategies can be used to reduce the psychological influence of concessions in order to put the negotiating process on a less stressful and more rational basis. However, aside from this, both principled and problem-solving strategies concentrate on expanding the pie and to a degree avoid the problem of having to divide it.

11.3.5 Bargaining tactics used in dealing with concessions

A number of tactics have been developed and used as bargaining techniques for dealing with concessions. They cover ways of seeking concessions from the other side (ie, putting demands or proposals to them), making offers/concessions and responding to concessions sought. Most of these tactics stem from the competitive strategy and are based on the psychological influences on negotiators when dealing with concessions. The range of techniques available is set out below to assist you to understand the techniques which may be used against you and how you should respond.

11.3.5.1 Precondition demands

A party may require a condition to be fulfilled or a demand satisfied before he or she will enter negotiations. This is an attempt to obtain an early concession without trading anything in return. It may be used to test the other side to see how easily he or she will concede. If used against you, be clear that this is the position and ensure that the demand is seen by both sides as included in the negotiation. Just responding to it may be seen as being prepared to capitulate too easily.

11.3.5.2 Extreme opening demand

Using an extreme opening demand (ie, at the very margin of what is credible) can influence how the parties see the 'bargaining range' (see **3.2.2**), putting it closer to the end which gives your client the most. It can also indicate that a competitive strategy is being used. It may create doubt in the opponent's mind about his or her assessment of the case. If too extreme, however, it undermines the maker's credibility, introducing distrust and competition into the negotiation which may then break down. When used against you, you can counter with an equally extreme demand (thus escalating the negotiation), label it as extreme, ignore it or move to non-positional bargaining, ie, to discussion of the issues, needs and interests of the parties (see **Chapter 17**).

11.3.5.3 Bunching

This tactic involves putting all the important demands together early in the negotiation. It has a similar impact to a high opening demand. However, it reveals more about your position than a mere high opening demand as it indicates which issues you consider important. If used by your opponent, respond to it in the same way you would to an extreme opening demand while absorbing the relevant information to use later.

11.3.5.4 Concessions early

Making early concessions is the sign of a cooperative negotiator trying to create trust, openness and reciprocal behaviour from the other side. It is a risky tactic as it may easily be exploited. It may also result in both parties swapping concessions without having considered the real issues in the case or the clients' interests. In responding to it be aware of the underlying ethos, which seeks reciprocation and may lead to soft positional bargaining which may not consider all of the options.

11.3.5.5 False demands

This tactic involves inflating the number and importance of issues or demands, and serves several purposes. First, it disguises the real position. Secondly, it gives the negotiator scope for making concessions at little or no cost. Thirdly, where there is consideration of how far each side has moved to reach agreement, it can create the perception of greater movement by the side making the false concessions. It may, however, backfire on the user by precipitating more demands from the other side or shunting the negotiation into irrelevant discussion. By asking for reasons to support the demands sought, you can attempt to guard against being taken in by this tactic.

(*Note:* in some books this technique is labelled the 'Brer Rabbit technique' because of his ploy of using pleas not to throw him into the briar patch to get his captors to do just that. Not strictly the same thing, but there are similarities.)

11.3.5.6 Escalating demands

Most negotiators 'open high', ie, start with the most they seek and move 'down' from that position. However, some, as a tactic, escalate their demands, increasing them either from what was expected from the papers and previous exchanges between the clients or from their opening position. Done with a view to determining the toughness of the opponent or the limits of what they will concede, it is a risky tactic likely to result in confrontation, escalation on both sides and complete breakdown. Where used against you, counter by increasing your demands (a dangerous response), labelling the behaviour, refusing to consider the demands or moving from positional bargaining (see **Chapter 17** below).

11.3.5.7 Split the difference or compromise

A negotiator may suggest that a way of settling either the whole substance of the negotiation or one issue may be to 'split the difference', ie, both sides compromise equally. This can in fact be a reasonable suggestion and produce a reasonable result for both parties. It is also a tempting solution because it is a 'focal point', ie, easy to identify and explain as a common position. However, it can be used inappropriately.

Whether splitting the difference is fair depends on where the parties started and how far each has moved during the negotiation. It is not a genuine compromise if one party has opened with an extreme or inflated demand and made fewer concessions than the other party who may have opened at a more reasonable level.

Also, splitting the difference may not be the solution which produces the best result. It may not satisfy either party's interests. Using it as a way of resolving differences may simply divert the discussion away from the parties' real needs and interests. Because the parties are speaking in cooperative terms, it can produce a sense of fair settlement where the settlement is in fact not fair because it does not reflect the parties' needs.

In responding to such a suggestion, acknowledge the apparent appeal to fairness but also weigh up what has already occurred in the negotiation to ascertain whether it really does represent a compromise. Also, move away from positions and towards consideration of the interests and needs of the client to see whether another solution or formula would be more appropriate.

11.3.5.8 Boulwarism or the single offer approach

Named after a man who negotiated an offer based on his perception of what was fair, it is a 'take it or leave it' approach which may be used to save time and cut through the ritual dance of positional bargaining. It may also give the user a sense of power and authority. The person using it may genuinely consider that what is proposed is fair. However, the other side may not believe this. In addition, such a tactic fails to recognise that it deprives the other negotiator of any participation in determining the settlement and gives him or her little control over the settlement reached. The other negotiator is left with no input and may react by straight rejection, even if the proposal appears to be reasonable. Where used against you, acknowledge the consideration which may have gone into the proposal and point out that there may be considerations on your side which have not been included and therefore need discussion, or ask for the reasoning behind the offer and how it has been assessed as fair to both parties.

11.3.5.9 Slicing/salami/nibbling

This tactic involves dividing issues up into smaller issues which can be used with demands or concessions. Used with demands, it consists of seeking and getting agreement on individual demands, on the basis that a series of small demands are more likely to be accepted and disguise the overall amount of the total demand. Used with concessions, it consists of dividing what you have to concede thereby increasing the number of concessions made (although not the overall amount conceded). Focusing the negotiation on the number of concessions made, rather than the amount both parties have conceded, produces the appearance of conceding more than has in fact been given. In both cases, insistence on no unconditional agreement until the whole package is on the table guards against this being used effectively against you.

11.3.5.10 Trade-offs/log-rolling/the overall package

Rather than dealing with items sequentially, ie, agreeing each one before moving to the next, negotiators can trade off items. Where parties put different values on different items they can log-roll, ie, trade off items of lower value for those of higher value. To do this effectively they need to consider all the issues before reaching unconditional agreement on any of them. Parties should weigh up the relative values of different items or issues, explore each other's preferences, and then consider the whole package. By making all proposals conditional or hypothetical until an acceptable overall package has emerged, the negotiators are able to discuss a variety of options to produce the best settlement. Research has shown that negotiators who agree only to the 'overall package' generally make better settlements.

11.3.5.11 Backtracking/reopening

Where a particular item or issue has been agreed and the negotiation has moved to other issues, a negotiator may backtrack and try to reopen the agreed issue with a view to increasing the gain either on the issue currently under discussion or the one already agreed. This is a risky tactic as it immediately creates distrust and may cause the negotiation to break down. When used against you, recognise what is happening and why, then label the behaviour and refuse to deal on the basis suggested.

11.3.5.12 Misleading concession pattern

As outlined above, most negotiators will reduce in size and number the concessions they make as they get nearer to their 'bottom line'. This tactic involves reducing the concessions well before the 'bottom line' and is used to mislead the other side as to the bottom line and therefore the potential settlement range.

11.4 Concessions distinguished from clarification; statements of law; admissions of fact

It is useful at this point to revisit one of the collaborative strategies discussed in **Chapter 7**, that of distinguishing between the parties' legal positions and their needs and interests (see **7.3.2**). While a court case is focused on and will make a decision based on positions (the merits), a negotiation should focus on and reach settlement based on interests (what the parties want—eg, money, an injunction).

Any case in which you are briefed to appear in court will contain instructions as to both what the client wants (the remedies) and the basis for their claim (the legal case). The court hearing is focused on establishing whether or not the client has the right in law to the remedy claimed. The decision that the court must make is whether the party claiming the right has established this right to the court's satisfaction. Once the right has been established, including a determination on the amount of damages legally proved or the extent of an injunction being legally justified, the remedy follows automatically and there is no argument or discussion about, for example, how much of the legally justified damages should be paid. As an advocate, most of your energy and focus will be on how to persuade the court that your client does have the right to the remedy (or, for the defence, how to persuade the court that the other side does not have the right). Any 'concessions' in court relate to the individual's legal right to the remedy. Thus, a client may 'admit' that an allegation of fact by the other side is true. You may 'concede' on a point of law that a case introduced by your opponent is 'on all fours' with the case under consideration and therefore should be followed.

In a negotiation the focus is the reverse of that in a court hearing. Much of the discussion will be about what the client wants, with the 'rights' of the parties being discussed only in the context of persuading the other side to give the client as much as possible of what he or she wants. The focus of the negotiators is on how much of what the parties want they will get. Negotiators should not attempt to act like a court to determine whether or not the rights have been established. Thus, concessions made by the negotiators should focus on how much of what each party wants he or she will get and not on the allegations of fact or state of the law.

In planning how to deal with concessions in a negotiation, it is therefore very important to distinguish between making and seeking concessions and:

(a) Clarifying what the issues are in the case and what facts are agreed and disputed. This is not conceding, merely assisting to clarify what is in dispute and what needs to be settled.

(b) Agreeing or seeking agreement on the interpretation of disputed areas of law or evidence. Agreeing with your opponent's view on areas of law in dispute can unnecessarily weaken your case. Seeking his or her agreement with your interpretation can make him or her more entrenched. While it may be a tactic to get your opponent to agree, it is not essential to reaching settlement on the items on which your client is seeking to settle (unless your client is seeking a statement from the opponent that he or she accepts a particular interpretation of the law).

(c) Making/seeking admissions of disputed fact. Making admissions can unnecessarily weaken your case. Seeking admissions from the other side can decrease your opponent's willingness to bargain because he or she may well recognise that this weakens his or her position and case. As with agreement on the disputed legal issues, while it is useful to get admissions from your opponent, it is not essential to reaching settlement (unless your client is seeking a statement from the opponent that he or she accepts a particular view of the facts).

11.5 Concession planning strategy

Planning how you will approach the difficult area of concessions may involve adapting parts of all three strategies, taking into account both the need for concessions to be made to reach settlement and the risks in making such concessions. Thus, where appropriate, one may adopt the collaborative approach of using information exchange to assist in expanding the pie or seeking to find imaginative ways for both parties to obtain a settlement which satisfies their underlying needs and interests. Equally, where appropriate, one may adopt a more competitive approach to concession-making, being very cautious and making only those concessions which you must make to achieve settlement.

Thorough preparation is essential to ensure that you use all the tools at your disposal to enable you to use concessions effectively, ie, to ensure that the negotiation moves towards compromise but that the compromise achieves the best possible settlement for your client. This involves three principal steps. First, ensure that you have thought carefully and broadly about what both parties might seek from the negotiation, ie, what 'items' are on the table for negotiation and what are the possibilities to achieve what both parties are seeking. Secondly, ensure that you have evaluated the case effectively and understand how this affects what is achievable for both parties. Thirdly, use this analysis and evaluation to consider precisely what proposals you will make, what concessions you will offer and what you will seek.

11.6 The whole list/thinking laterally

At this point, you need to review your preparation on objectives. Revisit your analysis of your client's and the other side's objectives. Check that, in light of your analysis of the arguments which may be used and the information that may be exchanged, you have a full list of all the items which may be sought by both your client and the other side. Also ensure that you have done the best you can with the information available to determine the parties' priorities on these items.

Are there any shared objectives, something which both parties want to achieve? Both may wish to continue in business with each other. They may agree on some of the terms but dispute others on how this is to be done. Consider how to introduce this into the negotiation and how it may impact on other objectives where there may be some distance between the parties' objectives (eg, how much one party seeks financially and how much the other party is willing to pay).

Reconsider all the possible options available by way of settlement. Are there possibilities for 'expanding the pie'? Are there options that offer mutual advantages to the parties, or an advantage to your opponent at no or very little cost to your client? There may be opportunities you missed on your first analysis of the objectives that are now apparent after a more in-depth analysis of the information. For example, it may be reasonably cheap and easy for your client to offer free advertising to the other side. However, be careful not to make offers that go beyond your instructions and are unlikely to be confirmed by your client or cause him or her problems.

Look for variables that give the most scope for negotiation. For example, your client may want a set price for a contract but also be open to payment by instalment or offering further contracts on terms favourable to the other side. Consider what variables the other side may have. Might he or she be happy to defer the start of the contract or have items delivered over time? Use these factors to trade.

As a result of this analysis you should be clear about what items will be the subject of negotiation. You may not have the full list so think how you want to check this in the negotiation. Do you set out what you think the other side wants and ask your opponent to confirm it? Or do you ask your opponent to tell you what his client wants? The first method risks alerting your opponent to matters which he or she may not have identified but enables you to present the items. This may affect how they are dealt with in the negotiation. The second method enables the opponent to present what his or her client wants and so perhaps influence the negotiation in that respect.

Be clear which items may be relatively easily settled because there will be more room for manoeuvre, more ways of settling which achieve a significant amount of both parties' objectives or potential opportunities for variables. Also be clear which items may prove more difficult to settle because there has to be a division of something which both parties want equally (eg, money).

11.7 Evaluating your case/what is achievable

Evaluating your case means assessing what is achievable for your client, having reasons to justify proposals. This was considered in **Chapter 9** (see **9.4**). It involves considering the list of the parties' objectives (ie, the items to be negotiated) and determining which issues underlie the different items, then, in respect of each issue, considering the strength of the arguments which may be used for or against you, and how likely it is that the court will find for or against your client on this issue.

Having done this, you then need to assess how likely it is that your client will get the items which rely on this issue and consider what settlement standard would be reasonable in light of this. This exercise is more akin to the principled approach of a BATNA (Best Alternative to a Negotiated Agreement) than to a true bottom line favoured by competitive negotiators as it is not completely definitive.

The process of determining your settlement standard involves considering the chances of success in court (ie, winning) and what the court will award (ie, precisely what will the court order). Using an example of a damages claim where breach, causation and proof of loss are in issue, you may determine that your client has a 90 per cent chance of winning on breach and, if he or she does win, a 50 per cent chance of winning on causation. He or she has evidence to prove the losses, so you consider this is virtually certain. Generally speaking, this means the client has roughly a 45 per cent chance of the court finding in his or her favour and ordering the full amount of damages. This will give you a rough standard against which to gauge offers. It does not mean that an offer below 45 per cent is unacceptable. Nor does it mean that the best you can expect to get from your opponent is 45 per cent. What it does mean is that you should seek something within a range of, say, 25 per cent to 65 per cent of the damages. Precisely where on this range will depend on a variety of factors including any information your opponent may possess which would affect your chances of success, how persuasively you and your opponent are in justifying your offers, etc.

Your opponent, doing the same exercise, will of course take into account that your chances of success are less than 50 per cent and that your client may get nothing. He or she may therefore open by offering nothing or something very low. Given this, you should consider where you will open. Your opening should be well above 45 per cent as, arguably, if your client wins, he or she is likely to get the whole sum. Your opening will also be based on how well you can justify it. Providing your reasons are put cogently, emphasising the aspects which favour your client, focusing on the breach and proof of loss which are your strengths and pointing out that if your client wins he or she will get the whole amount plus costs, you may be able to justify an opening at 100 per cent. Clearly, however, you will need to be prepared to move down. You should consider how to stage the steps down so that they are neither too small nor too big. Moving from 100 to 50 per cent is too big a step. Moving down by 1 per cent at a time is too small. Steps of 10 per cent may be right. If the sum is large (eg, £100,000), then moving in 5 per cent steps may be acceptable. If the sum is small (eg, £200), moving in 10 or even 15 per cent steps could be acceptable.

Where the issues under consideration are terms of a contract or an injunction, it may be more difficult to reach a clear settlement standard. However, you should complete the same kind of exercise. Thus, for example, if you act for a client who is seeking an injunction, the question will be how likely the court is to order the injunction as drafted. What is the risk the court will refuse the injunction? Even if the court grants it, will it grant it in the terms sought? These two outcomes may be intertwined in that the court may be prepared to grant the injunction on different terms. Although more difficult, you should try to assess what the court is likely to grant thereby understanding how to approach the negotiation.

11.8 Using your evaluation to plan concessions—justifying your proposals

The example above on damages works through the process of how to relate your evaluation to concession planning. You should do an evaluation on each item and plan your concessions so that you have some appreciation of:

11.8.1 Where should you open?

What is the most that you can justify to your opponent? What is the highest you could possibly argue on the basis of the merits of the case? How can you put the arguments to emphasise strengths and diminish weaknesses? On the above example, you could possibly justify 100 per cent in the way suggested.

11.8.2 The best possible outcome

What is the best you can possibly do for your client on this item, given your evaluation of the relevant arguments for and against you? So, on the above example, 65 per cent is probably the most you could realistically expect to achieve.

11.8.3 The lowest reasonable outcome

In the above example, 25 per cent was the figure. This is not necessarily a rigid bottom line. After all, if the client goes to court, he or she has less than a 50 per cent chance of winning and will get nothing if he or she loses. However, it is a standard against which to gauge offers. Something around this figure would be acceptable, albeit you should be aiming to get more.

11.8.4 Staging your offers

How can you stage concessions (ie, make small fall-back steps between your opening offer and the least you can accept) so as to increase the offer gradually (ie, not move directly from your opening offer to your bottom line) to ensure that the settlement you reach reflects as far as possible what your client is seeking? What reasoning/argument can you use to try to persuade your opponent to accept what you are suggesting? What arguments might your opponent use against you? In the above example, 10 per cent steps seemed to be reasonable.

11.9 Reviewing and using your client's priorities

11.9.1 What must the client have?

When planning your concessions you must be very clear about what your client *must* have, ie, what items will he not concede? If you are unclear, you must check. Most clients will say they want as much as they can get. Conversely, they say they are reluctant to pay anything to the other side. Both statements should be interpreted as doing your best to get the client as much as possible given the merits of the case. However, your instructions may set a money limit above or below which the client will not go and you must honour this. The client may require a particular term in a contract or an injunction. If what your client has laid down as a *must* is not achievable, you should tell him or her and seek instructions. Where it is achievable, you must note it and ensure that you respect it.

11.9.2 Using priorities to trade

Where there are several items on the table, you can use them to trade. Give more on an item to which your client gives little priority to get more on one to which your client gives high priority. For example, your client may be the defendant in a case where the claimant is seeking an injunction and a claim for damages. The injunction may be quite restrictive for the client's business and this is of real concern to him or her. The damages claim is of much less concern and, although reluctant to pay, he or she is prepared to pay something on the claim. Consider how you can trade money for fewer restrictions.

Even where there is only one item, eg, money, there are often different aspects of payment which can be traded. Thus, you could offer to pay earlier if the other side will accept less.

11.9.3 The overall settlement

Once you have done the detailed planning, you should stand back and look again at what your client wants globally. Given your evaluation, concession-planning and possibilities for trading, what do you think you can achieve for your client? What is the best overall settlement you can expect? What is the least that you should accept?

This can be difficult where there are a number of items for consideration, particularly where some are financial and others are not. Taking into account what the client *must* have on any item, try to decide/identify a point below which you will not go. Thus, for example, when negotiating both the terms of future dealings and past losses, what is the least you will accept on the future terms and how will that affect your 'bottom line' on losses?

11.10 Making a note

Having done the planning, make a note to ensure that you can follow your plans during the negotiation. Do not rely on memory. You may forget in the heat of the moment. You may become confused by your opponent. New information may be thrown at you.

The best way of ensuring that your planning is useful in the negotiation is to write out a note to include:

- an overview of what your client wants;
  - what must your client have;
  - what is the best overall outcome you could achieve;
  - what is the least acceptable overall outcome;
  - what items can you trade;
- in respect of each item:
  - your opening offer and how you will justify it;
  - what is the best you can achieve for your client;
  - what is the least you should accept;
  - how will you stage concessions and how will you justify them.

11.11 Summary

Planning concessions has concentrated on how you can plan to make concessions: what your opening will be, how you will stage concessions, etc. This is because you need to be prepared to actively make concessions. However, do not forget that seeking concessions from your opponent is the reverse side of the coin.

First, although your planning concentrates on what you are conceding, each proposal will include concessions by you and by your opponent. Thus, if you propose that your client pays 60 per cent of the other side's claim, you are seeking a concession from them of 40 per cent. The way this is viewed may depend on how you phrase your proposal (do you 'offer/concede that you will pay 60 per cent' or 'seek/demand a concession from the other side that they accept 40 per cent less than the claim').

Secondly, you can plan to deal with an item by asking your opponent what he or she is prepared to give. This has the benefit of gaining an indication of his or her range without revealing your own. It also has the potential disadvantage of starting the discussion on concessions at the opponent's end of the range rather than yours.

Once you have done the substantive planning you should consider which tactics would be useful. One which is extremely important is 'the overall package'. Keep your options open. Do not agree to separate parts unconditionally. Agree all items, subject to the overall settlement. Only when you are clear as to the overall settlement should you agree finally and then make it subject to your client's confirmation (see **Chapter 16**).

11.12 Application to Case Study A

Overview of what client wants

No specific limits by client—so get as much money as possible.
Would like to continue trading with C.
Try to use future custom (purchases as trades on C's losses).

Individual items

C's claim for the price £2,520 (£1,260 each instalment) plus interest (c£50).

Instalment 1—cannot really resist this—price or interest.
Instalment 2—have strong argument to resist paying 50 per cent of price; but some risk not proving; delay, etc.
Query deal with them together:

- Opening offer: £1,260—agree to pay 1/2 the claim; chocolate clearly faulty.
- Best outcome: as above (cannot resist paying 1st instalment).
- Least outcome: pay instalment 1 and 3/4 instalment 2 = £1,260 + £945 = £2,205.
- Staging: in £200/£250 steps—likely goods will be found to be faulty.

C's loss benefit of remainder of contract £4,100 (5,000 Kilo @ 82p kilo)

D weak on repudiation (given phone call *plus* failure to pay or respond) but C must prove D repudiated (burden on him).
C must prove loss—potential weaknesses here for C.
Need to get information about what happened to chocolate before offer (provided still has it and in good condition—use offers to buy it to offset claim). If not available—must get information about whether sold/steps to sell etc before offer; outcome *very* dependent on this.

- Opening offer: buy remainder at 500 Kilo per month at contract price—solves both parties' problems.
- Best outcome: the above.
- Least acceptable outcome and staging:
    - If buy any chocolate resist paying further money; if essential offer small per cent of loss claimed (notional sum 'goodwill'—start £200 work up to £1,000; *alternatively*: offer increased price per month eg £20 per month (ie 4p kilo) to 6p kilo (£30 per month) (£30 per month = £300 for whole contract) (query get client permanently into higher price range).
    - If no purchase of chocolate: dependent on whether chocolate sold or not/steps to mitigate; start small £200 (C produce problem; failure to mitigate); if sold—work through to 1/2 of remaining loss; if not sold—pay up to a maximum of 1/2 the claim = £2,000).

D's loss of profit on Chocaganza weekend (£2,000—got 2/3 contract price).

D's reasonable case on causation (see above) less good on remoteness; reasonable on mitigation.

- Opening offer: dependent on arguments on faulty goods; seek all (emphasise causation and proof of loss).
- Most get: 3/4 = £1,500.
- Least get: 1/4 = £500.
- Staging: reduce in small steps of £200.

D's loss of profit on shops.

D has reasonably strong claim.

- Opening: all = £1,500—clear causation, contemplation and proof of loss.
- Most get: all = £1,500.
- Least get: 1/2 = £750.
- Staging: £150 steps.

Costs

Normal order—D pay today.

- Open: C pay some of D's costs—C jumped the gun; no further investigation of difficulties; C cause legal cost.
- Least get: D pay C's costs of today; otherwise each pay own.

The case

Not subject to bargaining—assuming above items agreed; ensure get agreement that C discontinue case.

Overall outcome

This is dependent on whether or not chocolate still available to buy and/or been sold as this affects C's claim substantially.

Best possible outcome

- D buy chocolate at 500 Kilo a month at normal price/C drop claim for £4,100.
- C pays D money—D offset payment on 1st instalment for payment on his claims—most D likely to get is payment in region of £500–£1,000.

Least acceptable outcome

- Chocolate not available to buy.
- C and D's money claims therefore offset—but need to deduct price received for remaining chocolate/sum for mitigation and see concession planning above.
- D pay C—a maximum in the region of £2,500.

11.13 Application to Case Study B

Do the same exercise for Case Study B.

12 Planning your strategy

12.1 Introduction

As we have seen in the chapters so far on preparation, planning your strategy includes being aware of the strategic implications of the various aspects of the negotiation process, eg, information exchange and use of concessions. Once the detailed preparation is complete, you should pause to consider whether and how your planning so far creates an overall strategy that leans towards a particular type, eg, more competitive than collaborative. First, you need to be able to implement your strategy, ie, carry out what you intend to do. It is one thing to write on a piece of paper that you are going to adopt a competitive strategy, either overall or on a particular aspect, and quite another to carry that through with a difficult opponent. Secondly, the strategy used could influence the conduct of the negotiation bringing advantages and/or disadvantages for the use of a particular strategy. This chapter therefore looks first at how your own psychological make-up can influence which strategy you use naturally when negotiating. It then goes on to consider the pros and cons of the three strategies (competitive, cooperative and collaborative).

12.2 Behavioural aspects of negotiation—dealing with differences

As discussed in **Chapter 1**, because we have been negotiating all our lives we have all developed particular ways of negotiating of which we may not even be conscious. Negotiation is about resolving differences, real or perceived. The parties are apart and want to come together to reach agreement.

We all cope with differences in a variety of ways and our way of coping is related to our personality (eg, how assertive or conciliatory we are) and our self-image (eg, whether we pride ourselves on being leaders, fighters, sharp and tough, or being facilitators, problem-solvers, reasonable and fair-minded). Although there is a wide range of ways of coping with difference or conflict, the following attempts to categorise them into five basic reactions. These reactions can, to a degree, influence the type of strategy a person is naturally inclined to adopt. Being conscious of how different people react to differences, and your particular reaction to them, will enable you to decide whether you have difficulty in adopting a particular strategy or dealing with an opponent who uses a particular strategy, and how to deal with such difficulties.

12.2.1 Avoiding

'Avoiding' is to withdraw, not deal with, or ignore in the hope it will go away. It is a 'lose/lose' reaction. The person cannot cope with dealing with differences and tries to avoid doing so by denying the differences or withdrawing from the discussion. As negotiation is all about discussing and resolving disputes, avoidance is totally ineffective.

12.2.2 Accommodating

'Accommodating' does not deny the existence of the disagreement or conflict but resolves it by giving in completely to what the other side wants. It is a 'lose/win' reaction which leads to capitulation by the accommodator. Negotiation is about reconciling differences for both parties; therefore this reaction is also totally ineffective.

12.2.3 Competing

'Competing' involves dealing with the differences head on by 'fighting' it out on the basis that the strongest competitor wins. It is a 'win/lose' reaction which leads to confrontation. While it is useful in some circumstances (eg, our civil justice system is an adversarial one in which advocates are expected to compete), it has its drawbacks, (eg, where there is no independent judge of who wins), and it can result in deadlock.

12.2.4 Cooperative/compromising

The 'cooperative/compromising' reaction is to deal with differences on the basis that they can be resolved by cooperating with the other person on the understanding that both sides will compromise equally to resolve the differences. It is a 'win/win' reaction which does not produce the best results. If both parties react this way, it means that agreement will be reached but it will not necessarily be one which adequately or genuinely resolves the underlying differences.

12.2.5 Collaborative/problem-solving

The 'collaborative/problem-solving' reaction is to deal with differences as though they are a joint problem which can be solved by analysis and pooling of information and resources. It is a 'win/win' reaction which can lead to optimum results.

12.2.6 Know your reactions

No one has just one reaction to dealing with differences. We all react in a much more complex way which mixes these reactions in differing degrees in different situations. The reactions to any one situation may come from basic personality type, from feeling unconfident because of lack of expertise, or from being unprepared. You cannot plan your personality type, nor can you do much to change it. You also, probably, cannot alter some of your basic instincts and ways of coping which you have used since childhood. Thus, a naturally cooperative person cannot change overnight into a competitive one, and vice versa. However, you can become more conscious of your tendencies and basic ways of dealing with differences and learn to control and adapt them to assist you to become a good negotiator.

You can also ensure that you are properly prepared for a negotiation. The better prepared you are, the less 'reactive' and the more 'proactive' you will be.

12.3 Negotiation strategies

The three main strategies were outlined in **Chapter 3** and the use of specific tactics, such as use of argument, exchange of information and concessions, was examined in the chapters dealing with these aspects of preparation (**Chapters 8** to **11**). In this section we examine the factors which may influence your choice of strategy. We then consider the advantages and disadvantages of the three main strategies.

12.3.1 Factors influencing the choice of strategy

A negotiator does not choose a particular strategy in advance and then apply it throughout. It is unusual and counterproductive to apply one strategy across the board. Instead, you should adapt your strategy during the course of the negotiation depending on the case, the people involved, the issues being discussed, etc.

As noted above, negotiators may have predominant patterns and predominant behaviours, and so may be generally competitive or generally cooperative. However, they should be conscious of the risks involved in choosing a particular strategy. Even if you intend to adapt the strategy to the dynamics of the negotiation, starting with one particular strategy may limit later flexibility. Thus, starting with a competitive strategy and style may make it more difficult to change to a more cooperative or collaborative one later.

Depending on your personality, you may find you naturally tend towards a particular strategy. If you are naturally aggressive, you may automatically go into competitive mode. If you are naturally pragmatic, you may find you are inclined to a more collaborative or problem-solving approach. Be conscious of this and at least try to be more aware of the different strategies, the impact they have on the negotiation and their advantages and limitations.

There is some research on the effect of gender and culture on negotiations (in particular by the Harvard Negotiation Project). While some of this research points to there being differences in negotiating styles and strategies which may relate to gender and cultural or ethnic background, many other factors also influence an individual's style and strategy. This is a complex subject and it is difficult, if not impossible, to give concise but accurate summaries of the research covering these influences. We have therefore not attempted to cover it in this manual.

There is much discussion and some disagreement about which strategies are more effective and which the legal profession should adopt. You will find different authors have differing views and argue persuasively for the adoption of a particular strategy. Many 'How To Do It' guides on negotiation are written for sales or business people and in general promote a competitive strategy.

Many of the legal professional skills courses and books promote, virtually unaltered, the principled approach of Fisher and Ury, although some tend to collapse the principled and problem-solving strategies into one and label it as 'cooperative'. This strategy clearly has advantages over both the competitive and cooperative strategies but is not without its limitations, which means that adopting it religiously whatever the circumstances is not necessarily a good idea.

12.3.2 Competitive strategy

As we have seen, a competitive strategy seeks to maximise one's own gains by taking a strong stance. The negotiator seeks to persuade by being determined, unyielding, single minded (see **8.2.1.1**), seeks information but gives little (see **10.3.1**) and makes high opening demands and gives few concessions (see **11.3.2**) on the basis that this will force the opponent to move towards one. The goal is victory.

12.3.2.1 Advantages/when used effectively

Competitive strategy is more like simple bargaining than any of the other strategies and as such is used most successfully in those types of situations, ie, where there is only a single issue, a distributive, 'zero-sum' negotiation.

It may also be used where there is an imbalance of power by the person with the power. A power imbalance can stem from a variety of sources, eg, having an extremely strong case or being a repeat player negotiating against a one-off player (an insurance company negotiating against a claimant). The person with the power adopts a competitive strategy because he or she risks less if there is no settlement.

The use of pressure, hard stance, etc, in this strategy increases the tension and stress levels. The overall strategy of giving little by way of either concessions or information, maintaining control and pressure which may be coupled with a competitive style, attempts to undermine the opponent and cause him or her to 'give in'. Clearly, this will work only if the opponent is susceptible to manipulative behaviour and it could result in winning more concessions and a better outcome. It can be particularly effective with opponents who are inexperienced or have difficulty coping with aggression and conflict.

There is little chance of exploitation by the opponent because of the competitive negotiator's basic attitude of distrust of the opponent, giving of few concessions and selective, limited disclosure.

The strategy is relatively easy to understand and use providing the personality of the negotiator allows it. It has limited objectives and keeps consideration of issues to the minimum. It has a simpler and more obvious behaviour pattern and is less intellectually taxing because of the limited range of issues under discussion.

12.3.2.2 Risks and limitations/when not used effectively

A competitive strategy is not the most effective one in a multiple issue, integrative negotiation where there are a variety of issues, needs and interests on which agreement is sought. The hard stance, limited disclosure, and tension-creating behaviour mean that less information is exchanged. Both negotiators tend to become more rigid, retreat to their stated positions and 'play their cards close to their chest'. Communication is distorted. The exchange between negotiators becomes limited and unimaginative. They may fail to explore the full range of issues or options available with the result that the clients get a less attractive deal than they might otherwise have obtained. Common or compatible interests may not be explored, let alone form part of the settlement.

Even in a negotiation with limited issues to be negotiated, a competitive strategy tends to emphasise differences rather than common ground. It generally increases misunderstanding between the parties and leads them to believe that they are farther apart than they really are.

Many people are not susceptible to the manipulative behaviour of a competitive negotiator. They do not react to the increased tension, won't 'play the game', do not feel undermined or lose confidence and do not give in. Indeed, a fairly common reaction to the behaviour of a competitive negotiator is to do quite the reverse of the assumption and 'dig one's heels in'. This can be done either by avoiding behaviour (refusing to discuss the issue) or by retaliation (mirroring the behaviour of the competitor). In either case, deadlock is the result.

There is a real risk that the competitive strategy will escalate into really aggressive behaviour which irritates and frustrates the opponent. The client's interests are lost sight of and the negotiation becomes a battle rather than an attempt to settle. The parties may get stuck battling over trivial issues and fail to recognise the main issues which need to be discussed. It may take longer to reach agreement as both sides jockey for position and do not deal with the issues or need for exchange of information.

A competitive strategy is not effective if there is an ongoing relationship. Such a strategy can easily destroy it. Even where the negotiation is not carried out by the parties, eg, done by the lawyers, the stance of the negotiators may affect the client. The outcome may reflect the strategy (ie, win/lose) or be described by the lawyer or other party in competitive terms (ie, in win/lose language) which may undermine any ongoing relationship.

Those who negotiate regularly, particularly within a set community, eg, the Bar, develop a reputation based on their behaviour and what is relayed to others about their behaviour. A negotiator who uses a competitive strategy or style will become known as competitive. Studies show that those confronted by a competitive negotiator respond competitively. This may create a treadmill of competitive negotiations with less flexibility in choice of strategies.

Finally, some unprepared negotiators have a tendency to use a competitive strategy in an attempt to disguise their lack of preparation. As the strategy involves limited disclosure and strong positional stances which reveal little about the analysis and real position, it is tempting to take a competitive stance where insufficient analysis has been done or the real position is unknown. However, a competitive strategy depends on credibility. The negotiator using it must be able to carry it through. Using it to mask lack of preparation runs the risk of blowing one's cover and losing all credibility.

12.3.3 Cooperative strategy

A cooperative strategy assumes that both sides must compromise and, by being 'reasonable', one can engender trust in the opponent and thereby induce reciprocal behaviour by the opponent. The cooperative negotiator therefore persuades by being conciliatory (see **8.2.2**), shares information (see **10.3.2**) and makes a number of reasonable concessions (see **11.3.3**). The goal is agreement.

12.3.3.1 Advantages/when used effectively

A cooperative strategy can be effective in situations where the continuing relationship is more important than what is achieved for each of the parties in the settlement. This continuing relationship may be in business (eg, two parties wish to continue trading despite a past dispute) or personal (eg, a divorce where the parties do not want to affect the relationships of both parents with their children). The strategy is unlikely to damage the relationship as it emphasises the importance of reaching agreement while building and maintaining a relationship.

Given that the main focus is on agreement, a cooperative strategy means there are fewer risks that the negotiation will break down. Additionally, a cooperative strategy may result in the parties reaching agreement faster than would be the case in a competitive situation, particularly where both sides are cooperative.

Where both sides use a cooperative strategy, it is likely to result in the parties reaching an agreement which is seen as 'fair', as they will feel not only that the terms of the agreement are fair but that they have been fairly treated in the negotiation. Provided both parties use a cooperative strategy, it can be much less stressful than a competitive one.

12.3.3.2 Risks and limitations/when not used effectively

To make unilateral concessions is risky as the behaviour may not be reciprocated and it is difficult, if not impossible, to retract a concession once made. The negotiator may have reached the bottom line and have nothing left to trade in the negotiation.

A strategy which relies on making concessions to create an open, trusting atmosphere means that too much may be conceded too early. The negotiator gets too close to the bottom line too early and is left with little room to manoeuvre during the negotiation.

Making concessions is interpreted as a sign of weakness by competitive negotiators. It is seen as soft, done only because of a lack of ability to compete. It also reinforces for competitive negotiators the belief that their strategy works, ie, they are getting movement towards themselves. They will continue to use their strategy, possibly pressing even harder for concessions. They will take advantage of what they perceive as lack of ability by the opponent on the basis that they will get what they deserve.

It is clear that a cooperative strategy is vulnerable to exploitation. But, surprisingly, many cooperative negotiators do not recognise when they are being exploited. They continue to use their strategy (ie, making concessions and volunteering information) even though they are getting nothing in return. Many cooperative negotiators work on the assumption that their behaviour is being or will be reciprocated even when it is clear that this is not the case. Because they fail to check whether their strategy is working, they are open to exploitation.

The underlying ethos of a cooperative strategy is to create an open, trusting atmosphere and reduce any sense of conflict or aggression. This means that cooperative negotiators tend to avoid the confrontational or more challenging aspects of a negotiation. They may try to deal with competitive techniques by being conciliatory and open, rather than recognising, and possibly drawing attention to, the disruptive competitive technique used. They are also less likely to test the opponent's statements, or probe for reasons behind proposals or evidence to back up statements of fact. This, again, leaves them open to exploitation.

Cooperative negotiators' main aim is to reach agreement. There is therefore a risk that they will focus too much on reaching agreement and concede too much to achieve it. They may lose sight of the client's objectives: they may undervalue the strength of their case and simply not pursue them. Alternatively, they may mistake an easy option (ie, one easily agreed) for the correct one (ie, in the client's interests). This is a risk and a weakness even where there are two cooperative negotiators; where a cooperative negotiator is against a competitive one, he or she may lose a substantial amount.

A cooperative negotiation strategy is based on mutuality of concessions and shared information. Cooperative negotiators may react emotionally to competitive ones. The moral element of the cooperative strategy (both negotiators reciprocating and having a sense of 'fair play') means that there is room for cooperative negotiators to see competitive ones as unfair and selfish. The cooperative negotiator may react with a sense of moral indignation which is then introduced into the negotiation. They may then misread the situation and assume there is more disagreement than in fact exists.

From the above it is clear that using a cooperative strategy against a competitive negotiator is highly risky and very open to exploitation, eg, when negotiating against someone with more power, someone with a much stronger case or a repeat player, or where the negotiation is zero-sum.

12.3.4 Collaborative strategy

A collaborative strategy assumes that the parties can work together (ie, collaborate) to reach agreement. The negotiator approaches the negotiation on a rational basis: separating the people from the problem (**7.2.1**), exploring the underlying interests of the parties (**7.2.2**), being creative in the options considered (**7.2.3**), judging any settlement against some agreed test or criteria (**8.2.3**) and sharing information (**10.3.3**).

12.3.4.1 Advantages of the collaborative approach

The collaborative approaches as represented by both principled and problem-solving strategies have enormous advantages over both the competitive and cooperative approaches in that:

(a) they increase focus on the parties' real needs and interests;

(b) rather than focusing on the division of resources on the basis that they are limited, they encourage techniques to expand the resources;

(c) rather than assuming that the parties' needs and interests are directly opposed so that resources are wanted equally and exclusively by both, they encourage negotiators to distinguish between genuinely conflicting needs and those which may be shared or compatible;

(d) they encourage a more rational and reasoned approach to negotiation whereby the two negotiators use information constructively and focus on resolving the issues rather than swapping concessions.

Where both parties use a collaborative approach, they are more likely to have genuinely considered the parties' objectives, to have considered a far greater range of options for settlement, to have considered whether the options satisfy the objectives and therefore to reach a settlement which is more satisfactory to both parties.

Clearly, the greater the range of interests and needs of the clients, the easier it is to use this approach. However, even where the scope for 'option creating' is limited, some aspects of the strategy are useful, eg, separating the people from the problem.

12.3.4.2 Limitations of the collaborative approach

There are practical limitations on the use of the collaborative approach for those negotiating at the court door. Both collaborative strategies require:

(a) time to explore interests, needs and options;

(b) sharing and maximising available information on which to reach a settlement;

(c) investigating the client's underlying interests and needs to reach a settlement to achieve these;

(d) looking at options with both parties being open-minded and having a genuine interest in expanding the pie and exploring the options.

The circumstances of court-door negotiations (set out above at **4.3.2**) create some potential difficulties because of time pressure, lack of access to information or knowledge of the client and limited opportunities to expand the pie.

Negotiators who use a collaborative strategy are open to a degree of exploitation by a competitive negotiator if the collaborative negotiator does not assess what is happening. An opponent may use a cooperative style and many of the phrases taken from principled or problem-solving strategies, eg, 'objective standard', 'fair and reasonable', 'underlying interests', 'joint benefits', etc, but in fact be using a competitive strategy, revealing little information and making few, small concessions.

Finally, while both principled and problem-solving strategies have a test against which to judge whether the settlement is fair, these tests are not in fact as certain as one might think.

(a) Principled negotiation relies on the use of 'objective' criteria. As Condlin points out in his article 'Bargaining in the Dark: The Normative Incoherence of Lawyer Dispute Bargaining Role' (1992) 51 *Maryland Law Review* 1:

Objective can mean neutral or non-partisan, in the sense of treating each side's interests equally... or it can mean fair and legitimate, in the sense of respecting recognised entitlements of the parties and reconciling conflicts between them through the use of principles, procedures and substantive norms that are accepted as authoritative.

(b) Problem-solving relies on solutions which are 'fair or just' where 'no party can gain without hurting the other party' (Carrie Menkel-Meadow, 'Towards Another View of Legal Negotiation: The Structure of Problem Solving' (1984) 31 *UCLA Law Review* 754–842). But even the author recognises that this produces problems in legal negotiations. 'When might the negotiator choose to pursue less gain for his client or actually cause his client to suffer loss so as to benefit or not hurt the other side?' In discussing this, the author observes, 'In considering the acceptability of a particular solution, both lawyer and client might engage in a dialogue about the fairness or justness of their proposals'. As Condlin (above) points out (p 41, note 118), 'Menkel-Meadow expresses a hope that justice will take care of itself in the needs ascertainment dialogue between the lawyer and client'.

Even using these strategies, the negotiators are left to define 'objective' or determine what is 'fair or just' in the circumstances in which they are negotiating. For those negotiating at the court door, the way in which the court is likely to view the merits will most likely be the appropriate standard (ie, a good settlement is one in which the merits of the case matter). How much does this conflict with the 'ethos' of the problem-solving strategy in particular?

12.4 Summary of strategies

There is much discussion and debate about the different strategies and what is and is not effective. This debate is carried on, not only in the context of which strategy achieves the best result for individual clients, but also which are best for the civil justice system overall. The discussion has taken on an added dimension with the rise of the concept of Alternative Dispute Resolution (see **Chapter 20**) and the increased use of mediation. Thus, over the course of your professional life, you may find that attitudes change towards what is effective and acceptable in negotiation strategies.

13 Planning the structure

13.1 Can a negotiation be structured?

13.1.1 Phases of a negotiation

As we saw in **Chapter 2**, although there are no set rules on how a negotiation should be structured, research has identified recognisable patterns of behaviour which many negotiations follow. These patterns do not set out a particular structure, rather they are a series of developmental phases through which many negotiations pass:

(a) opening/orientating/positioning: in this phase the negotiators assess each other and set the scene including setting out how they expect the negotiation to proceed;

(b) exploration/discussion: in this phase the negotiators use information exchange, argument, etc, to assess the relative strengths of the parties' cases and begin the process of narrowing the differences by seeking and making concessions;

(c) bargaining/convergence: in this phase the negotiators, on the basis of their assessment and initial suggestions for compromise, make more serious efforts to bridge the gap to reach settlement through concession-seeking and making;

(d) settlement/breakdown: in this phase the negotiators either reach settlement or acknowledge that settlement cannot be reached.

These phases do not dictate a particular structure as they may overlap or repeat. The phases may take more or less time and be of more or less importance, depending on the negotiation. However, having an understanding of them can assist you in recognising why particular behaviours are more prevalent at some stages than others and how you can use that to plan your structure.

13.1.2 How planning a structure helps

As with advocacy submissions and conferences, a good structure can improve the conduct and outcome of a negotiation. A clear structure to a negotiation can assist you to:

- use the time available efficiently and effectively;
- ensure that you cover all the things you need to;
- work more coherently to achieve your client's objectives;
- argue your case in the most effective way.

The risks of not planning a structure for the negotiation are that you are more likely to:

- make poor use of time;
- slip into repeating points or reach a deadlock;

- forget to make some of the positive points you had planned;
- fail to achieve all you need to and fail to cover all appropriate details;
- fail to present coherently and consistently and persuade your opponent.

Planning the structure of a negotiation can therefore assist you to be efficient and persuasive and ensure you cover everything you must to reach a beneficial and complete settlement for your client.

13.1.3 What does planning a structure mean?

You cannot plan and stick to a structure for negotiation in the same way that you can for an advocacy submission or conference. When making an advocacy submission your opponent does not, or should not, interrupt you. It is your submission and you make it as you plan, subject to interventions from the judge. There is likely to be a logical order for your submission given the test to be applied and the order in which the judge will apply the elements of it. Similarly you control a conference and, subject to accommodating specific concerns of your client, can adopt and follow a logical structure to ensure that you get all relevant information from the client before you advise.

As a negotiator you do not have such control. First, there is no inherently logical order to follow. Although most negotiations will go through the phases set out above, they may be repeated or overlap. Thus, for example, there may be a number of items on which compromise is sought, eg, how past losses will be resolved and how future dealings will be conducted. The negotiation may go through these phases several times as each item is considered. One negotiator may have a tactic of opening with an offer, before any discussion or exchange of information. This offer may be so good that you accept it. Alternatively, it may not be sufficient so you begin to explore and discuss the parties' positions. Secondly, the order in which matters are discussed is itself open to negotiation and the two sides may have different views on which structure is more likely to be effective. Thirdly, a negotiation may take unpredictable turns and unforeseen problems or issues may arise which impact on how it is conducted. You may find that some of the items are more difficult to agree than others.

Planning the structure of a negotiation therefore means considering different aspects of the negotiation and planning how you will deal with them. It also means being prepared to be flexible, knowing where you can give and where you wish to remain firm with regard to the order in which matters are discussed. Your plans will depend on the type of case you are dealing with, and what you find works best for you. The two areas to consider prior to the negotiation are:

- how you wish to start the negotiation;
- the order in which you would like to discuss matters in the negotiation.

13.2 Planning how to start

The start of a negotiation is of great importance. Your energy is likely to be at its highest at this stage, and you will be setting the tone for what comes later. Each negotiator is giving key messages to the other as to what he or she hopes to achieve, which approach he or she will take, and how strongly he or she intends to argue. It is possible to make a real impact at this stage and show from the start that you are fully in command of the case. You miss a great potential impetus if you do not give careful thought to how to start the negotiation. As with all aspects of a negotiation, you should plan the start that you feel is best for the case and do what you reasonably can to achieve what you want. However, both negotiators may have very clear but very different views about who should start and the overall structure to be used. You may find that the first thing you need to negotiate is how to start! Be prepared to be flexible.

13.2.1 Considerations when planning

How should you start a negotiation? Who goes first and what does he or she say? The answers to these questions will depend on a variety of factors including the type of case, you and your opponent's analysis of it, the order in which you wish to cover matters, etc.

In planning how to open you should take into account your overall view of the negotiation and how you want it to proceed. What tone do you want to set? What needs to be covered in the negotiation, taking into account the phases that are involved in most negotiations and the items that will have to be discussed to reach settlement? In what order do you want to cover the matters?

The way in which a negotiation starts sets the atmosphere that influences the remainder of the negotiation. A competitive stance at the start will create a different tone than a reasoned, rational and pragmatic suggestion that a principled approach be adopted. Both negotiators will try to determine the approach being adopted by their opponent. You could wait and see what your opponent does, thereby letting him or her set the tone, at least initially. Alternatively, you could state the approach you wish to take with a view to influencing the atmosphere and committing the other side to the desired approach.

The way in which a negotiation starts may also impact both on the overall structure of the negotiation, the order in which matters are covered, and the use of time, whether or not it is used effectively. The matters to be covered include dealing with all items on which settlement is sought, argument, information exchange, seeking and making concessions and clarifying and finalising what is agreed. It may be that time is not a pressing factor and that there are very few matters to discuss. Equally, time may be of more concern and there may be a number of matters to discuss. Even where time is not an issue, you need to be conscious of how the opening you choose will impact on the structure and use of time.

13.2.2 The options

There are numerous options for starting a negotiation. As noted above, the way in which the negotiation opens will affect the tone of the negotiation and its structure. We set out below some of the options.

13.2.2.1 Setting an 'agenda'

You could start by listing the matters which you consider need to be discussed and the order in which you wish them to be considered. Doing this can set a pragmatic tone, and assist in focusing the negotiation so that time is used efficiently. Setting out at the start what needs to be covered and an order for doing it ensures that both sides know how the negotiation is likely to progress and are able to gauge whether it is progressing (assuming the suggested order is followed, even if loosely).

In setting an 'agenda' or order for the negotiation, you need to ensure that the order is one that will assist you to negotiate effectively. If time is a factor, your structure should allow you to use it efficiently. If you want to present your client's case strongly, you should suggest a structure which enables you to do this (eg, putting items with the merits on your side first). You should also consider how the structure you suggest could influence how your opponent sees you and the tone of the negotiation. Thus, by suggesting a structure which deals with the strengths of your case first, you may be seen as competitive and induce similar behaviour in your opponent.

You could plan to set the 'agenda' unilaterally or by agreement. Thus you could start by just setting out the order in which you would like to conduct the negotiation. Alternatively, you could open by saying, 'I thought it would be a good idea to agree an order in which to discuss the matters, the order I think would be best is... What do you think?' Clearly the second option takes a more cooperative stance and sets a different tone than the first, even though the practical outcome may be the same (ie, the negotiation follows the structure you suggest). Either option shows that you have a good grasp of what needs to be covered and have taken the initiative by setting out how this could be achieved. Even if done in a cooperative manner, it could put you in the driving seat.

13.2.2.2 Starting with your view of the case

You could start by simply outlining your view of the case. If you start this way, you need to decide what to cover. You may wish to stress what your client is expecting to achieve in the case and go on to say something about your confidence in achieving your client's objectives and how the merits of the case justify your confidence. Alternatively, you may decide to set out the strengths of your client's case and, possibly, the weaknesses of your opponent's case.

Setting out your case enables you to adopt a strong stance which may impress your opponent. However, the more you stress the strengths of your client's case, the more competitive you will appear to your opponent. This could produce the result that most competitive negotiators seek, ie, causing your opponent anxiety about the strengths of his or her own case and how he or she will seek compromises from you. Alternatively, it may have the opposite effect and produce a competitive response.

You could of course temper the opening to make it less competitive by injecting phrases about settlement. However, avoid overplaying your hand by stressing how keen your client is to settle (even if he or she is). This may give your opponent the impression that you are desperate to reach agreement. An alternative way of reducing the competitive impact of setting out your version of the case is to suggest that your opponent also sets out his or her view of the case and what it is that his or her client wants.

One risk of this opening is that you say too much about your client's case before your opponent has had a chance to speak. This could give your opponent ideas about how to attack your case. There may be things you do not know about your opponent's case or information about which he or she has evidence which it would be wise to explore before revealing too much. Another risk is that, by launching into arguments about the merits of your case, no structure will be determined and the negotiation may not proceed efficiently.

13.2.2.3 Getting your opponent to start

It can be a useful tactic to get your opponent to start. This may help you to evaluate your opponent's likely negotiating strategy, view of the case and what he or she hopes to achieve. It may assist you to gauge whether your strategy will work effectively or should be adjusted. It may be clear that your opponent is weak and likely to take an almost exclusively cooperative approach to the negotiation. You could gain more by appearing to be cooperative than by being obviously competitive. You may also get more information about your opponent's case before revealing your hand. Your opponent may reveal weaknesses in his or her case of which you were unaware. Alternatively, he or she may reveal information which affects your client's case and calls for a readjustment of how to respond and/or what compromises you consider realistic. Once your opponent has outlined his or her case, you may decide to seek further information on the points raised, to outline your case in reply or to attack the case your opponent has set out.

This type of opening may be beneficial where you want to take decisions on structure after you have seen your opponent's approach to the negotiation. This could be useful in strategic terms if your case is weak or if you have limited information and need to find out more from your opponent.

The risk of this type of opening is that your opponent may interpret it as showing weakness on your part because you are giving him or her the chance to set the tone with the strengths of his or her case. Unless handled carefully, you may find that your opponent takes control of the negotiation. You could find it difficult to reestablish credibility and control. Finally, although you may plan to ask your opponent to start, you cannot compel him or her to do so (unless you are prepared to use silence effectively). Nor can you compel your opponent to start in the way you want him or her to, ie, by setting out his or her case. Your opponent may start by setting out his or her own agenda or attacking your case.

13.2.3 Summary

However you decide to open the negotiation, you should consider how it will affect the tone of the negotiation, the conduct of it and how your opponent views you. In addition, it may have an impact on the overall structure of the negotiation. You need to know which issues you wish to cover during the negotiation and the order in which you want to cover them. If no structure is expressly stated or agreed, the risk of the negotiation being unstructured and therefore less efficient is greater. During the negotiation, you should assess whether you are getting through what needs to be discussed in the time available and whether the matters are being discussed in an order which is beneficial or detrimental to you. Whatever you decide to say by way of opening, setting out or agreeing a structure early in the negotiation is the clearest and easiest way for both negotiators to be clear about where they are going.

13.3 Planning the structure

13.3.1 What should you consider in planning your structure?

Whether or not you decide to set out or agree a structure for the negotiation, you must plan both what you want to discuss and the order in which you wish to discuss it. You therefore need to be clear about the matters which you consider need to be discussed. In deciding the structure you wish to adopt, consider what the main thrust of the discussion should be. What do you want to achieve? How can this be done most effectively and efficiently? You should also consider the 'phases' of a negotiation and how these are likely to affect the discussion to assist you in achieving what you want.

The two main areas of discussion in a negotiation to resolve a legal dispute are:

(a) the parties' objectives and how these can be achieved through compromise: what they want out of the negotiation (ie, setting a list of all the items to be negotiated); and suggestions for compromise and consideration of the practicalities of any suggestions;

(b) the merits of each party's case: what issues are in dispute; and where the merits lie on those issues (including consideration of the substantive and procedural law, and allegations of fact and evidence). There may, of course, be several issues before the court and the merits of the case may not all be on one side.

The discussion in both areas will include information exchange and argument. Only the first topic should include concession-making and seeking. However, concessions should be made and sought on the basis of information exchange and argument on the merits. Given this, it is impossible to divide the negotiation into distinct sections, eg, of information exchange, argument, etc. It is equally impossible to divide it into discussion on the objectives and discussion on the merits.

13.3.2 What are the options?

The structure envisaged by the problem-solving approach is investigation of interests and needs, followed by option-creation and allocation. This could also be applied to the principled approach. Somewhere in this process will be consideration of the objective criteria or what is fair or just. Thus, these approaches recognise that discussion of the parties' needs from the settlement is of prime importance. However, they focus on option-creation and do not recognise explicitly that allocation may be what takes the time. The problem in most legal negotiations is getting the balance right between discussion of the objective criteria (ie, the settlement standard/merits of the case) and the parties' needs and interests.

The prime purpose of a negotiation is to reach settlement on the items that the parties want, not the merits of the case. Nor is it to ensure that all parties have full information. Given this focus, it makes sense to have a structure that enables the negotiators to deal with the items efficiently and effectively. Where there is only one item to be resolved, eg, a claim concerning the price of goods on the basis that they are not of satisfactory quality, it may be possible to follow the stages identified in the research. However, where there is more than one item, which is invariably the case in legal dispute negotiations, all the items have to be discussed and any structure must take this into account.

The decisions on structure may therefore come down to whether you structure the whole negotiation around the items to be negotiated (ie, set them out in order and work your way through them one at a time) or deal with other matters before you deal with these. Other matters that may need to be discussed are:

13.3.2.1 Merits of the case

Discussing the merits of the case means both sides putting forward their arguments about their clients' chances of success in court. The reason to do this is to justify seeking a settlement to satisfy the client. When considering whether or not to discuss the merits first outside the context of considering proposals, remember that the best use of argument is to justify concessions sought and proposals put.

Discussing the merits of the case before the items may be useful where you have a strong case overall that is weak on some minor issues on which some claims are based. It may also be appropriate where all or a substantial percentage of the items are dependent on one or two issues and determining where you stand on those issues will assist on the majority of the matters which need to be negotiated. Thus, in a claim for damages for a single breach of contract, where you have a strong claim on the cause of action that is weaker on proof of the amounts claimed, you might suggest starting with a discussion of the merits of the claim. This gives you an opportunity to present the whole case strongly up front. This may put you in a stronger position from which to discuss the losses.

The risk of discussing the merits first, out of context of the items, is that when you do get to the concessions you will be repeating arguments you used previously. This will be the case where there are several items with different underlying issues. Thus, in a claim for damages for several different breaches of contract, discussing the case as a whole means discussing the different breaches. If this is done out of the context of the claims, you are likely to repeat your earlier arguments when you discuss the individual claims for damages. Not only does this waste time, it also reduces the impact of the arguments and makes them less persuasive.

13.3.2.2 Checking the information each side has

In considering whether or not this exercise would be useful, remember to check what documents you and your opponent have in common. The further along in the litigation process you are, the more shared documents there will be and the clearer it becomes to both lawyers when preparing precisely what information is shared. Where this is clear, going over it in the negotiation may just be a waste of time.

Where you have a case prior to issue, it may not be as clear what information is shared. Your instructions should give you some indication of this, eg, correspondence exchanged and statements of what has been said in conversations between the parties. From this you are quite likely to have a reasonable amount of shared information about both parties' views of the case. Checking what information is shared will generally be a useful step only where you have real doubts about what the other party wants or the material facts. Generally, less major gaps in information held by the other side will become apparent during discussion of the items and be more usefully filled at that point.

13.3.2.3 Agreeing what is in dispute

In considering whether or not this would be useful, you need again to remember where in the litigation process you are. The further along, the more the issues will have been defined and the less useful this discussion will be. Disputes as to individual facts and/or evidence are likely to come out during the discussion of the items and your arguments to justify the proposals on the basis of the merits of the case.

13.3.3 Items to be negotiated

Where there is more than one item to negotiate, whether or not you decide to have some preliminary discussion about the merits or what is disputed before dealing with the items, you must still decide the order in which you want to discuss the items. Matters to take into account when deciding this include:

13.3.3.1 Are items linked by a common underlying issue?

It may make sense to deal with these items together. Discussion of the underlying issue can then be used efficiently to assist in determining what is a reasonable settlement on all those items.

13.3.3.2 Where do your client's priorities lie?

You may want to deal with the high priority items first as the others will fall into place once you know where you stand on your client's most important objective. The dispute between the parties may involve an ongoing commercial contract. It may involve both the terms of the contract and claims for past losses that are also dependent on a variety of other issues, including causation, remoteness and mitigation. Your client's priority is to maintain the commercial contract on the terms he or she alleges were agreed. The past losses are of less priority.

13.3.3.3 What items are most arguable?

Where there are several areas of dispute, different items may be dependent on different issues. You may then prefer to determine the order in which the items are covered on the basis of the strength of your case on the underlying issue. Thus you may wish to start with the items based on the issue on which you have the strongest case to gain a strong position in the hope that, by the time the negotiation has reached the issues on which you are weaker, the other side has been worn down. This is, of course, likely to produce a competitive tone to the negotiation.

13.3.3.4 Are there items which can be agreed easily?

Are there items on which agreement would be easy to reach either because both parties want the same thing or want such different things that there is no real need for negotiation on them? For example, in a divorce case, in dividing up the assets, it may be that there are a number of items wanted only by one of the parties. Starting with these could assist. First, getting them out of the way quickly may clarify what really does need to be negotiated and leaves time to do it. Secondly, it may introduce a cooperative tone to the negotiation which could assist even where items must be negotiated.

13.4 Summary

Whatever opening and overall structure you choose, use of time will be important. In practice, you will have to be able to carry out complex negotiations in less than half an hour outside the court. You should develop the ability to work at speed even though you will often have more time than this in chambers. Negotiations tend either to start with a lot of energy but then slow down after 10 to 15 minutes, or take a long time to get going and only become useful after 10 to 15 minutes. This is not necessarily a bad thing, but try to plan a structure which uses time well and does not result in losing too much momentum or in taking too long to build momentum. Always make sure that you spend the most time on the most important issues.

The order in which you deal with the matters to be discussed in the negotiation is itself subject to negotiation. Never simply agree an order suggested by your opponent. Be ready for your opponent to object to your suggestions. Where there is discussion about the order, ensure that your client's objectives and matters you want to discuss are included and that the order is as favourable as possible to your client. However, you also need to be flexible about this. Spending time negotiating how you will negotiate is not efficient. Remember, too, that the order can be altered if it proves impractical.

13.5 Application to Case Study A

Opening: D likely to have judgment set aside—in hospital and strong case; both here to settle, limited time—items to be discussed; set out order as follows:

- C's claim for instalments 1 and 2 and D's claim for losses:
  - try to link them
  - deal with instalments 1 and 2 together
  - show how D's claim larger than C's claim for price.

- C's claim for loss on remainder of contract:
  - link to offers to buy chocolate
  - consider future trading.
- Costs.
- What will happen to the case—if settle?
  - Judgment set aside
  - C discontinue claim.

13.6 Application to Case Study B

Do the same exercise for Case Study B.

14 Considering possible tactics

14.1 Introduction

As explained in **Chapter 3**, 'tactics' are the different behaviours and specific actions used in the negotiation to achieve the negotiators' desired ends. There is an overlap with strategy in that certain tactics, in particular those which relate to concessions and information exchange, are more likely to be used within a particular strategy. We have seen some of the tactics used in these specific aspects of the negotiation in **Chapters 10** and **11**.

14.2 Specific tactics

In addition to the tactics which underlie certain strategies (eg, use of high demands, small concessions, etc, by competitive negotiators), there are a number of common specific tactics used in negotiations. Most stem more from the mindset of positional bargaining than from the principled or problem-solving approaches. Like strategies, there is not necessarily agreement on terminology or on the details of some of these tactics. They may be given different labels or approached differently. We have attempted to categorise the main tactics you are likely to come across in negotiating. Some have been included in the appropriate chapter and this is indicated below. The remainder of this chapter introduces you to some additional tactics with guidance to assist you in understanding when and why they may be used, the risks attached to their use and possible responses you might have to them.

14.2.1 Information exchange

The tactics used by negotiators in relation to the exchange of information which can affect (increase or decrease) the accuracy and/or flow of information exchanged were discussed when we considered how to plan this aspect of the negotiation in **Chapter 10** (see **10.4**).

14.2.2 Concessions/demands/offers

The tactics used in seeking concessions from the other side, making offers/concessions and responding to concessions sought were explained when we considered how to plan the concession-making aspect of negotiation in **Chapter 11** (see **11.3.5**).

14.2.3 Structure/order

Negotiators may set up a structure for the negotiation or alter its order to assist them to get the most out of the negotiation or to cope with difficulties. How the negotiation is started and the way in which negotiators open is one of the tactical considerations that can have a real impact on the whole negotiation. These have been considered in **Chapter 13**.

14.2.3.1 The agenda

By setting or suggesting an agenda, you determine the order in which issues will or are likely to be discussed. This tactic was discussed in **Chapter 13** when dealing with planning your structure.

14.2.3.2 'Moving on'

Negotiators may discuss issues sequentially, agreeing them as they go along. Even where they agree to settle only once all the issues are on the table and have been discussed, negotiators must discuss each individual issue or item. It may be more difficult to reach even provisional agreement on some items and the negotiators may therefore decide to 'move on' to other items and come back to the one causing difficulty—an efficient suggestion for keeping the negotiation moving. However, a negotiator who sees a weakness in his or her case or is suddenly confronted with new information may also use this tactic as a device to avoid discussing it, either until later when he or she has decided how to deal with the issue, or altogether. It is surprising how many negotiators move on from items never to return to them, particularly where they appear to be, but are not necessarily, unimportant items such as costs or date of payment. Recognise that this may be the case but be prepared to be flexible as insistence on discussing one item until agreement is reached may produce deadlock.

14.2.3.3 'Just one more thing'

This tactic introduces a new demand near the end of the negotiation, at the point the negotiators are reaching or actually agreeing the outcome: 'Oh by the way, just one more [often, but not always, small] thing.' Done to test the resolve of the other negotiator on the basis that, in sight of agreement, he or she will give on this (little?) matter, it is a risky tactic which may undo what has already been achieved. When used against you, label the behaviour and refuse to respond to it. Clearly, where the negotiation has been on the basis that it is conditional until the whole package is agreed, this additional demand becomes part of the package. You could require the opponent to put the full package on the table and expressly confirm that there are no more 'add-ons' before you decide whether to continue.

A variation of this is adding an item or condition after agreement has been reached on the basis that it had been forgotten or a mistake was made. This is a highly dubious tactic. Refuse to react to it. Once agreement has been reached, provided it satisfies contractual principles, it is enforceable as a contract. Additional terms cannot be added unilaterally. If, however, the agreement has been insufficiently specific then it will not be enforceable as the terms will be too uncertain. The potential use of this tactic is another reason why it is essential when negotiating to finalise the terms fully and precisely.

14.2.4 Setting the parameters/fixing the focus

There are several devices which may be used to set the negotiation into the context, settlement range or parameters favourable to one of the parties. The underlying ethos is the same for all of them. The person using the tactic gets the negotiation centred around his or her view of the issues.

14.2.4.1 The drafts

This tactic is the easiest to understand and identify. The negotiator brings a draft agreement to the negotiation and suggests the discussion proceed by going through the draft. This puts him or her in a powerful position. First, the text of the draft will dictate the agenda, both what issues are discussed and the order in which they are covered. Secondly, a solution to each of the issues is already set out in the text, leaving the other party to counter it. While working from an existing draft by one party can have advantages, eg, saving time, you should think carefully about the implications if it is suggested by an opponent.

14.2.4.2 The objective standard

While principled negotiators genuinely try to use objective standards in a negotiation to enable them to negotiate on the basis of principles rather than pressure, not all negotiators suggest using objective standards for this reason. As pointed out above, 'objective' can mean different things and there can be different standards against which to judge settlements, eg, precedent, norms, business practice, etc. The standard used may have an impact on what each of the parties get. A negotiator may suggest applying an apparently objective standard in the knowledge that this particular one favours his or her client. Where an 'objective' standard is suggested, do not just assume it is objective. Check it out. Consider whether it really is objective in your case. Take time to consider what other standards might be equally or more 'objective'.

14.2.4.3 Anchoring

This tactic is more subtle than the two above but has the same purpose. By making a particular statement, the negotiator fixes the focus of the negotiation in a way beneficial to him or her. By discussing the issues using a hypothetical figure or set of facts, the parties 'anchor' or focus on that figure or those facts and this can influence their thinking. For example, if the parties discuss a case 'hypothetically' on the basis that the defendant is liable, the fact that this focus has been introduced, and the statement probably repeated, may influence the outcome against the defendant.

14.2.5 Reframing your approach

The ability to put a case persuasively is an important part of a lawyer's tool kit. What is persuasive will depend on the circumstances. A negotiation, particularly a legal dispute resolution between lawyers, is done within a litigation framework. The lawyers speak from an adversarial perspective using adversarial language. (Contrast this with the framework and language of other professions, particularly those in the caring professions, such as social workers whose whole approach is conciliatory, eg, 'sharing concerns'.)

The way in which proposals are framed and the language used has an impact on the negotiation process. One can learn to 'reframe' or use language to affect the process. Using more conciliatory language, while not in any way altering the substance, may produce an atmosphere more conducive to agreement. Alternatively, using adversarial language and framing may increase the sense of competition and stress to which the opponent may react (by giving in or possibly by deadlock). The following paragraphs (**14.2.5.1** to **14.2.5.3**) illustrate some specific examples of 'reframing' or using language to effect.

14.2.5.1 Seeking proposals/making demands

In many negotiations the negotiators 'make demands' of each other, ie, each puts what he or she wants to get out of the negotiation in the expectation of being beaten down (ie, having to make concessions). The two then focus on how far each has moved from the initial 'demand'. Another approach is to ask your opponent what he or she 'proposes' by way of settlement. This moves the focus from what that side is seeking to what he or she considers reasonable.

14.2.5.2 Reasons or requests first

When asking for something from someone, one can either put the request and then say why it is wanted or set out the reasons why something is needed and then put the request. Putting the request first in a negotiation may mean that the other side does not hear the reason because he or she is busy thinking about how to respond. Putting the reason why something is needed first means the other side is more likely to be listening throughout to find out precisely what is wanted.

14.2.5.3 'Yes but. . .'

Responding to a proposal or demand which is not either wholly unacceptable or wholly acceptable requires an indication of some agreement with qualifications. Often this is done by saying 'yes but. . .'. The 'but' acts as a signal that a negative is to follow and many negotiators hear only the part from 'but' onwards, ie, the qualifications, the negatives, the parts on which there is disagreement. (This is also a well-known phenomenon in teaching, where in the comments, 'You did x, y and z well but you need to work on a, b and c', the student hears only a, b and c. By substituting 'and' for 'but', ie, by joining the qualifications to the agreement rather than separating them, the whole proposal is heard.)

14.2.6 Psychological

There are a number of tactics using behaviour and/or words which are not directed at substantive or procedural issues but affect the negotiators' thinking, emotions and confidence.

14.2.6.1 Aggressive tactics

There are a wide variety of tactics which can be used to introduce an emotional element into the negotiation, to wear the opponent down or cause loss of confidence or self-image, eg, aggression, confrontation, anger (feigned or real), sarcasm, ridicule, blame or fault-finding, guilt, put-downs, and unpredictability through sudden change of mood (which many people have difficulty coping with partially because they assume they have somehow caused it). When used against you, do not react. If necessary, take time to consider how to respond in a rational way to get the negotiation back to the relevant issues. Consider labelling the behaviour and refusing to negotiate unless it is altered.

14.2.6.2 Positive emotions/strokes

We all like to be liked and are, generally, well disposed towards those who are friendly to us. We also like to have the positive aspects of our self-image confirmed by others (eg, that we are clever). As in all human interactions, giving people positive strokes in negotiations—being friendly, flattering them, etc—can make them more predisposed to persuasion and to making concessions. While a friendly demeanour or positive statement may be genuine, it may also be used as a tactic. Being conscious of your reactions to such use of emotions/strokes (whether conscious or not) means that you are able to identify them more easily and limit your response to a rational discussion of the substantive issues.

Being amused, or finding something humorous, generally creates a positive atmosphere. Although different people find different things amusing or humorous, there is also much humour which is shared and can be used to lighten the atmosphere when it has become too tense. This may induce people to feel more predisposed to one another, and more able to work together. While it may be used as a positive tactic (eg, to break deadlock), be aware that it may also be used negatively (eg, to disguise a move away from an issue under discussion or make the opponent feel more predisposed to make concessions).

14.2.6.3 Silence

In any interaction between people in Western culture there is little room for silence. We find silence difficult and react automatically to fill it by speaking. This cultural behaviour can be used in a negotiation. Remaining silent can put pressure on the opponent to speak. Thus, where the opponent has put a proposal with the reasons for it, remaining silent may produce more information or a variation of the proposal, possibly a further concession. To avoid being the victim of such a tactic, learn to resist the automatic response to silence. Being silent yourself is fine but both negotiators cannot remain silent for long. Think carefully about what you say if you break the silence and ensure that it is guided by the substance of the negotiation and not the pressure to speak.

14.2.6.4 Tit-for-tat

This tactic is one whereby the negotiator mirrors the strategy adopted by the opponent. He or she responds to cooperative behaviour by being cooperative and to competitive behaviour by being competitive. The tactic may also be used with concessions, matching the size and frequency of concessions to those of the other side. This reinforces the desired behaviour (ie, the cooperative) by rewarding it with concessions and punishes the undesired behaviour (ie, the competitive) by withholding concessions. A basic strategy which is completely positional has been shown in experiments to produce concessions even after the negotiator has stopped rewarding the behaviour.

14.2.7 Increasing the competition

Some tactics are used to increase the apparent competition for particular items. Thus, a negotiator may state that there are other people who want a particular item, hence their unwillingness to go below a certain point. A negotiator may also indicate that what the opponent wants is a scarce commodity thereby increasing the competition for it and possibly its desirability for the person seeking it. The other person and the scarcity may be real or fictitious. Check it out.

14.2.8 Using time

Even negotiations between solicitors while the case is trundling its way through the litigation process will be subject to the pressure imposed by court time limits or the wishes of the clients. The pressure exerted by lack of time in negotiations at the court door is very apparent.

There is research to show that negotiators make lower demands, increase concessions and lower their expectations under pressure of time. Negotiators can use time to try to press their opponent into reducing demands and making concessions.

(a) The Deadline: Negotiators may create false deadlines. Where there is a genuine deadline, eg, at the court door, they may repeatedly refer to the shortage of time.

(b) Brinkmanship: Negotiators may delay dealing with the main issues or introduce new ones very close to the deadline to test the opponent and increase his or her anxiety that settlement will not be reached unless he or she concedes. A risky tactic, it may backfire and result in no settlement.

Being conscious of the effect of time pressure on most negotiators, being aware of the real time pressures, checking any additional ones suggested by the opponent and taking some control of the structure of the negotiation to ensure best use of time may safeguard against succumbing to these tactics. Remember your reservation points and bottom line or BATNA and that you can walk away.

14.2.9 Forcing the issue

Some negotiators make it appear that the negotiation stands or falls on the opponent's actions to induce anxiety and force concessions from him or her to reach agreement. Two common tactics used to force the issue are:

(a) The final offer: The negotiator states a final offer as an ultimatum. Whether settlement is reached then depends on the opponent's response. This tactic attempts to transfer responsibility for reaching settlement to the opponent and to force him or her to accept the offer because of anxiety that failure to do so might cause the negotiation to break down. The negotiator may or may not give reasons why it is the final offer. He or she may also make an additional concession when making the statement. It is a risky tactic unless it is genuine, ie, you actually are prepared to discontinue the negotiation if it is not accepted. When used against you, think carefully about the offer and your bottom line or BATNA. The fact that it is stated as a final offer does not make you responsible for any breakdown which may follow. That is determined by the overall conduct of both parties throughout the whole negotiation. If you have been unreasonable during the negotiation, maybe what is offered is reasonable, far better than your BATNA. On the other hand, it may be far worse.

(b) The walkout: A version of the above tactic, the negotiator threatens to discontinue negotiations unless his or her proposal is accepted. It has the same risks as the final offer and when used against you should be handled in the same way.

14.2.10 'I am only the representative'

Representative negotiators can separate themselves from the person whose case is being negotiated. Clearly, it is important to have a professional approach to the negotiation and not see it as personal. A professional, not directly experiencing the problem, has a more objective view of the issues and possible settlements. A representative must ensure that he or she has the authority to negotiate for the client and be clear exactly what that authority empowers him or her to discuss and agree.

However, this separation can also be used artificially by employing the following tactics.

14.2.10.1 Lack of or limited authority

Making it clear that any agreement is subject to the client's approval at the start of the negotiation is a statement about the limits of the negotiator's authority. It enables the client to have the final say on what is agreed. However, a negotiator may unnecessarily claim lack of or limited authority. The lack or limit may have been specifically sought or may not in fact exist. The claim may come near the end of the negotiation when the other side thinks that final settlement has almost been achieved. As a device, lack or limit of authority can be used to obtain information from the other side while reserving your position, for buying time to think or for obtaining more. Ensuring you are clear about the other negotiator's authority at the start of the negotiation prevents this device being used against you later.

14.2.10.2 'My client won't agree'

A representative negotiator may be sympathetic to what is being proposed but state that he or she cannot agree because the client will not. This may in fact be the true position. However, it may also be a device whereby the negotiator appears to be negotiating in a reasonable and sympathetic way while in fact being tough. A variation of this tactic is for the negotiator to present the client as insisting on a particular issue, as being 'locked in' to a position despite the risks attached because the client will not or cannot move. The negotiator may express views about the unreasonableness of the client's approach while insisting that the demand be met. Alternatively, the client may be presented as being reasonable but subject to forces 'beyond his or her control'. When used against you, press for more details (exactly what is the client committed to and why) or deal with the issues on which there may be agreement to produce a package which persuades 'the client' to agree on this issue.

14.2.11 Where there is a team

Lawyers may negotiate in teams. At the court door, where barristers have been instructed, the negotiation will generally be 'between counsel' and therefore rarely in teams. However, there may be circumstances where there is a team (eg, leading and junior counsel or the solicitor takes an active part in the negotiation).

A negotiation team may play 'good guy/bad guy'. One negotiator is friendly, sympathetic and apparently cooperative and the other is overtly aggressive and competitive. The opponent begins to see the 'good guy' as an ally and assume that he or she is more cooperative than is in fact the case and as a result is more disposed to make concessions. When used against you, deal with the substance of what is said by each negotiator and use some of the tactics from principled negotiation, eg, separate the people from the problem.

14.3 Dubious tactics

14.3.1 General

Some tactics are clearly dishonest and unethical, eg, deliberately misleading your opponent by pretending to have evidence you do not have. This is against the Bar's Code of Conduct and, even if the statements do not amount to an offence (eg, fraud), using them can result in being debarred.

Even when behaviour comes within ethical boundaries (which are often difficult to determine), the tactics you use will invariably affect the reputation you build. If, for example, you use aggressive tactics, you will get a reputation for being confrontational which may be difficult to get rid of.

Some tactics, particularly the more competitive ones, although not blatantly unethical, may fall over the line. There are many grey areas and different views as to where the line is drawn between acting ethically and unethically. Two areas covered above where this difficulty lies are:

(a) Aggressive behaviour which may become sufficiently insulting or rude to amount to a breach of your professional duty to act courteously.

(b) Managing or manipulating information which may become sufficiently 'tricky' or misleading to amount to professional misconduct. A barrister's job is to promote the client's case as an advocate. You may quite properly pitch the case at its highest when trying to reach a settlement, even though you may not necessarily succeed in proving the whole case in court. There is not always a clear line between doing the best for your client and misleading or unfair tactics. But you must not pretend that you do know a fact or have particular instructions if this is simply not true.

14.3.2 Threats

'Threat' is defined, in Donald G Gifford's book, *Legal Negotiation: Theory and Applications* at p 143, as 'a conditional commitment by a negotiator to act in a way that appears detrimental to the other party unless the other party complies with a request'. Threats demonstrate commitment by the person making them and attempt to induce concessions from the opponent. Many negotiation tactics, although not phrased as threats, implicitly involve them, eg, 'the final offer' is basically a threat to end the negotiation if the offer is not accepted.

Two questions arise in considering the use of express open threats:

(a) How effective are they? To be effective, the threat must be believed. To be believed, it must be credible. The size of the threat must relate to the issue involved; if it is disproportionate, it is less likely to be believed. The negotiator must also be believable. Issuing a number of threats, none of which is carried out or which the negotiator is clearly not in a position to carry out, reduces his or her credibility. Finally, the reaction to a threat may be to counter with a threat, escalating the aggressive behaviour and leading to deadlock.

(b) Are they ethical? It is unprofessional and unethical to introduce improper threats. On the other hand, it is quite legitimate to point out potential consequences. The dividing line between a legitimate statement and an unethical threat is difficult, and is dealt with in the Professional Conduct Course and the Negotiation Course.

There are a variety of ways of responding to a threat depending on the circumstances under which it is made. You could ignore it. You could label it and refuse to deal on the basis of threats, treat it with derision, 'If making a threat is your best line of argument. . .', or express surprise at such behaviour. You could discuss the content of the threat to ascertain what lies behind it and whether it could be carried out. You could divert the discussion to another topic. Making a counter-threat is generally not a good idea as it escalates the hostility and increases the chances of deadlock.

14.4 General attitude/preparation for tactics

The best protection against being overwhelmed by your opponent's tactics is thorough preparation, ie, knowing the issues, the facts and the law, the objectives, the options, the arguments which could be used for and against you, and planning your concessions and your bottom line or BATNA. This cannot be emphasised too much. Knowing the strengths and weaknesses of your case well will assist you to respond rationally to any tactic and reduce the possibility of reacting in the manner intended by the user.

The knowledge that you do not have to settle is another safeguard. Having considered the alternatives your client has to settlement, you are able to measure this against proposals and make rational decisions about whether or not to accept them. Using protective tactics makes you less vulnerable to buckling under pressure (see, eg, **11.3.5** on concessions). Remember, you do not need to agree unconditionally to any one issue until you have the full package (including any costs or procedural issues) on the table.

Being professional and detached is also a safeguard. The negotiation should not become personal. Control your reactions. Do not show surprise unless used as a tactic. Maintaining control means you are less likely to give things away unintentionally. Work at maintaining this mindset. Remind an opponent who acts unprofessionally of his or her duty as a barrister.

Respond to specific tactics by recognising them, appreciating your natural response to them and controlling your reaction. Do not feel you have to respond immediately; if necessary, take time to consider the best response. You may wish also to label the tactic, identify the behaviour and ask why it is being used or explain that you will not continue unless it is stopped. If you consider that your opponent is acting unethically, make this clear.

Where relevant, take into account anything you know about your opponent personally. The Bar is not a large profession, and when you have been in practice for a few years or if you work in a specialist area it is likely that you will know your opponent. Even if you do not know your opponent personally, another member of Chambers may do so, and some barristers build a reputation for the way they approach negotiations. Personal characteristics should not, of course, have any impact on the outcome of the case for the client, but knowing something of an opponent's likely approach to a case can properly be taken into account in planning strategy and tactics.

15 Communicating effectively

15.1 Introduction

This chapter discusses how to communicate effectively in a negotiation. First, it considers how behaviour and psychological influences can impact on communication. Secondly, it looks at ways you can increase your persuasiveness in speaking and effectiveness both in questioning and listening in the negotiation. Thirdly, it gives examples of how you could present aspects of the negotiation visually. Finally, it looks specifically at the two activities of presenting and responding and gives hints on how to use them most effectively.

15.2 Behavioural and psychological influences

Before we look at the more obvious communication skills (speaking, questioning and listening), we consider some of the behavioural and psychological influences that may impact on them. We have already considered some of these psychological influences in previous chapters.

Your manner or style of speaking can have a huge impact on how your message is received. Style is the manner of delivery, a person's attitude and demeanour. A person's style includes a range of factors, such as use of language, tone and volume of voice and physical presence, eg, the way of sitting or standing. Style can extend to particular types of statements (eg, making personal remarks about the opponent or being sarcastic or condescending, all hallmarks of a competitive style). An argumentative style will produce a very different psychological reaction in the listener and this in turn may affect how the listener responds. In **Chapter 8**, we saw how negotiators use this to make their opponent more open to compromise. Thus, for example, a competitive negotiator may use an argumentative style to wear the opponent down. A cooperative negotiator may use non-threatening, reasonable language to engender trust and reciprocity in their opponent.

Our expectations and preconceptions may lead to selective filtering of information and mean that we do not hear accurately what has been said. In **Chapter 10**, we saw how this phenomenon can influence the exchange of information.

Our fear of losing credibility may influence how we deal with concessions, which we considered in **Chapter 11**. Finally, in **Chapter 14**, we looked at tactics, many of which use underlying psychological influences to gain an advantage in the negotiation.

We now turn to look more closely at two important behavioural influences on effective communication: non-verbal communication and mirroring behaviour. Both can impact on what the negotiators say and how they hear what is said to them.

15.2.1 Non-verbal communication

Non-verbal communication is the way we transmit information through our behaviour. In discussion with another person, in addition to speaking, we also communicate using physical gestures (ie, body language). Our physical gestures (eg, how we sit, hold our heads, arms, etc) convey information about our attitude to the other person (eg, that we are attentive and want to agree, that we are annoyed and not listening, that we feel superior, etc). This can play a significant role during negotiation. An ability to understand what information facial expressions, hand gestures, or other movements of the body may be revealing assists a negotiator to respond in a more effective way if the message is correctly read. Equally, being able to manipulate your own non-verbal behaviour can be very useful in a negotiation.

Learning how to interpret someone's behaviour is complex and riddled with possible dangers. When interpreting someone's body language, there is an obvious danger of misinterpretation, particularly when you do not know the individual concerned. The solution is not to ignore a person's behaviour but to consider with care what it could mean. If someone does not make eye contact, there could be a number of explanations. It may be they feel intimidated by a point being made or alternatively that they are disinterested. Equally it could be that they are simply considering a point with care and cannot look, listen and think at the same time. Having thought about what their behaviour could indicate, you should create opportunities to check what you think they are indicating by their behaviour. For example, you could ask what they think of the point being made, or whether they have anything they wish to add or any comments to make.

Many negotiators concentrate on how their opponent is behaving and what their body language could be revealing and are unaware of their own behaviour or the reasons for it. Many people fail to appreciate the impact of their behaviour and continually adopt patterns of behaviour that have a negative effect on negotiation. It is also common for lawyers who negotiate to adopt a particular style of negotiation which they use for all negotiations, whatever the context and whoever the opponent, and give no thought to alternative ways of negotiating which may be more suitable to a particular context.

You need to be aware of and be able to evaluate not only your opponent's behaviour, but also your own, if you are to have any degree of control over a situation. This will assist you to learn what works, and why, and what does not work, and why. This information can only be gained through careful observation during the negotiation and critical reflection after the negotiation. One way of achieving such detachment is to mentally remove yourself from the negotiation and try to observe it critically as a non-partisan spectator. Another way is to video a negotiation and then watch it. Often when we view a video of ourselves, we are shocked that we do not look, act or behave as we imagine ourselves. Be aware of possible negative effects of your behaviour. A good starting point is to consider what you dislike in someone else's behaviour and consider carefully whether it could apply to you and under what circumstances. Many features that are commonly disliked are those that tend to indicate that the listener is disinterested. Consider what it feels like to be at the receiving end of someone who constantly looks over your shoulder, will not make eye contact, is fidgeting, looking at his or her watch, does not smile, or who slouches. Consider how such behaviour has a negative effect upon the negotiation. Part of persuasion is showing that you are interested, listening and attempting to understand the other side's point of view. If your behaviour is read as a lack of interest, you may have a problem if you are not aware that this is the message you convey.

Be conscious of the impact of behaviour on negotiation, but do not get carried away and focus on it too much. You are not a psychologist. There are also dangers inherent in trying to simulate certain behaviour. As a lawyer you must act ethically and speak plainly. Experimenting with certain behavioural techniques to evaluate their effectiveness as a negotiation tactic should never be at the expense of the proper representation of your client. Finally, simulating behaviour for particular effect could end up with you looking ludicrous and your opponent thinking that you are simply 'a little odd'. Alternatively, you may be conveying unintended messages.

15.2.2 Reciprocal or 'mirroring' behaviour

When two people are involved in discussion, they often unconsciously 'mirror' the behaviour of the person to whom they are talking (eg, adopt the same or similar gestures demonstrating attentiveness, annoyance, etc). This mirroring behaviour can be limited to physical gestures but is often extended to other areas, eg, tone of voice or even an attitude taken on an issue (eg, both becoming heated or aggressive). This mirroring behaviour also takes place in negotiations and can influence the behaviour of both negotiators.

Although much mirroring behaviour may have no major impact on the conduct of the negotiation, it can be 'destructive' or 'constructive'. Behaviour that is 'destructive' to the negotiation and escalates conflict is akin to 'an eye for an eye and a tooth for a tooth'. If your opponent makes positional statements, aggressive arguments, and generally behaves in a hostile manner, it is tempting to 'reward' such behaviour in kind. Unwittingly, an escalation of conflict may occur that could have disastrous consequences for the negotiation. Yet negotiators who exhibit mirroring destructive behaviour will often cling to the notion that such behaviour is justified on the basis that the opponent started it, and that their response was reasonable in the circumstances. Curiously, if negotiators are privately consulted, both will consider their actions as reasonable whilst citing the opponent's as unreasonable. Being aware of the possibility of mirroring your opponent's behaviour, and remembering that both you and your opponent are likely to feel justified in what you do, is the basis for avoiding destructive mirroring behaviour.

The alternative is for mirroring behaviour to be 'constructive', leading to an escalation of concessions, with both negotiators trying to reward each other's 'good' behaviour. We saw earlier how to some degree cooperative negotiators may rely on this mirroring behaviour to induce reciprocity. Where there is true mirroring behaviour, it is likely to lead to a settlement which is achieved quickly and painlessly. Whilst reciprocal concession-making due to mirroring good behaviour is acceptable, in as much as it leads to settlement rather than deadlock, this does not always mean that the settlement reached is appropriate for either or both clients. Caution is required to ensure that the concessions made are in the client's best interests.

A key feature of mirroring behaviour is that it is unintentional and occurs as an unconscious reaction to the way your opponent behaves. It is precisely because it may occur without a negotiator being aware of it that a negotiator needs to be able to identify if it is happening. One of the key elements of negotiation skills is the ability to understand the process as it occurs and know what is happening, and why, as this brings control and informed decision-making.

15.3 Speaking, questioning and listening effectively

A substantial component of being an effective and persuasive advocate or negotiator is good communication skills. A good communicator is aware of and uses various methods of communicating effectively. These include being aware of the above factors which may influence communication and being able to present persuasively, question effectively and absorb and evaluate what the opponent is saying efficiently.

15.3.1 Speaking persuasively

Although negotiations do not involve the formalities of courtroom advocacy, the techniques of persuasive presentation in court are equally persuasive in a negotiation. This includes both what you say and how you say it.

Dealing first with what you say: you have done your preparation so will know the arguments you wish to use, concessions you wish to seek, make, etc. These should be clear in your mind. As with presenting in court, the words you choose to articulate an argument can render it more or less persuasive. To be persuasive, you need to ensure that your listener understands your words and attaches the same interpretation to them as you intend them to have. Being concise and precise in your choice of words will produce clear persuasive argument. Using too many words and being vague is not persuasive. The message loses impact because your opponent will have difficulty ascertaining what your argument is. He or she is also likely to misunderstand it.

Consider the following statement:

> I feel compelled to point out to you the obvious mistake in what you appear to be saying, as my client could not possibly have failed to observe the warning signs on any version of events, let alone the ones you seem to be presenting, despite the obvious distractions at the time.

Consider by contrast how much more powerful the following statement is:

> My client saw the warning sign despite the distractions present at the time.

The manner in which you speak will also affect how persuasive you are. Speaking with confidence is as important in a negotiation as it is in a courtroom. Looking at your listener, taking care in your pronunciation, speaking at a reasonable pace, etc, will all increase your persuasiveness. Frequent use of 'um', 'er', 'ah', will weaken the impact of what you say and convey a lack of confidence. This is also irritating to the listener.

Negotiators who speak hesitantly, use too many words or are repetitious risk diluting the impact of what they are trying to say. They also risk the listener becoming bored, frustrated and irritated. Such speech also requires the listener to expend more energy deciphering what it is that is being communicated. Unless these consequences are desired for tactical reasons, it pays to speak plainly and confidently.

Finally, remember the tactic of reframing what you say (**14.2.5**), choosing your words carefully to alter the impact of what is said: 'offering a proposal' rather than 'making a demand'; putting reasons before your request; saying 'yes and' rather than 'yes but'.

15.3.2 Questioning effectively

Questioning an opponent can be a persuasive technique to use in a negotiation. Skilled use of questioning techniques can assist you to gain information on a variety of matters, from the strength of the opponent's case based on specific questioning about the facts and evidence, to a greater understanding of the other side's underlying non-legal motivation for settlement.

Questions can also be useful in establishing an atmosphere you consider appropriate. The focus of what is asked can be inherently confrontational (eg, questions to test your opponent on the evidence) or inherently cooperative (eg, seeking information from your opponent as to what his or her client genuinely wants from the negotiation). However, the manner in which a question is put can make it more or less confrontational, or more or less cooperative. Thus, asking in an assertive tone, 'On what possible basis do you make that claim?' is more confrontational than asking in an inquiring tone, 'Why does your client feel his claim is strong?'. Alternatively, inquiring about what your opponent's client wants by saying, 'So your client's total claim consists of X, is that right?' is more confrontational than saying, 'Is there anything else you think I ought to know about how your client has been affected by this accident?'. The tactic of reframing (see **14.2.5**) is as useful in questioning as it is in making statements.

Effective questioning can affect the balance of knowledge and information available to the negotiators and the relationship between them. It is as important in a negotiation as it is in advocacy and conference skills to understand the distinctions between different types of questions and what they can achieve.

15.3.3 Listening effectively

Listening is a vastly underrated skill. It is a stereotypical view that a barrister is paid to talk. In fact, this is often not the case. A major part of a barrister's job is to listen, and listening skills play a vital role in any negotiation. Negotiation is a process of information-exchange that occurs on at least three different levels: the explicit spoken word, the 'subtext' or hidden message in what someone does not mention, and the non-verbal information conveyed. Very often, listening occurs at the first level only and even at this level, negotiators do not 'hear' what is being said.

Listening effectively is essential to being persuasive given the intense levels of concentration required, particularly during a negotiation. You must be able to absorb and monitor what your opponent says and react to it appropriately. This involves digesting what is said as well as what is not said. Particular care should be taken when interpreting the 'subtext' of what is said. It is easy to make mistakes when listening to someone in a negotiation. The process lends itself to a rapid exchange of information. It may help if you check your understanding with your opponent, particularly about what has been expressly stated. Equally, if you have found a more obscure message in what has been said, try to test your views before making any major decisions about it.

Apart from the obvious benefit of enabling you to obtain information, listening is also a powerful tool of persuasion in its own right. Often a persuasive negotiator will be marked out by his or her ability to make the opponent feel that what is being said is being heard. Contrary to the notion that saying nothing gains nothing, if used correctly, listening can do the opposite. Showing that you are paying attention and hearing what your opponent has said conveys a variety of positive messages to the opponent. It shows interest and commitment. It can inspire trust, respect, even honesty. It is also very reassuring for your opponent. All of which may help you to get what you want from a negotiation. However, unsubtle and deliberate 'active listening' may have a very destructive effect. Demonstrably not listening, eg, blatantly appearing bored or uninterested, can also be a powerful tool, although of more limited use and with the risk of alienating your opponent.

Understanding some of the obstacles to listening should help you to develop the ability to listen effectively. One of the main obstacles to effective listening in a negotiation is your internal dialogue as you process the information received and consider what your next move should be. You will need to practise disciplining your own thoughts so that they do not preclude you from listening to important verbal and non-verbal messages which you may receive from your opponent.

Another obstacle you face is that listening can appear to be contrary to the culture of the Bar. It is tempting to think that if you are not doing the talking in a negotiation you are somehow missing an opportunity and appear weak. Yet saying nothing and doing nothing are two different things, and by listening carefully you obtain information which may be of great assistance in the negotiation. It takes confidence and patience to become a good listener, but remember that, when you are not saying anything and simply listening, you are receiving information, whilst your opponent is giving it away. Silence is itself a valuable tool and you should learn to resist filling the void in conversation/dialogue if you find yourself tempted to do so.

Finally, at a more simple (but no less distracting) level, external factors also militate against effective listening, and this is particularly true in a crowded corridor trying to negotiate a settlement with the clock ticking and the pressure of an impending hearing if settlement is not achieved. Under these circumstances, it is easy not to hear the subtle messages and fragments of important information that your opponent may be giving you.

15.4 Presenting argument and information visually

Most of the arguments in a negotiation are presented orally. However, you could consider how you might physically present information or argument to your opponent to assist you to 'anchor' or fix the focus of the discussion (see tactics at **14.2.4.3**). Some examples are:

(a) Figures: you could, for example, prepare a schedule of figures in a format that suits you and hand a copy to your opponent, which may pull your opponent into arguing about the figures on the basis you have chosen, and which may even confuse him or her into making concessions.

(b) Evidence: if you have evidence that you think the other side does not have and it is clearly favourable to you, you may choose to photocopy it to hand to your opponent. This could have the effect of making your evidence seem more real. This may in turn lead to a concession. On the other hand, where the evidence is open to different interpretation or has weaknesses, you may choose to provide your opponent with only a swift glance. This means that your opponent does not have the chance to analyse the evidence in full or to take it away.

(c) The law: if you are arguing on the basis of a statutory provision or regulation, you could consider taking a copy for your opponent as well as for yourself. This could be a good tactic to use if you have a particular legal strength. It can be more difficult for your opponent to refuse to argue a legal point if you have thoughtfully provided him or her with a copy.

15.5 Effective presentation and response

A negotiation should be a dialogue with both negotiators presenting their case, proposals for settlement, etc, and listening and responding to what has been said. We consider the main ingredients of effective presentation and response in turn.

15.5.1 Presenting effectively

Effective presentation is very important, and can indeed be decisive. A well-prepared case may fail to achieve the client's objectives if it is not effectively presented. An effective presentation can sometimes work wonders for a weak case. In a negotiation there is no judge to intervene, so a strong presentation of a mediocre case may achieve more than a weaker presentation of the same case (subject to the skills of the opponent).

The most important factors in effective presentation are as follows. Some of the factors are those required for good advocacy, but they may be more difficult to achieve in the faster and less controlled atmosphere of a negotiation.

15.5.1.1 Persuasive use of argument

Argument can be used to create a number of different effects. Competitive negotiators use it in a confrontational way, to appear aggressive and wear their opponent down. The risk of using this approach exclusively is that it is likely to induce deadlock in the negotiation. Argument may also be used rationally to explain what you want and why you think you should get it. Arguing for argument's sake is not persuasive. Ensure that you have a purpose. Use argument to test your opponent or to justify what you are seeking. When putting a proposal to your opponent, justify it: 'Payment of 75 per cent of the damages claimed would be fair because, although the issue will be determined on the oral evidence of the parties, and therefore on which of the parties the judge finds more credible, the burden of proof is on your client.'

15.5.1.2 Clarity and conciseness

As we saw from the example given earlier, it is more persuasive and effective to make your points as clearly and concisely as possible. Your opponent is more likely to understand the impact of your argument or precisely what you are proposing. This assists in keeping the discussion focused and is likely to limit argument to specific points and lead to more efficient progress. Making a point at length can be used as a tactic to wear down or confuse an opponent. However, it should be used sparingly and with caution as it also has the disadvantage of making you appear confused and/or inarticulate.

15.5.1.3 Coherent presentation

Presenting your arguments and proposals coherently is more likely to be effective and to persuade your opponent to consider them seriously. Presenting a proposal with the reasons to justify it means that your opponent has to consider and respond to the reasons you have given. Making proposals without justification or reason does not present this difficulty for your opponent and is therefore less persuasive. Considering one issue or item as thoroughly as possible before moving to the next builds a clear picture of your case or item based on several arguments. The opponent gets the impact of the cumulative effect. Jumping about and using surprise points means you lose the cumulative effect of your arguments. Indeed, the impact of individual arguments may be lost because a new and unrelated point is raised. While jumping around may be more useful on an issue on which your case is weak, or may confuse your opponent into making concessions, it is a risky tactic to use given the disadvantages.

15.5.1.4 Confidence and conviction

It is not only what you say but also how you say it that makes you persuasive. As a barrister, part of your skill in being persuasive is your ability to present confidently and with conviction, even when you feel neither confident nor convinced by your client's case. Looking and sounding confident depends on making eye contact with your opponent, not being hesitant in your manner or speech and speaking at an appropriate volume. Showing conviction in your client's case means choosing appropriate words. Thus, stating that, 'the balance of evidence favours my client's case on this point because . . .' shows more conviction than saying, 'I feel that the evidence may be more strongly weighted for my client on this point because . . .'. Both statements make the same point, but the first statement shows more conviction because it uses objective language and is more categorical than the second.

15.5.1.5 Appropriate use of language

When negotiating with another lawyer, it is appropriate to use legal terminology which you might not use with a client. You can often present legal issues simply by using the appropriate terminology, for example, 'your client is clearly in breach of an implied term' or 'I can't see that there is any problem with foreseeability here'. Where the legal concepts are more obscure and your opponent is confused, you may have to do more. The way you express things can also underline your approach to the case, or can be used as a tactic, for example saying, 'I don't think my client would accept that', rather than saying, 'I won't accept that'. Reframing what you say may also alter the impact of what is said (eg, using 'offers' or 'demands').

15.5.1.6 Pace

Pace is important, especially if you have limited time. Practitioners negotiating at the door of the court will often get straight to the main issue in the case and negotiate in a form of legal shorthand because both are familiar with the case and both anticipate the points the other is likely to make. Speed is not necessarily a virtue if it means that an important issue is not properly explored. However, generally speaking, if your case is well prepared, you should be able to deal with it at a reasonable pace and use time effectively.

15.5.1.7 Flexibility

Being flexible is vital. You will rarely find that a negotiation goes exactly as you wish. You will inevitably have to adapt to the approach and style of your opponent, to new issues, new facts, new evidence, a different approach to the law, and/or an alternative version of the figures in the case. Flexibility does not mean that detailed planning is of little use. It means that your planning must be capable of adaptation as the circumstances require.

15.5.2 Responding effectively

Responding effectively can be more difficult to achieve than presenting effectively. When you present your case, you are to some degree in control. You have chosen the point to present. Responding is about listening to your opponent, absorbing what is said and then replying appropriately. You have less control because you have not chosen the point on which you are being asked to speak. Some of the aspects of responding effectively are set out below. As with presenting, many of the points are equally relevant to advocacy but are more difficult to achieve in a negotiation which moves faster and in a less structured way than a trial.

15.5.2.1 Effective listening

We saw earlier how effective listening can be more difficult than it first appears to be. A number of things can interfere and mean that you do not hear what your opponent is saying. First, you may want so desperately to say something yourself that you cut your opponent off mid-flow. Not only is this rude, but it also means you do not hear what he or she was about to say (eg, you may have missed a very good offer). So be polite; do not speak over your opponent. Where you feel it is appropriate for you to cut in, wait for a pause and then indicate that you are conscious of cutting in and why. Secondly, you may be so busy concentrating on what you will say next that you miss an important point made by your opponent. Thirdly, you may be guilty of selective filtering, hearing only those points you want to hear. Be aware of these potential interferences and try to guard against them.

15.5.2.2 Precise and accurate responses

Responding accurately and precisely to any point made by your opponent using fact/law/evidence as appropriate is persuasive as it shows that you are well prepared and on top of your case. Being obtuse is a tactic which may occasionally have its uses but on the whole is ineffective.

15.5.2.3 Responding effectively

Generally trying to respond as quickly as possible to what your opponent has said will keep the momentum going and show the opponent that you are on your toes. However, do not be pressed into responding at speed where this is not appropriate. Where the purpose of the opponent's question or point is not clear, check you have understood it correctly. Where you wish to check figures, etc, if you need it, take the time.

15.5.2.4 Rational responses

Your response should move the negotiation forward and assist you to get the best for your client. Ensure that it does this. Your responses should keep a clear focus on your client's objectives and your picture of the case. Your response need not mirror what your opponent said. Thus, you do not have to respond to an argument with an argument if this is not appropriate. Equally, you do not have to respond to a concession with a concession. Think what response is most appropriate. Finally, just because your opponent asks for information does not mean you have to give it. Think about whether you should. Remember also that silence can be an effective response (see **14.2.6.3**) although, clearly, remaining silent frequently and for more than a few seconds is ineffective and inefficient.

15.5.2.5 Testing your opponent

In a negotiation, what you present will include setting out what your client wants and why you think it is justified. What you say will, of course, be positive and put your client's case in the best possible light. When your opponent presents, he or she will do the same: present the most positive aspects. Remember this and test your opponent. Make him or her justify proposals, set out reasons, etc. Ask 'why'. For example, responding when your opponent seeks a concession with, 'why should my client accept this', requires your opponent to justify what he or she has proposed. Asking for evidence to support an allegation of fact tests your opponent and the case. If he or she says that a standard is objective, ask for the rationale; how is it objective?

15.5.2.6 A poker face

Your opponent may say something which surprises you. This could be making an offer well beyond what you expected to get for your client. Alternatively, it could be something that exposes a weakness in your case. Do not show your elation in the first instance, nor your panic in the second. Accept the offer and move on.

15.5.2.7 Weaknesses exposed

It is difficult to deal with responding to an opponent who has exposed a weakness in your case, particularly if your opponent is aware of both your surprise and the weakness revealed. Your preparation may assist you in reducing the impact (eg, if it is an allegation of fact, asking for the evidence may expose a weakness). Alternatively, you may be able to deflect it.

15.6 Summary

Communicating effectively is as important in a negotiation as it is when acting as an advocate in court. It can have a huge impact on the conduct of the negotiation and the outcome of the negotiation. Communicating effectively is also generally more complex and difficult in a negotiation than in court. In court you speak to an independent arbiter who usually, though not always, listens to what is said and makes a decision about who wins on the basis of what you and your opponent have said. Although you need to respond to your opponent and to interventions from the judge, there are some conventions covering who speaks and when and your sole role is to persuade the decision-maker. However, in a negotiation, you not only have to present in a way which will persuade your opponent, you also have to jockey for position to speak and have to listen to what is said and make decisions about offers and settlement.

16

Conducting an effective negotiation

16.1 Introduction

A negotiation is a dynamic interactive process which involves a variety of activities. Each negotiation is different and presents different problems depending on the type of case and the approach you and your opponent take. There is no single blueprint or model for how to conduct a negotiation. In earlier chapters we considered how you should prepare to deal effectively with the various aspects of a negotiation.

This chapter provides a practical guide on how to use your preparation to conduct a negotiation effectively, taking into account your professional duties, the psychological and emotional factors which will influence you in the negotiation, the circumstances in which you are negotiating, and the different activities involved in a negotiation.

16.2 Acting professionally

Professional conduct is as important in negotiation as in any other aspect of a barrister's work. The Code of Conduct applies equally to your conduct as a negotiator and your conduct as an advocate. The ***Professional Conduct*** manual considers this in some detail which is not repeated here. In this section we highlight the aspects which are of relevance during the negotiation.

16.2.1 Making the limits of your authority clear

In **Chapter 7** we covered the importance of identifying your client's objectives and the professional conduct issues that arise when dealing with your client. When dealing with your opponent, remember that you are acting as the client's agent and have the apparent authority to bind him or her to what you agree with your opponent. Binding your client to something which does not meet with his or her approval is acting beyond your instructions and is a breach of your duty to your client. Where there is any risk of this happening, it is important that you make it clear to your opponent that anything agreed between you is subject to your client's approval.

Where you have been asked to negotiate a settlement at the court door, your client will also be at court and will be available to make the final decision on the acceptability of any settlement you reach with your opponent. You will generally conduct the negotiation with your opponent without your client present and you must ensure that you make it clear that any agreement reached is subject to your client's approval. You will rarely be asked to negotiate a settlement without your client being present at court unless it is a minor interim hearing not involving the client where that client is a corporate client and the dispute is purely about money. You may therefore not be able to put any settlement you have reached with your opponent to your client to make the final decision (although checking by phone would be a wise precaution). You must therefore have clear instructions from your client as to precisely what is acceptable before you negotiate with your opponent. If you have any doubt at all as to the acceptability to your client of what is agreed, make it clear to your opponent that the settlement is subject to your client's approval.

16.2.2 Respecting privileged discussion

Discussions to reach settlement are generally conducted 'without prejudice' to indicate that what is said between the lawyers is privileged and cannot be revealed in court. This is subject to exception once agreement is reached, in which case the agreement is treated as an enforceable contract on which evidence may be given. Thus, if agreement is not reached, you must not repeat what was said in the negotiation and you must warn your client of this rule as well.

16.2.3 Respecting client confidentiality

Negotiations between barristers, particularly at the court door, are frequently done out of hearing of the clients. The discussion may therefore be less formal and the barristers may say things which might not be said in the clients' presence (eg, that the client is currently very upset, stressed, etc). However, you should always remember that your primary duty is to your client and that your duty of confidentiality means that you should not reveal anything to the other side that your client would not wish the other side to know. It also means not disparaging your client in conversation with your opponent. Whatever you may feel about your client or his or her objectives, in discussion with your opponent you should be as respectful as possible about your client and his or her concerns.

16.2.4 Professional behaviour towards your opponent

You have a duty to your client to do your best, to present his or her case in the best possible light and to use any legitimate tactics to achieve success. However, you should be aware of the line between what is and is not ethical. This was considered in **Chapter 14** when we looked at dubious tactics.

You have a duty to be honest with your opponent. This means being truthful and not misleading your opponent about the facts of the case, your own instructions or the relevant law. Thus, for example, although you may pitch the case at the highest possible level, you should never say that you know a fact or have evidence when you do not. On the other hand, you have no duty to disclose information and you should consider whether it is in your client's interests to reveal information that does not have to be revealed. For example, you are not obliged to answer questions from your opponent about the facts of the case or your instructions, and you could refuse to answer, or simply move on to another topic, if this is in your client's interests.

You also have a duty to be trustworthy and not to go back on your word. Never pretend that you have said something you did not or did not say something which you did. If you made a mistake, admit it.

Finally, you have a duty to treat your opponent with courtesy. This does not mean that you cannot be assertive or take a competitive stance in the negotiation. However, it does mean that you should not be rude, insulting or overly aggressive.

16.3 Recognising the impact of stress

A barrister's job is to win cases for his or her client. Feeling that the case stands or falls on how well you perform can be stressful. This applies to acting as an advocate as well as negotiating a case. Negotiating a settlement for your client may, for some people, be even more stressful than acting as an advocate because of the uncertainty stemming from the lack of rules of procedure and an independent arbitrator to make the decision. Never underestimate the effect that stress may have on your performance and the impact this may have on the most careful preparation. In previous chapters we have looked at some of the psychological and behavioural influences which may have an impact on the negotiators and the negotiation. When under stress, you may find these have more of an impact on you and/or you are less aware of the impact. As a number of the tactics used in negotiation rely on these influences, you need to be conscious of the potential impact on you and how it can be used by your opponent. It may be that you find that you too use them in the negotiation, consciously or unconsciously.

16.4 The context of the negotiation

The first step in your preparation should have included consideration of the context in which the negotiation would take place (see **Chapter 6**), which includes taking into account the circumstances of the negotiation. Although these circumstances include negotiation by correspondence or phone, this chapter looks at the conduct of face-to-face negotiations between barristers, although most of the principles apply to other types of negotiation too. Face-to-face negotiations can range from a negotiation to be arranged by you or the solicitors to take place over a whole day (or several days) in either chambers or the solicitor's offices, to having a few minutes with opposing counsel before you go into court.

In the first situation, your preparation will have included a variety of considerations (see **6.1.2**) such as who should attend the negotiation, where it should be held, the seating arrangements, etc, all of which may influence the process. Thus, for example, the more people who attend, the more people who will want to have their say, which may slow down the process. You should be ready to take this into account during the actual negotiation.

In most cases, particularly in your early years, you will negotiate outside the court door, having been instructed to appear at a particular hearing. The circumstances here will equally effect the process and you need to take these into account. A negotiation at the door of the court may simply have to take place in the nearest bit of corridor. Although many courts now have small 'interview' rooms that you may be able to use, there is frequently great demand for them and you may find that there is nowhere to negotiate except in the corridor, which may be noisy or busy.

In addition, where the client and solicitor are at court, you will have to decide whether either or both should be included in the negotiation. Generally, court door negotiations are strictly between counsel without the client or solicitor participating. This is because the time pressure means the negotiation must be conducted efficiently as well as reducing the possibility of the client's more personal involvement interfering with the negotiation. However, even where the client does not participate, you may find that they are a short distance away, possibly within hearing and are also watching you. This may make negotiating awkward and you should consider finding somewhere a short distance from the client.

Negotiating in a corridor may also present problems for dealing with papers if there is no opportunity to sit down, or if there are seats but no tables. You need to be ready to cope with being unable to refer to papers easily and to avoid dropping everything when you are trying to make your best point! Needless to say, all these additional factors invariably add to the stress.

16.5 Dealing with the different phases of the negotiation

In this section we look at the different phases of a negotiation and those aspects that may cause you concern or trip you up in a negotiation.

16.5.1 Opening/structuring the negotiation

In **Chapter 13** we considered how the opening can set the tone of the negotiation, affect the process and efficiency with which it is conducted and give the negotiators a feel for their opponents' potential objectives, strategy and behaviour in the negotiation. We considered how you might plan to open by taking into account the impact and by setting out some of the options and the pros and cons of each.

However you have planned to open, you will have to take on board the actual circumstances in which you find yourself negotiating (eg, you have less or more time than you thought or your opponent appears to be much more cooperative or competitive than you expected). You need to be flexible and may need to rethink your opening. Time may have become an issue and it may be important to start the negotiation in a way that will focus on using the time most efficiently. Your opponent may greet you with a fairly competitive statement about the strength of his or her client's case and you may feel that you should respond to this to establish your own credibility as a negotiator.

The need to be flexible in how you open does not mean that you jettison the whole of your plans for setting out what needs to be discussed and the order in which you consider it should be discussed. Both of these are themselves subject to negotiation. Take stock of the situation and decide whether, in light of the opening statement, your planned content and structure is still, in your view, the best for you. If so, make this clear to your opponent. You may find that your opponent disagrees with you. Decide how flexible you could be on the content and/or structure. For example, you may consider that, given the time, you cannot afford to have a general discussion on the merits of the case before dealing with the specific items which are sought by the parties (eg, money, terms of a future agreement, etc). However, you may be happy to discuss those specific items in the order suggested by your opponent. You should to make this clear to your opponent and negotiate accordingly.

16.5.2 Information exchange

In **Chapter 10** we set out some of the factors that may distort information, how the different strategies use information exchange and some of the tactics adopted by negotiators actively to distort or avoid providing information. We also considered how you could use this aspect of the negotiation most effectively by considering what information to seek from your opponent, how to deal with requests for information and how to propose to deal with gaps which neither party is able to fill. Careful preparation should go a long way in ensuring that you deal with this aspect well when in the negotiation and do not get caught out by being anxious or by clever tactics used by your opponent.

One of the considerations in planning the structure of the negotiation is deciding when to exchange information. You can plan to have a section at the start to check what information each side has. This may include filling in gaps in the information held by either side. Although this may be useful where there are substantial gaps, in most cases you are likely to have sufficient shared information to make this unnecessary (see **13.3.2.2**). In addition, it is potentially risky and unhelpful. The information exchange is to help you to find a good settlement. It might be useful where a straight exchange of information is simply about what the individual parties want from the negotiation and there is a real prospect of reaching an agreement which gives both parties more because their needs do not directly conflict. Thus, in the example given at **13.3.3.4**, in a negotiation about a divorce settlement, having a section in which each side sets out what items they want could be very helpful. Having a section to swap information about the allegations of facts or evidence is unlikely to be helpful. Such exchange of information relates to the strength of the parties' claims to the remedies, or various items, and using it is part of determining concessions. Generally, seeking information as the gaps arise in the discussion is much more likely to be both useful and persuasive. In a straightforward swap of information, out of context of argument, neither party will have an incentive to reveal information which is anything other than 100 per cent supportive of their case. Therefore a swap is likely to make both negotiators more confrontational (ie, adopt a more competitive stance). In the context of argument, seeking the information may be useful as it may be more difficult for the person with the information not to provide it.

However information exchange takes place, most negotiators, even those who are carefully prepared, still have some concern about how much they should reveal in a negotiation (see **10.2.3**). Particularly when dealing with information which is clearly not strengthening the client's case, they find it difficult to gauge how much to reveal and when and how to do it. It is important to achieve the right balance, not being overly cautious nor overly cavalier about what is revealed. Where it is unclear how much information is shared by the parties (eg, where proceedings have not been issued or are still in the early stage of litigation), making these decisions is likely to be even more difficult. Use the fact that your opponent is likely to reveal any weaknesses they are aware of in your case. Thus, when in doubt about what your opponent knows about the weaknesses in your case, before you say anything, ask your opponent what his or her client has said happened. Where he or she provides an explanation, check the evidence to support it.

Try to gauge your opponent's strategy or tactics on information exchange. If he or she is adopting a competitive stance, give information which is clearly not harmful to your case and then ask your opponent for his or her client's view. Make it clear that the negotiation can proceed only if both sides are prepared to exchange information. Check also whether your opponent is using tactics to distort or evade giving information. Listen carefully to responses to your questions, check that your opponent has answered the question as posed and given you the information you asked for. For example, if you have asked for evidence on a particular aspect, your opponent may have repeated the allegation by his client. Ask again. What is the evidence?

Do not forget to use information you have which is persuasive as it reinforces the merits of your client's claim. Where you have information or evidence, eg, a copy of a document that appears to have been sent to the other side, do not assume the other side is aware of its existence. Although in your analysis you may have seen this as shared information, ensure that you raise it in the negotiation. It could be that it is new to your opponent and will require him or her to re-evaluate his or her case.

Your opponent may equally have information about your case which comes as a surprise to you. Particularly in the early stages of a case, but also in cases approaching trial or at trial, information comes from the other side which alters your view of the case. Clients are not always as forthcoming with information as they ought to be, and even those who try to be as helpful as possible forget or fail to realise the significance of a piece of information. The result is that you learn it for the first time from your opponent. We dealt with this to an extent in **Chapter 15** when we looked at responding (see **15.5.2**). Keep a poker face, do not react, and absorb the information. Think laterally how to challenge it and undermine the effect in the same way you did when evaluating the arguments and preparing to respond to your opponent's arguments (see **9.5** and **9.6**). Thus, for example, if it is an allegation, press your opponent for evidence; if it is evidence to support an allegation, consider how the burden of proof impacts on this. If you cannot think of an effective way to challenge it, consider using one of the tactics on information exchange (see **10.4**) to distract your opponent or appear to respond.

16.5.3 Using effective argument

The purpose of the negotiation is to reach a settlement which achieves your client's objectives, eg, payment of money, transfer of property, etc. This should be the focus of what is said. While in a dispute-resolution negotiation the merits of the case are likely to be influential in determining what is a reasonable settlement, the negotiators' role is not to determine the outcome of the case on the merits. The purpose of the discussion of the merits of the case in the negotiation is not to agree on the interpretation of the law or areas of disputed fact. The purpose is to use the merits of the case as one of the tools to gauge a reasonable settlement standard and to justify the proposals. Sometimes it is easy to lose sight of this in the negotiation. Arguing your case is fun! For many barristers it is why they chose to join the Bar. In the heat of a negotiation it is easy to get carried away with this aspect and find that you and your opponent are simply arguing for the sake of it.

In any negotiation you should constantly monitor whether or not exchanging argument with your opponent is serving a useful purpose for the negotiation. Is it getting you anywhere? Are you repeating arguments? Is your opponent repeating him- or herself? If so, why? Generally, there is no need to repeat points already made.

Is the problem that you and your opponent are trying to agree the law or the facts or the evidence? This is not necessary, nor is it advisable. Is the problem that there really is ambiguity and the law or the facts could be interpreted as either you or your opponent see them? If so, this means that it is not clear which party will win on this issue. Thus the chance that either party will win may be 50/50 (depending on whom the burden of proof rests). This should inform your view of the case. If, prior to the negotiation, you had considered your client to have a very strong case, maybe you overestimated it and now have to re-evaluate it and either seek or make proposals for compromise.

Is the problem that your opponent's view of the law or facts is wrong but that he or she is convinced of the merits of his or her client's case and is refusing to make concessions as a result? This is more difficult. You should not concede just because your opponent refuses to budge based on a faulty analysis. It may be that moving to another issue or item will help, stating that, given there appears to be no movement on this particular item or issue, it would be efficient to move to something else where there is more prospect of moving towards settlement. Leave this item or issue on the back burner and come back to it when, perhaps, your opponent has had time to think or later discussions have made him or her more amenable to making compromises on this item.

Is the problem that neither you nor your opponent want to move to making concessions because you are worried about precisely what to offer and/or that you will lose credibility by making the first offer. First, your preparation should have enabled you to plan your opening offer. Rely on that. Secondly, bear in mind that making the first offer may put you in a strong position. Your opening will be as close as can reasonably be argued to what your client wants. This will focus the discussion around what your client wants. This is a form of anchoring (see **14.2.4.3**). Where the discussion starts may influence the content of it, which in turn may influence the point at which settlement is reached.

16.5.4 Concession-seeking and making

Many negotiators find this aspect of negotiating the most difficult, and rightly so, because it is the area which can do the most amount of damage if done badly. In **Chapter 11** we considered the psychological influences on negotiators in respect of concessions (**11.2**) and a number of tactics used in making and seeking concessions, many of which are based on these influences (**11.3.3.1**). The fear of conceding too much (ie, that the opponent would have accepted less), and that making concessions will be seen as a sign of weakness, can impact on how you perform in this aspect of negotiating. Being naturally competitive can also impact on your behaviour. The desire to win, to feel victory over your opponent, can outweigh rational thought and affect how you respond to suggestions of compromise. Feeling uncomfortable with conflict and confrontation (ie, being naturally accommodating or compromising) may mean that you seek to reduce it by agreeing with what your opponent says. This could result in conceding too much. In these situations your behaviour in the concession-seeking and making may be overly influenced by your emotions. As a result you may refuse to make concessions or make concessions too quickly and unnecessarily.

Expectations and preconceptions may also interfere. If the opponent opens with a competitive statement about the case, or an extreme opening demand (see tactics at **11.3.5.2**), you are likely to expect that he or she will follow a competitive stance throughout and seek a much higher sum than he or she may intend. Your response may be to react to this emotionally, forget your analysis and take a competitive stance yourself, refusing to make any of the concessions you planned, even small ones. Alternatively, you may find the competitive opening so worrying that you make more compromises than your planning indicated were appropriate. Your expectation of the pattern of behaviour in concessions may also influence what you do. A noticeable pattern of behaviour in negotiations is that concessions are usually larger at the start and decrease in both size and frequency over time, and as negotiators get closer to their bottom line. This pattern sets up expectations—the negotiators reading the behaviour pattern assume a level of closeness to the bottom line. Your opponent may use this as a tactic (see **11.3.5.12**) and you may react accordingly.

Many of the tactics used in concessions depend on the opponent responding emotionally or on the basis of expectations rather than on rational thought. Where both sides are responding emotionally rather than rationally, or reacting on the basis of expectations or preconceptions, the result may be deadlock or reaching an agreement very quickly that does not reflect what either party wants or the merits of the case.

Planning your concessions carefully will enable you to approach this aspect in a rational way. Remembering that you are not negotiating to determine the outcome of the case, whose version of the facts is believed or whether the claimant or defendant wins should take some of the heat out of the situation. In respect of the legitimate areas for compromise, knowing where you will open, being conscious of the least you should expect and how to stage concessions will give you a sound rational basis for making and seeking offers. However, putting your plans into practice also requires that you understand your own expectations and fears and anxieties about concessions to ensure that you are not, either consciously or unconsciously, reacting in response to these rather than on a rational basis to the actual content of your opponent's proposals.

Set out below are a few things to bear in mind in the negotiation to assist you to undertake this aspect on a rational basis, first, when you are making proposals and, secondly, when you are responding to your opponent's proposals.

16.5.4.1 When making concessions

It will be a very rare negotiation indeed where you reach settlement without having to make any concessions/proposals yourself. The following list sets out things to bear in mind when making concessions yourself.

Get the whole list

Before you start to make offers, know what the potential settlement will have to cover. Even if you have an idea from the papers what the other side are likely to want, check it out (see **11.6**).

Get information first/test the case

Your preparation should have made you aware of the gaps in the information you have. In some cases, it may be essential to fill these gaps before contemplating making a concession (eg, has the other side sold the goods for which they are claiming loss of profit from your client because he or she rejected them). In most cases it is helpful to assist you to gauge whether or not your assessment of your opening offer is the best you could achieve. By getting your opponent's view of the merits of the case, you may find that he or she has not seen some of the strengths in his or her case that you have seen. Similarly, by getting your opponent to state what his or her client wants, you may find that he or she has lower expectations than you thought. In addition to getting the information, where appropriate, test the case before making any concessions. If your opponent sets out what his or her client wants, ask him or her to justify it. If your opponent says his or her client has a very strong case, the justification being based on allegations of fact by his or her client, ask for the evidence. Once you have the relevant information and a feel for whether you can press your opponent further, you can then move to making concessions.

Give persuasive reasons for your proposals

As we saw in concession planning, any proposal you make is likely to include both a concession by your client and the other side (an offer to pay 50 per cent of a claim means you are asking the other side to forgo 50 per cent). When making a proposal for settlement, justify it. Give your opponent a good reason to agree to your proposal (ie, a way he or she can justify to his or her client why the proposal is reasonable). Link your proposal to your justification. Use 'because'. 'Payment of 80 per cent of the sum sought would be justified because. . .'

Your concession planning should help you here (see **11.7** and **11.8**). Your evaluation of the case gives you reasons to justify what you are accepting to your client (this is all that is achievable). Your preparation should also have included formulating arguments to persuade your opponent that what you offer is the best he or she can achieve for his or her client. Although these two are based on the same issues and facts, they are not quite the reverse side of the same coin. Your evaluation of the case will be a realistic view of what is likely on the facts and the law. The arguments you use with your opponent will be putting the best possible gloss on both the facts and the law, presenting your case at its highest.

Phrase your proposals persuasively

Always make sure that the wording of a concession or offer is clear and sufficiently detailed to avoid any misunderstanding. Also, consider putting your reason first, followed by the proposal. By putting the reason first, your opponent is more likely to hear it than if it is put after the proposal (see tactics at **14.2.5.2**). It also gives you a chance to hear your argument/reasoning spoken aloud. Given what has happened in the negotiation, it may sound more persuasive than you originally thought or you may feel that it will be more persuasive with this particular opponent and result in an adjustment of the proposal. Consider also whether you want to 'make a demand' or 'put a proposal' as the phrasing could have an impact on your opponent (see **14.2.5.1**).

Do not offer ranges

When making proposals, it is best not to give a range of offers (eg, 'if we were to pay between £1,000 and £2,000. . .'). Your opponent is likely to accept the most favourable to him or her and you will have difficulty retreating from it.

Make offers conditional

You can rarely retreat from a concession once made. Do not get locked into making a concession before you know what you are getting in exchange. Make conditional offers, eg, 'If my client were prepared to. . . would yours?'.

Do not agree to separate parts

A good settlement is one which meets as many of the client's objectives as possible. You should keep all the items on the table until you see the overall package. Make any agreement on an individual item 'subject to a satisfactory overall package'. While you may discuss individual items in turn and trade off on different items, only agree unconditionally once all of the items have been provisionally agreed.

Stage concessions

Your planning should put you in a good position to do this (see **11.8**). You may have to reassess how you stage the concessions, but resist the temptation to move straight from your opening to your bottom line in the heat of the negotiation.

Seek trade-offs

Again, your planning should have prepared you to seek trade-offs (see **11.9.2**). Depending on your client's priorities, you could make an offer on something of low priority to your client in exchange for getting something of high priority (albeit not making your client's priorities known to the opponent). Your offer should explicitly be made provisional on your opponent also making a concession. When doing so, make the provision on your offer clear.

Consider the timing of offers

If you genuinely have only one offer to make (very rare indeed!), then do not make it too early and use it to secure the best advantage for your client. Also avoid making consecutive concessions. There is no rule that you have to respond to a concession with a concession. You could also refer back to concessions made earlier as a reason not to move further. Thus, for example, if you have given a substantial amount on the terms of a future agreement, you could remind your opponent of this when he or she is seeking concessions on past losses.

Think carefully before you just 'split the difference'

This may be fair and could be a good tactic (see **11.3.5.7**). However, your offers should be based on sound analysis of what your client wants and what is achievable. Splitting the difference may achieve neither of these.

Making the first offer can be a strength

As explained above, there are some advantages to making the first offer. It can focus the negotiation nearer to your end of the settlement range. The opponent's reaction may also provide information about his or her position. The disadvantage is that it gives your opponent some information about your range.

Avoid using 'final offer' threats

Avoid using phrases such as 'this is my final offer/the lowest we are prepared to go' unless it really is. If you then retreat further, your credibility will be greatly reduced and you may find your opponent pressing you even when you have genuinely reached your bottom line. Quite reasonably, your opponent does not believe you.

16.5.4.2 Responding to proposals/offers/demands from your opponent

You need to think carefully when responding to proposals by your opponent, however they are phrased. The following is a list of matters to consider when deciding how to respond.

Take time/check it out

Take sufficient time to respond to an offer or concession made to you. If the opening offer made by your opponent is very good, ie, the most you expected to get or more, it is generally right to accept it. However, you may wish to pause briefly to consider whether or not you could get a little more. If an offer seems very generous, consider why. It may be that your opponent is aware of a weakness in his or her case that is not immediately clear to you. If you do not understand what your opponent is offering, then pause to consider it. If necessary, ask your opponent to clarify it. Consider whether you would like the offer modified in any way before you accept it. The pause is likely to be extremely brief: a second or two. The point is not just to jump in and accept an offer without thinking about it at all.

Test your opponent/make him or her justify the proposal

Most offers from your opponent will be nowhere near the most you expected to get. Make your opponent justify the reasonableness of the offer. Ask him or her why you should agree to the offer. Test your opponent and the case. Are there genuine reasons why this offer is a good one for your client? Is your opponent able to persuade you? How strongly is he or she going to resist a counter-proposal from you suggesting something better for your client?

Be wary of suggestions to split the difference

For the same reasons that you should not offer merely to 'split the difference', be wary of a suggestion by your opponent to do this. If you have the better case, your client should get more than half. Also beware of an offer which simply trades off claims by each side which on the face of it are of equal value. Your client's claim may be much more soundly based than your opponent's.

Do not interrupt your opponent

When your opponent is making an offer, do not interrupt. You may be tempted because what is being said sounds initially as though you could counter it. Don't! The offer may be better than it sounds initially. You may get information about what the other side wants, which assists you in your assessment of how to proceed.

Be aware of tactics

Remember that your opponent may use any of the tactics set out at **11.3.5**. Precondition demands, an extreme opening demand, false demands and escalating demands are all signs of a competitive negotiator. Remember why they are used. Be conscious that you may respond in kind. Separate the strategy from the content of what is being offered. Respond as though you are treating the demands as genuine proposals. Ask your opponent to explain why your client should accept the proposal.

Some tactics are used to obscure the amount your opponent is offering by way of compromise (see **11.3.5.9**). If your opponent points out the number of concessions made, check it out. Are they real concessions? Is he or she in fact using one of the tactics set out at **11.3.5.9**—slicing/salami/nibbling—to make it appear that he or she is offering more than is actually the case? Although there is some cross-over with staging concessions, the two tactics are not identical. Staging offers is a genuine attempt to move slowly towards a reasonable middle ground. These tactics try to make what is offered seem more than it is.

Your opponent leaves out an item

It can be very difficult to know how to deal with the fact that your opponent has clearly forgotten to include an item which, according to your instructions, his or her client wants. Do you remind your opponent or keep quiet? You have no duty to ensure that your opponent gets all that his or her client wants. On the other hand, if the failure to agree on this item is likely to mean that the other side will not agree to the settlement, it is pointless letting your opponent walk away without reminding him or her about it. You will have to judge where along this spectrum the item lies.

16.5.5 Making progress

Making progress means moving through the matters to be discussed with reasonable efficiency. This may be achieved in several ways.

16.5.5.1 Focus on the main items

The discussion should be well focused, and you should be spending time on the matters which need it and not on those which do not. While it is worth spending a reasonable amount of time on the issues or items which are central to reaching settlement (ie, items of genuine importance to the client or of large financial value), you should not spend too long on aspects which are peripheral to settlement (ie, items of small value either in money terms or to the client), especially if you are negotiating within a limited time.

16.5.5.2 One thing at a time

Most negotiations involve several underlying issues on the merits of the case and a number of items that the parties want from the settlement. Ensure that the discussion is well-focused and that you are moving forward in seeking a compromise, both overall and on the individual items. Deciding a structure for the negotiation and making this explicit can help. However, just setting out a structure at the start is not enough. During the negotiation you should monitor whether or not the structure is working and whether you really are making progress. Moving from one item to another can be a way of getting 'unstuck' if you cannot reach compromise on a particular item. However, jumping around too much can be inefficient and confusing.

A common reason for inefficiency in negotiating is that the negotiators deal with items partially and then move on to another item. As soon as they reach a slight impasse on seeking compromise, they move to another item. This means that the negotiation jumps around from item to item and little is resolved, even provisionally. The result is that arguments and proposals are repeated and both negotiators become confused about what has been discussed and agreed and what has not. To be efficient, a more methodical approach is required. The negotiation should move forward to settlement with as little repetition as possible. You should also be getting a clearer idea of what an overall settlement will look like.

It is helpful to discuss each item separately in an attempt to reach provisional agreement on it before you move to the next item. This means working through the arguments on both sides to gauge possible settlement standards, linking arguments to suggestions for compromise and going as far as you are able to reach agreement on a particular item. Where agreement is reached, ensure that, at least on your part, it is provisional on the overall settlement being satisfactory to you. If you cannot reach agreement on an item, even provisionally, note the disparity (eg, 'we have reached a point where I am suggesting your client pays 50 per cent of my client's losses and you are suggesting he pays 30 per cent'). You can then move on to other items and return to this item later. Do not forget to return to the item (it is surprising how many people do, forgetting that agreement has not been reached)!

Trading concessions on items may involve discussion of more than one item at a time. It may be that you cannot deal with each item independently as some are interlinked, eg, how much your client will pay for future deliveries is dependent on when and how they are delivered and on guarantees about quality. Discussion of these items together could be useful. However, you still need to confine the discussion to matters that could be agreed together. Lumping in discussion about payment on past losses may just obscure and confuse. Consider which items could usefully be discussed together and then, in the same way as you would if it were one item, work through the arguments, suggestions for compromise, etc, and move as far as you are able towards agreement on these interlinked items before moving on to other ones.

16.5.5.3 Using a formula

Sometimes you cannot reach a final agreement because you need further information or instructions from your client. Again, try to get as close as you can to an agreement. Using a formula may help. For example, there may be a dispute over ownership of an item but neither party knows its value. You could still agree who will keep the item and who will pay money. You could also agree how the amount of money will be calculated, eg, it will be a quarter of the value as determined by an independent expert. The formula then needs to include detail to make it workable, eg, how is the valuer found, who pays, etc.

16.5.5.4 Is there really agreement?

Where you are making progress, it is important to be clear about both whether there is agreement and what precisely has been agreed. All too often there are misunderstandings about this. One lawyer may assume that a particular issue has been finally resolved, whereas the other may think that the agreement is only provisional and will lapse if other issues are not resolved too. A whole negotiation can collapse as a result of misunderstandings about what has been agreed. Make sure that you are always clear about what has been agreed and whether it is final, and that you make an unambiguous note of it immediately.

16.5.5.5 Getting bogged down

Even with the best preparation, you may get bogged down at some point. Every negotiation is likely to have parts which go well, where you and your opponent make progress, and parts which go less well, where you do not seem to be able to progress. When this happens, recapping can help to get the negotiation moving again. Summarise the progress to date and what still needs to be achieved. Recap:

- the items which need to be settled;
- the items on which you have reached provisional agreement;
- the items on which you cannot agree and the difference between you;
- the items which have yet to be discussed.

This will give you and your opponent an overview of where you are and what you have provisionally agreed and should help you to decide how to proceed. You may want to move to another item. Or it may become clearer how you can proceed on the item under discussion in light of where things stand.

Where you really are stuck, either because of your opponent's behaviour or because you have reached deadlock, then use the tactics set out in **Chapter 17** (dealing with difficulties).

16.5.6 Concluding the process

Finalising a negotiated agreement and enforcing it are dealt with in **Chapter 18**. This section simply deals with bringing the negotiating process to an end, though inevitably the two are closely linked.

16.5.6.1 Check before you agree

When you have been through all the items and appear to have reached provisional agreement on them, before you agree to the overall settlement (which you should in any event make subject to your client's instructions) ensure that this is a good settlement for your client. It is quite possible in the heat of the moment to agree to something which will not work. Ensure you take a little time for reflection before you finally agree. Check what has been provisionally agreed. Once the agreement is finalised, even where it is subject to your client's approval, it will be difficult to retreat from what is agreed if you have made a mistake. Both your client and your opponent will, quite rightly, feel they have been misled. You need to check that:

(a) The agreement covers all items, including matters such as costs, what will happen to the case, etc. Do not assume agreement on anything. If in doubt, check it out.

(b) The agreement is within your instructions, meets your client's objectives as closely as possible, and is likely to be acceptable to your client. This includes consideration:

(i) of the overall outcome—eg, where the agreement includes both parties paying some of the other party's damages, where does the balance of payment lie? Who will pay and how much will he or she pay?

(ii) of the overall impact of the agreement—even if your client is getting a good deal on some individual items, is the overall agreement in line with his or her priorities?

(iii) whether the settlement is within the limits set by your client—no item that the client insists on having has not been included and no money limit has been breached.

(iv) whether the agreement is practical and realistic—can your client do what the agreement requires, eg, pay a specific amount of money by a particular date or keep the noise to a particular level?

(c) All the terms are clear and agreed in sufficient detail. This means that you are certain that you and your opponent have the same understanding of what was agreed, both generally and on the detail. It is surprising how many times negotiators think they have agreed when they have not. Gaps are frequently left in the agreement. It is agreed that one party will pay the other a sum of money, but not when or how. Equally the negotiators may not have agreed on an item. For example, having agreed the hours for work to be included in an undertaking, one negotiator thinks those hours include the weekend and the other thinks they include only weekdays. It is essential that you check that you really are in agreement with your opponent as to precisely what will be put to the parties as the settlement reached. The best way of ensuring this is to write down what has been agreed, either jointly or by one person reading out what has been written, to check it is the same as the other person's understanding of what has been agreed.

16.5.6.2 Recording what has been agreed

Writing down what has been agreed is not only the best way to ensure both negotiators are walking away with the same agreement, but it also ensures that you have an accurate record on which to base what you tell the judge in court and that your solicitor also has an accurate record on which to write up the agreement. In addition to ensuring that the agreement is accurately and fully recorded, you need to decide what form this should take. There is a variety of options:

(a) Simply endorsing the agreement on your brief. This will be appropriate where the agreement is straightforward and will be presented by you or your opponent in court either as a simple agreement or the wording of a simple order.

(b) Writing out the agreement in detail on a separate sheet of paper. Where the agreement is not straightforward, you should write it on a separate sheet of paper. If you are seeking an order from the court, you should have a copy to give to the judge. If the agreement is one which does not need to be endorsed by the court, it is likely that the solicitors will confirm it by an exchange of letters. They will need to know precisely what has been agreed. Even if they were present in court, it is your duty to ensure they are clear about what has been agreed. Giving them a written copy of this is the only way to be sure that this has been done.

(c) Sometimes, agreements need to be more formally recorded than by exchange of letter. It will be the solicitor's task to make sure this is done. However, you should be aware of when such formality is needed and include this in your explanation to the solicitor about what has been agreed.

This aspect is discussed more fully in **Chapter 18**.

16.5.6.3 Agreement on some but not all items

Where you cannot reach an overall agreement but have reached agreement on some items, whether provisional or not, you need to ensure that you are clear precisely where the agreement stands and that you explain this to your client and solicitor. This includes covering:

(a) Which items have been agreed and the basis of the agreement. Is it final or provisional? On what basis is it provisional? Are there any aspects on which agreement has not been reached? For example, the amount to be paid has been agreed but not when or how.

(b) What items have not been agreed and why. Was any movement made on this item? What was the disparity between you and your opponent on this item (eg, on hours of opening of the business, you had suggested 8.00 am to 5.30 pm and your opponent was seeking 8.00 am to 6.30 pm).

(c) What, if any, practical difficulties were identified in the negotiation of the items not agreed (eg, does the opponent not have the money to pay now). Have you made an assessment of where the real difficulties lie in reaching agreement on these?

(d) Has any agreement been reached on the case itself? Will it proceed or is there agreement to stay it pending further negotiation?

16.5.6.4 Where no agreement is reached

Even if you have not reached agreement on any items, the negotiation is likely to have been useful in some respects. It is likely that you have a clearer idea on a number of matters which you may wish to check with your opponent if appropriate, but which should certainly be recorded (for future use) and passed on to your solicitor. For example, you are likely to have:

(a) further information about what the other side wants from the settlement. This may assist you to re-evaluate your concession planning and compromises that could be suggested in any future negotiation;

(b) better information about the case, where the strengths and weaknesses lie on both sides and how your opponent plans to run the case. You can re-evaluate your case in light of this and adjust both your plans for future negotiations and how to present the case in court.

16.6 Summary

This chapter has highlighted those aspects of conducting a negotiation which you may find difficult, despite careful planning. It deals only with those matters likely to arise in the normal course of events. **Chapter 17** covers in detail how to deal with specific difficulties which you may encounter.

17

Dealing with difficulties

17.1 An overview

Some opponents are more difficult to deal with than others, eg, a particularly aggressive and entrenched one or a weak and ill-prepared one. It can be less satisfying to deal with a particularly difficult opponent, but the test for the negotiation is whether the lawyer has done the best for his or her client under the circumstances. The remainder of this chapter covers difficulties you may encounter in negotiating and gives suggestions for how to do the best for your client given the particular circumstances.

The first section sets out a summary of a strategy ('Getting Past No'), devised by one of the creators of the concept of 'principled negotiation', which sets out a number of techniques which could be used in dealing with difficult opponents. The next section covers how to deal with an opponent who adopts a competitive strategy. We then set out how to deal with what is potentially the most difficult type of opponent: the weak, unprepared, overly cooperative opponent who fails to understand his or her role of acting for and seeking to satisfy his or her client's objectives. We then set out suggestions for dealing with a negotiation which has reached deadlock, not necessarily just because one of the negotiators is taking a competitive stance. Finally, we deal with difficulties which may arise where emotions get the better of you.

17.2 Techniques for getting past no

The various techniques for dealing with awkward negotiators identified in the book, *Getting to Yes*, such as separating the people from the problem, focusing on interests not positions, inventing options for mutual gain, and insisting on objective criteria and developing a Best Alternative to a Negotiated Agreement (BATNA), used by principled negotiators (see **4.5.3**), have been expanded in a further book, *Getting Past No: Negotiating Your Way From Confrontation to Cooperation*, by William Ury (1991), again a relatively short paperback. Although many of the ideas and techniques have been discussed or referred to in earlier chapters, it is useful to set them out here in their entirety.

The strategy suggested is based on breaking through the five barriers to cooperation (ie, getting past no) which Ury has identified.

(a) Your reactions: we all react to what other people say and do.

(b) Their emotions: the other side may have negative emotions which influence what they say and do. They may be angry, nervous or defensive.

(c) Their habits: they may know only how to negotiate positionally.

(d) Their doubts about the agreement: they may have difficulty seeing how an agreement which satisfies your client actually benefits theirs.

(e) Their perception of the negotiation as a power game.

The five steps in the strategy are set out below.

17.2.1 Do not react

Give yourself space to evaluate the position and distance yourself from any impulsive or emotional response. Ury suggests using a psychological trick to create a mental image which gives you this space: 'go to the balcony'. This enables you to:

(a) recognise the tactic;

(b) recognise how you feel and 'know your hot buttons', ie, those things to which you have strong reactions, eg, criticism or rejection;

(c) buy time to think by:

  (i) pausing and saying nothing. Do not be afraid of silence and do not be pushed into responding by rantings from the other side. Think what good it is doing to let off steam! Clearly this will buy limited time;

  (ii) rewinding the tape. When you can pause no longer, slow the process down by reviewing what has been said. This may help to clarify it;

  (iii) taking time out. If you need more time, take a short break if possible. If you cannot do this by physically leaving the negotiation space, do it by changing the topic;

  (iv) not making important decisions on the spot. Where a matter is sprung on you and there is no need for an immediate response, do not respond. Where an immediate response is needed, give yourself the time you need to consider it. Check deadlines imposed to see if they are real;

  (v) remain focused on your objectives. 'Don't get mad, don't get even. . . get what you want!' That is why you are negotiating.

17.2.2 Defuse the other side's emotions

Create a favourable climate for the negotiation. Disarm the other side by being conciliatory, acknowledging and by trying to understand their feelings. The psychological trick suggested by Ury is that you 'step to their side', which means:

(a) listening actively by:

  (i) giving the other side a hearing. Remain focused, do not interrupt and encourage them to explain;

  (ii) paraphrasing and asking for corrections. Sum up your understanding of what they have said and check whether you have got it right;

(b) acknowledging your opponent's point. This does not mean you agree with it. It merely means that you understand how he or she sees things. It may also be appropriate in some circumstances to acknowledge your opponent's feelings or offer an apology. This can be seen as exhibiting strength if done with confidence;

(c) agreeing whatever you can. No need to concede; simply focus on the issues on which you do agree, the common ground. Look for ways of saying 'yes' rather than 'no'. Tune in to your opponent's wavelength; watch the non-verbal cues and the manner of speech;

(d) acknowledging the other person. Treat him or her with respect. Acknowledge authority and competence. Try to build a working relationship. By doing this, you may change his or her perception of you and become more of an ally than an adversary;

(e) expressing your views without provoking. Use language which reconciles rather than accentuates differences, eg, 'yes and', rather than 'yes but' (see **14.2.5.3**). Acknowledge differences and be optimistic about resolving them.

17.2.3 Do not reject: reframe/change the game

Some people know only how to negotiate using positional behaviour, seeing the negotiation as a ritual dance in which both parties state their positions repeatedly with a view to making the other side change their position. Alter this perception by probing their position and asking for more information to enable you genuinely to understand what it is that they want. Use the psychological technique of 'reframing' to turn their position into an attempt to reach a solution by:

(a) asking problem-solving questions, ie, ones which require more than a 'yes' or 'no' answer, which seek reasons, information, etc. Why? Why not? What if?;

(b) asking for advice. How would you explain this offer to my client?;

(c) using silence. Do not automatically fill the silence if your opponent is having trouble answering a question. Give him or her time to think, possibly to feel uncomfortable and to come up with a proposal;

(d) ignoring or reframing positional statements and attacks;

(e) negotiating the rules of the game: where tacit tactics do not work to change the behaviour, deal with it explicitly. Label the behaviour without attacking the person.

17.2.4 Do not push: draw the other side towards you

A negotiator may reject a proposal because it is not his or her idea, it does not satisfy all his or her needs, because of a fear of losing face or because it has come too quickly. Pushing your opponent to agree may simply increase resistance. Ury's suggestion is to 'build a golden bridge' by:

(a) involving your opponent in the proposal. Do not 'tell' him or her the solution. Ask for ideas and build on them. Ask for criticism. Offer choices. Make the proposals joint proposals;

(b) satisfying unmet interests. Ensure all interests have been explored. Try to see the rationale behind them. Do not overlook basic human needs. Try to expand the pie;

(c) helping your opponent to save face. Find reasons which justify accepting the proposal.

17.2.5 Educate: bring the other side to their senses, not their knees

Some negotiators may resist all the above tactics and continue to play a positional power game. Resist the temptation to respond. Show your opponent that *this* negotiation is

not win/lose but win/win, and that the only way he or she can win is for you both to win by:

(a) letting him or her know the consequences of the behaviour. Ask reality-testing questions, such as 'What will you do if we don't agree?'. Explain in an objective way what you will do (ie, warn, do not threaten). Demonstrate your BATNA and use it if necessary.

(b) giving him or her space to decide, to choose whether to settle or lose.

17.3 How to deal with competitive negotiators

17.3.1 Generally

Many of the techniques of 'Getting Past No' can be used with competitive negotiators. However, this section focuses on assisting you to understand the main risks involved when you come up against a competitive negotiator and to understand and use the mentality of a competitive negotiator to deal appropriately with the strategy.

Competitive negotiators' strategy is based on appearing to be inflexible in order to manipulate the opponent into moving. However, in fact they are prepared to make some concessions and to give limited information. Be aware of the strategy, refuse to be manipulated, be proactive and not reactive, do not get emotional and take a firm but conciliatory stance. Try to see why they are acting like this—do they have a naturally aggressive personality? Are they in a position of power? Are they simply unprepared and bluffing? Are they responding to you—ie, are you using a competitive strategy?

First, check whether it is the negotiator's style which is aggressive, eg, using an argumentative tone of voice, speaking over you, etc, and making you feel uncomfortable. If so, is this in response to your style? Are you speaking over your opponent, in an aggressive tone; have you adopted an aggressive body stance? If so, adjust your behaviour and tone of voice and adopt a conciliatory stance. If you do not feel that your opponent is reacting to your behaviour, but for some other reason has adopted a competitive style, listen to the content of what is being said. It may be that the style is masking the content and that the opponent is actually making offers. If so, deal with the content and ignore the style. Do not get emotional; take a firm conciliatory stance. If the style is exceptionally aggressive and genuinely interfering with the discussion, eg, your opponent is talking over you and not letting you speak, then label the behaviour and explain how it is interfering with the negotiation.

Secondly, focus on the objective merits of the arguments used. If your opponent repeats his client's demands, ask him or her to justify the demand, eg, to explain how the merits of the case justify your client giving his or her client what is sought. Thus, for example, if the opponent repeats that his or her client will accept nothing less than 50 per cent of the damages claimed, ask him or her to explain how the merits of the case justify this (eg, does his or her client really have a 50 per cent chance of winning). Alternatively, explain your reasons why you consider that his or her proposal is not objectively justified and link this to an alternative proposal setting out your reasoning to show that it is objectively justified. For example, explain that, as the burden of proof is on your opponent and the evidence for that party is weak, your opponent stands a less than 50 per cent chance of success, so, although you are not prepared to accede to payment of 50 per cent of the claim, you will offer to pay 20 per cent.

Thirdly, try moving to another item. If you do this, you should ensure that you have noted with your opponent the range of proposals on this particular item so that, when you return to the item, you do not need to start again from the beginning.

Finally, remember that you can always say no. If you are getting nowhere at all, you can always walk away. This is a measure of last resort (see tactics at **14.2.9**) and not to be used lightly.

17.3.2 Not 'mirroring' competitive behaviour

In **Chapter 15** we dealt with the phenomenon of 'mirroring behaviour' (**15.2.2**) which is fairly common in negotiations. In particular, it is common with competitive behaviour (both of style and substance). Therefore, when dealing with an opponent who is competitive, one of the risks you run is that, if your opponent makes positional statements and acts in an adversarial way, you will respond with similar behaviour with the result that the negotiation ends up in a cycle of positional statements by both sides.

It is one thing to say you will resist this temptation, and quite another to do it. In the heat of the moment, with the stress of the negotiation, you may succumb, particularly if you are naturally competitive (which many who choose to be barristers are). The main technique suggested, again by the authors of the principled negotiation strategy, to avoid this is to break any such cycle by refusing to react in an adversarial way and by not using similar behaviour. They label this technique 'negotiation jujitsu' because it adopts the same basic strategy of stepping aside and using your opponent's strength to your ends.

If the other side:

(a) set out their position strongly: do not be drawn into argument; do not reject or accept it; treat it as a genuine attempt to solve the problem; look behind what is said to see which principles it reflects and what interests it might satisfy. Ask them to explain how it solves the problem;

(b) attacks your suggestions: do not get defensive; invite criticism and suggestions;

(c) attacks you: allow them to let off steam; do not react; reframe it into an attack on the problem.

On the basis that replying to a statement with a statement is more likely to escalate the confrontational stance, to produce resistance, the authors recommend the use of:

- questions which produce answers, instead of statements which produce resistance; and
- silence, which may also produce answers as many people feel uncomfortable with it and may, to fill the void, continue by giving explanations.

17.4 Dealing with the weak/ill-prepared opponent

Without doubt the most difficult type of opponent to deal with is the one who fails completely, or almost completely, to negotiate for his or her clients. He or she gives you everything, or almost everything, you ask for. He or she accepts virtually everything you say about the case and has few, if any, arguments to support his or her client, either on the merits of the case or on what is or is not practical.

The difficulty is that, while it is not your job to make up for the weaknesses of another lawyer, there is no point in reaching a settlement which your opponent's client will not accept. The tension that this creates arises from the conflict between doing the best for your client while recognising that the other side must agree to it and this means some compromise on the part of your client. How do you deal with the fact that your opponent is not basically seeking any compromise or the compromises being sought are clearly insufficient to satisfy his or her client?

Just making further concessions, ie, to the point where you think the opponent's client will accept the settlement, is not the answer. Although you may have some idea of what the other client wants from the negotiation from your papers, you have no real insight into the detail of why he or she wants what is stated in your papers or where he or she may settle on the various items. You need to make your opponent think! Ask him or her to explain why his or her client is likely to accept the offer as stated. Will the client have difficulties with what has been offered? What are those difficulties? Doing this may enlighten you as to what might be acceptable as well as make your opponent consider realistically what his or her client will accept.

How far you go down this route is a matter of judgement. You cannot negotiate against yourself. You cannot do the job for your opponent. If it is clear that you are going to get nowhere, it may be best to quit while you are ahead. If your questions do result in kick-starting your opponent into thinking and making realistic suggestions, then get the best workable settlement you can.

17.5 Dealing with failure to move/deadlock

It is not uncommon for a negotiation to 'get stuck' at some point during the process. Given the tension for both negotiators between doing the best for the client and making compromises to reach settlement, it could happen even if you have made every possible effort to pursue an effective structure. In **Chapter 13**, which dealt with the conduct of negotiations generally, we covered some of the situations which could prove 'sticky' in a negotiation, explaining how you might get stuck and ways of moving forward. Here, we deal with the more specific problem of reaching a dead-end or deadlock. Most of the techniques suggested have already been discussed in earlier chapters; this section pulls together the techniques which could be used in such a situation.

17.5.1 How it can happen

The negotiation may appear to reach a dead-end, having run through all the arguments for both sides, with neither negotiator making any further suggestions for compromise. The negotiation is stuck! Repeating the arguments for either side is not getting you anywhere. You have reached deadlock!

Deadlock occurs where the two sides are, or appear to be, unable to agree. It can arise from a variety of circumstances. Some tactics, eg, 'the final offer' or 'walkout', can produce it. Some negotiators can produce it by simply being intransigent, unreasonable or unrealistic. Alternatively, the negotiation may just be going round in circles with no progress being made or may have come to a complete halt because both parties have run out of ideas. In any of these cases, it may be that there is no option but to break off the negotiation. However, you should at least try to break the deadlock or get the negotiation moving again. The following are suggestions for trying to get constructive discussion going again. Different circumstances will lend themselves to different methods.

17.5.2 Ways of dealing with it

17.5.2.1 Review progress

One way to solve the problem is to review what has been discussed. Go over the progress made so far. Redefine the issues. Check whether all the issues and possibilities have been fully explored. Write a list of interests and issues. Writing them down may clarify where both parties stand and show that the differences are not as great as had been originally thought. You may find that exploration of one issue provides a possible way forward.

17.5.2.2 Discuss reasons for breakdown

Discuss why the deadlock or breakdown has happened. See if emotions have interfered in the negotiation. Try to empathise; see the difficulties in reaching agreement as a joint problem. If appropriate, acknowledge your feelings explicitly and attempt to get the opponent to do the same.

17.5.2.3 Disadvantages of breakdown

Focus discussion on the disadvantages of breakdown. Look at the impact of failure on both sides. Just articulating the negative results of failing to reach settlement may produce the incentive to continue negotiating with more purpose.

17.5.2.4 Advantages of agreement

Focus discussion on the advantages of settlement for both sides. Articulating the benefits of an agreement for the future and the difficulties which might be avoided may produce the incentive to continue negotiating. If appropriate, raise past positive relationships either between clients or negotiators. Create a positive mood.

17.5.2.5 Look for common ground

Restate the common concerns of the clients. Revisit the shared and compatible interests and try to build on them. Seek agreement on one issue and move on from that.

17.5.2.6 Give to get

Think of any information which you could disclose which may assist in movement. Make a planned conditional concession. Give something to get something, to get the negotiation moving again. However, do not offer a concession which is not justified or does not benefit your client simply to break the deadlock.

17.5.2.7 Move to the hypothetical

Ask a hypothetical question to get both parties thinking of alternatives, 'What if. . .?'. Explore hypothetical concessions which both parties could make, eg, 'if my client were prepared to do X, would your client be prepared to do Y?'. In adopting this strategy, you must be clear that the suggestion is hypothetical and consider new concessions to be made by both parties as, once you suggest a concession on behalf of your client, even hypothetically, the opponent will register that it has been made and use it.

17.5.2.8 Take a break

Suggest a break. Where appropriate, this could mean suggesting a further meeting at a later date. Where this is not possible, eg, at the court door, even a short break can be sufficient to change the atmosphere. Do not be afraid of simply being quiet for a moment or two while you review the situation.

17.5.2.9 Recognise that settlement may not be possible

If you have fully explored the options for settlement, the reasons for the proposals and why the proposals are not acceptable, then it may be that you cannot reach a settlement that is justifiable and acceptable to your client. You may have no alternative but to stop negotiating. You should be slow to do this and it is relatively rare to reach deadlock of this kind (unless you are negotiating with a truly entrenched opponent). If it appears that settlement cannot be reached, stating this as explicitly and as neutrally as possible to your opponent, and setting out the reasons why you feel this is the case, may assist. It may be that your opponent does not realise the full impact of what is happening and, being alerted to the risk of failure to settle, may see a way forward. Even if this does not happen, you and your opponent can review where you have reached by way of suggestions for compromise and lay the foundation for future negotiation. You may have narrowed the gap between the parties in what may be acceptable and the future negotiation can move from here. It may also be possible to agree future conduct of the court case in light of the discussions in the negotiation (eg, the issues may have been narrowed, which may mean rethinking the evidence required).

17.6 Emotions interfering

17.6.1 The role of emotion

We have seen how what happens in a negotiation could be affected by psychological influences, unconscious behaviour patterns and emotions. The more intense the circumstances of the negotiation, the more likely the negotiators will feel stress, even if they are not conscious of it. In addition to being aware of the impact of this on the negotiation, you should be aware of the impact on you and when you are at risk of your emotions seriously interfering with your conduct of the negotiation.

17.6.2 Personality clash

Sometimes, without intending confrontation, you simply do not get on with the negotiator for the other side. Personality and emotions may influence this. Try some of the tactics from principled negotiations to reduce the impact, eg, separating the people from the problem. See **17.2** above.

17.6.3 Feeling cross/irritated

In theory, if you are negotiating in a professional way, emotions should not surface. In practice, you will occasionally find that an opponent brings you close to losing your temper, for example because your opponent refuses to shift position on an issue even though you feel that your arguments are overwhelming. Sometimes an opponent may try to make you lose your temper as a tactic, to undermine your presentation of your case. The more frequent problem is that you find that something about the way your opponent presents his or her case is rather irritating.

If there is any risk that your emotions may affect your performance, remember that it is vital to stay as calm as possible, so that nothing you have planned is lost. You need to be patient, and to persevere in your attempt to achieve your client's objectives (though you may need to modify your approach slightly to get away from the thing that is irritating you). There are many ways to deal with emotion, depending on the circumstances. For example, it may help to discuss with your opponent why he or she is taking the approach that is irritating you, it may help to focus on the positive rather than the negative aspects of what is being discussed, or you may need to move to another issue.

17.6.4 Feeling vulnerable due to inexperience at the Bar

In practice, particularly in your early years, you will negotiate with more experienced practitioners. Your assumptions about this disparity of experience could influence how you negotiate. Most of us assume that with experience comes expertise. We therefore enter the negotiation with the expectation that the experienced opponent will know more and be more skilled at negotiating. Thus, if you and your opponent have a conflict over the interpretation of a legal principle or the merits of the case, you may assume that there is less chance that you are right due to your lack of experience. You may not be able to differentiate between concessions made because of your feeling of lack of experience or because your client's case is less meritorious. When your opponent makes suggestions as to how to conduct the negotiation, you may be tempted to agree because you assume it is a better way than you have planned to conduct the negotiation.

Although lack of experience may make you feel vulnerable, particularly when negotiating against a more senior member of the Bar, do not assume that this experience automatically makes your opponent a better negotiator. From the small amount of empirical research carried out, it would appear that most lawyers are not sophisticated negotiators. Be professional, remember your preparation, watch and try to determine what (if any) strategy your opponent uses. Focus on your preparation and knowledge of strategy and tactics rather than the difference in years of experience at the Bar.

17.6.5 Feeling you cannot cope

Negotiating is a complex skill which requires considerable concentration, self-discipline and hard work if it is to be done properly. Arguably, it has the fewest rules and guidelines in the litigation process as a whole. Even if you are well prepared, you may have to digest considerable amounts of new information in an already complex case. Some of this information may require you to alter radically your evaluation of the merits and reflect that in your proposals, whilst dealing with your opponent's strategy, tactics and points and considering your revised plan of action. You may have to do all this in a very short space of time. You may feel that you 'can't cope' with all this and want to throw in the towel and accept the proposals on offer without giving them due consideration. Alternatively, you may 'not cope' by just resorting to a pre-planned strategy and arguments, ignoring new information and proposals put forward by your opponent in the negotiation.

Sound preparation can minimise the extent to which this is likely to occur, but even that is sometimes not enough. Recognise that this may happen, in particular where the negotiation has been going on for a while and you may be tired and have lost your concentration. If appropriate, take time out. Do not be afraid to ask your opponent for time to deal with new information arising during the negotiation. Even a pause of a minute or two may assist you to collect your thoughts. Step back from the issue under discussion. Review your analysis of your client's objectives and the merits of the case and get an overview. Recap progress in the negotiation and think how you can adjust your plans to be more flexible. Try to ascertain whether your opponent is equally overwhelmed and, as a result, the negotiation is going nowhere. If so, it may assist to acknowledge explicitly that the negotiation seems to have gone off course. Take a step back from the negotiation and implement a plan for dealing with the complexities in the case that are causing difficulties, such as redefining or categorising what is on the table for negotiation and what are the related issues.

17.6.6 Feeling panic—dealing with the unforeseen

You enter a negotiation with, on your papers, a strong case. Your strategy, tactics and analysis of what can be achieved in the negotiations is based on your case being strong. Your opponent makes a statement which substantially alters the strength of your client's case, undermining it completely. While thorough analysis of the case prior to the negotiation should alert you to possible gaps and ambiguities, there may be times when the client has failed to reveal important aspects which alter the position. PANIC!!

Do not react. Keep a poker face. Stop and think. Check precisely what your opponent has said. Is the statement merely an allegation? Ask your opponent for the evidence to support it. If necessary, move the negotiation on to another topic. Give yourself time to absorb the information and reassess the case.

17.7 Summary

Thorough and effective preparation, a knowledge and understanding of the dynamics of negotiation and the unconscious elements which may influence these dynamics will go a long way towards ensuring that you are rarely unable to deal with difficult opponents and that you virtually never feel unable to cope. This does not mean that you will always reach settlement or that you will always get precisely what you want from a negotiation. Both of these are dependent on a number of factors beyond your control, such as the merits of the case, the client's position, the skill of your opponent, etc. The guidance in this manual is to assist you to be ready for any eventuality and to negotiate as effectively as you can in the circumstances.

18

Recording and enforcing a negotiated agreement

18.1 Introduction

Chapter 16 on conducting an effective negotiation included a section dealing with concluding the process with your opponent. This chapter gives guidance on the steps you must take to complete your job as counsel where you have negotiated a settlement or 'compromise' of a dispute, either before or after proceedings have been issued. In addition to some formalities, such as endorsing your brief, this includes ensuring that any settlement agreed with your opponent is properly recorded, that your client understands the settlement, in particular the consequences of it, and accepts it and, where appropriate, informing the court of or seeking the court's permission for the agreement.

18.1.1 Compromise is a contract

Where parties are in dispute, they have a choice of resolving the dispute through adjudication (largely by the courts) or compromise (resolving it themselves). If adjudicated, the court's decision is final on the matters disputed and a compromise is as binding and final as adjudication. The compromise is made 'in full and final settlement' of those matters which it resolves. Any rights of action in relation to the dispute are replaced by rights under the 'contract of compromise', to which the ordinary principles of contract law apply.

A compromise may resolve all or only some of the disputed matters. The compromise will only be final in respect of those matters covered by the compromise. The remaining matters may be litigated or the subject of a further negotiation.

18.1.2 Endorsing your brief

When you have completed any task for which you have been briefed, you must return the brief to your instructing solicitor with the enclosed documents and an endorsement on the back sheet of the work done (see the ***Case Preparation*** manual on endorsements generally). Where you have been briefed to represent a client in court and an order is made, you will have to endorse the order on your brief. Similarly, if you reach a settlement, you will have to endorse the brief to this effect. The primary purpose of the endorsement is a statement of the work done.

18.2 Methods of recording

There are a number of different methods of recording a compromise. A compromise may also be recorded using more than one method, with different issues being recorded by different methods. The method of recording a compromise will affect how it is enforced. It is therefore a matter which you will need to negotiate with your opponent (see **7.4.1.7**). You need to ensure that you choose the most appropriate method for your client in the circumstances in which you are negotiating.

The methods of recording divide into two main groups: those which do not involve the court and those which do. The distinction is important because, generally, those which involve the court may be enforced by returning to court within the existing proceedings to enforce the compromise. Those which do not involve the court require the party seeking enforcement to issue fresh proceedings for breach of contract.

18.2.1 Methods which do not involve the court

Where settlement is reached prior to issue of proceedings, the court will not be involved unless court approval of the settlement is required (ie, a settlement in respect of a child or mental patient). Any compromise made post-issue will have to take into account that the case is being litigated. The court will have to be informed of the settlement both as a matter of courtesy and as required by the Civil Procedure Rules. In addition, in most cases, any court proceedings will also be terminated, usually by the case being discontinued or withdrawn. However, there may be no need or wish by either party to involve the court in the recording of the compromise.

The following methods may be used in cases which settle pre-issue or, although post-issue, there is no reason to involve the court. If one party fails to abide by the agreement, the other party will have to issue fresh proceedings for breach of contract.

18.2.1.1 Only the endorsement on the brief

In addition to being a statement of the work done, an endorsement on your brief may also serve as the written record of what was agreed. Where the settlement is very straightforward, no additional written record of the agreement may be needed. In this case, you will need to ensure that the endorsement on the brief sets out fully and accurately what was agreed. Where used, the usual practice is for the lawyer for each party to sign each other's endorsement signifying agreement to what is written on the brief. This also prevents difficulties arising because the lawyers have recorded different outcomes on their briefs. The parties may also sign, again to signify their agreement to the terms recorded. Your brief is returned to your solicitor who may or may not write an additional letter to the lay client confirming the agreement, relying on your endorsement on the brief. Both your endorsement and any subsequent letter to the client are merely evidence of what was agreed.

Relying on the endorsement is clearly the cheapest and quickest method. However, as each party relies solely on the endorsement on his or her counsel's brief, and there is no exchange of written documents between the parties as to what was agreed, it is only appropriate for very simple cases with few very simple settlement terms.

EXAMPLES OF ENDORSEMENTS ON BRIEFS

1. In a case where one substantial issue is in dispute (like the ownership of beneficial interests in real property) a smaller issue might be settled by endorsement on a brief rather than by separate argument in court.

JAMES BROWN

V

AMANDA SMITH

It is hereby agreed that:

(1) The claimant shall have ownership of the dining room table and chairs.

(2) The defendant shall have ownership of the painting known as 'Conflict Rationalised'.

(3) The collection of silver teaspoons shall be sold and the proceeds divided equally between the claimant and the defendant.

Signed (client) Signed (client)

Signed (barrister) Signed (barrister)

Dated

2. If an interim order has been made or a case adjourned the parties may record an agreement on claims pending a further order in the case.

RANJIT SINGH

V

QUICK SUPPLIES LIMITED

Upon the adjournment of this matter by consent, it is agreed that pending a further hearing in this case:

- the defendant will continue to make supplies of stationery material to the claimant upon the terms of the contract dated 1st April 2006
- the claimant will pay for all such supplies within 28 days of invoice.

Signed (client) Signed (client)

Signed (barrister) Signed (barrister)

Dated

3. If a court makes a general order, such as that contact with a child should be as agreed between parties, detailed terms can be endorsed upon the brief.

DARREN JONES
V
TRACEY JONES

In pursuance of the order herein, whereby it is ordered that contact with the child Jeremiah Jones should be as agreed between the parties, it is hereby agreed that the defendant should have contact with the said child on alternate Saturdays, commencing on the Saturday immediately following the making of this order. The precise times and places of such contact shall be agreed by the parties by telephone at least 24 hours in advance.

Signed (client) Signed (client)

Signed (barrister) Signed (barrister)

Dated

18.2.1.2 Exchange of letters

The compromise may be recorded by an exchange of letters, usually written by the parties' solicitors. One solicitor writes a letter setting out the full terms which have been agreed, and the other replies accepting the terms. The solicitor will draft the letter on the basis of the endorsement on the brief and/or discussions with and/or notes by counsel about precisely what was agreed. As with an endorsement on counsels' brief, this is merely evidence of what was agreed.

An exchange of letters will be used where no proceedings have been issued. It may also be used even where proceedings have been issued where the agreement is not sufficiently short and simple to rely on counsels' endorsements on their briefs and there is no need for court involvement or a formal contract.

The solicitors will charge both for writing and reading the letters. Although this charge may not be high, it should be taken into account both when deciding whether an exchange of letters is needed and who pays the costs.

4. Letter setting out terms of a negotiated settlement.

16th March 2009

Dear Sir,

Megadell Foods Ltd v Angus Warley (t/a Choc Folie)
I am writing to you to record the terms of negotiated settlement of this case reached by counsel for the parties on 6th March 2009, the detailed terms being subject to client approval.

I understand the terms agreed to be as follows:

1. That there should be a new contract for the supply of chocolate by the claimants to the defendant, to commence within 28 days of the date of this letter. It has been agreed that this contract will last for a minimum of two years, and will provide for a minimum delivery of 500 grammes of chocolate per month. The defendant and a representative of the claimant will meet within one month of the date of this agreement to agree full detailed terms for this contract.

2. On the basis that approximately half of the Luglian Chocolate held by the claimant has already been sold to an alternative purchaser, and the rest will be used to meet the new contract with the defendant, no payment will be made with regard to loss of profit by the claimant, save for that provided in (3) below.

3. The defendant will pay to the claimant the sum of £1,890 in respect of one and a half deliveries of chocolate plus interest of £150. This sum is to be paid within seven days of the date of this letter.

4. The chocolate from the second delivery remaining in the possession of Angus Warley will be inspected by an independent expert within one month of the drawing up of this agreement. If the chocolate is found to be of satisfactory quality Angus Warley will retain it and pay for it forthwith. If it is not found to be of satisfactory quality Megadell Foods Ltd will collect the chocolate forthwith and no payment will be required.

5. There will be no payment with regard to the defendant's alleged loss of profits. However, the claimant and the defendant will discuss the possibility of a joint advertising promotion of the Luglian chocolate products manufactured by the defendant.

6. Each party will pay their own costs, save that Megadell Foods will pay the costs of drawing up this agreement.

I have discussed these terms with my client and he is prepared to accept them. I look forward to hearing from you that your client is also prepared to accept the terms.

Yours sincerely

(Solicitor for the claimant)

5. Letter accepting the above terms.

20th March 2009

Dear Sir,

Megadell Foods Ltd v Angus Warley (t/a Choc Folie)

I am writing in reply to your letter dated 16th March setting out proposed terms of agreement for this case. I have confirmed with my client that he is prepared to accept these terms in full and final settlement of the case. Indeed my client is looking forward to a more positive commercial future with your client.

Yours sincerely,

(Solicitor for the defendant)

18.2.1.3 Simple contract or deed

The terms of the compromise may be recorded in a simple contract or a deed drafted by you or the solicitor. The contract or deed is a legally enforceable document. In the event of a dispute over the terms or failure to abide by the agreement, the court will consider the contract/deed and apply the general law of contract, including the parole evidence rule. When drafting a contract or deed to record a compromise, you therefore need to ensure that you have observed the ordinary principles for drafting such documents. In addition, to avoid uncertainty as to what the compromise covers, it is common to include a preamble setting out the disputed matters which are compromised by the settlement contained in the document.

A contract or deed will be used either where proceedings have not been issued, or where they have been issued but there is no need for court involvement and the matter is sufficiently complex or requires more formality than an exchange of letters. For example, it may be appropriate in a dispute between an employer and employee, or between businesses involved in trade, for the compromise to be enshrined in a new contract. Whether a simple contract or contract by deed is used depends on the requirements to ensure enforceability of the compromise and the level of formality appropriate to the subject matter of the compromise. Where there is doubt as to whether one party has given consideration, a deed is required to ensure enforceability. Where the agreement relates to rights over property, eg, a boundary dispute, a deed may also be more appropriate.

EXAMPLE MEMORANDUM OF AGREEMENT

(This example is an alternative to the exchange of letters above. A further alternative might be to have a new contract between the parties, which would probably be based on a standard form contract used by Megadell Foods Ltd rather than being a wholly separate document.)

THIS AGREEMENT is made on 16th March 2009 between Megadell Foods Limited of the one part and Angus Warley (trading as Choc Folie) of the other part.

WHEREAS the aforesaid Megadell Foods Limited and Angus Warley have been in dispute regarding alleged breaches and alleged repudiation of a contract for the supply of chocolate by the claimant to the defendant in a contract dated 11th July 2008.

NOW IT IS HEREBY AGREED by way of compromise of the said dispute as follows:

1. A new contract for the supply of chocolate by Megadell Foods Limited to Angus Warley will be entered into within 28 days of the date of this order. This contract will last for a minimum of two years, and will provide for a minimum delivery of 500 grammes of chocolate per month.

2. Angus Warley will pay to Megadell Foods Limited the sum of £1,890 in respect of one and a half deliveries of chocolate plus interest of £150. This sum is to be paid within seven days of the date of this agreement.

3. Each party will pay their own costs, save that Megadell Foods will pay the costs of drawing up this agreement.

IN FURTHERANCE OF THIS AGREEMENT:

1. Angus Warley and a representative of Megadell Foods Limited will meet within one month of the date of this agreement to agree full detailed terms for continued delivery of chocolate by Megadell Foods Limited to Angus Warley.

2. The chocolate from the second delivery remaining in the possession of Angus Warley will be inspected by an independent expert within one month of the drawing up of this agreement. If the chocolate is found to be of satisfactory quality Angus Warley will retain it and pay for it forthwith. If it is not found to be of satisfactory quality Megadell Foods Ltd will collect the chocolate forthwith and no payment will be required.

Dated:

Signed Signed

In the presence of In the presence of

18.2.2 Methods which involve the court

Where the settlement of a case is negotiated at the court door, the negotiation and compromise must include what is to happen to the matter in court (see **7.4**). Counsel will then inform the judge that the parties have settled, what the parties have agreed should happen and seek an order from the court which reflects this agreement.

A compromise at the door of an interim application need only deal with that application, although the parties may also want it to deal with the case as a whole. A compromise at the door of the final hearing must deal with the case as a whole. The court may deal with an interim application by making an order dismissing or adjourning it or by making an order on the application in the terms agreed by the parties. The court may deal with the case as a whole by making an order discontinuing or dismissing the claim, adjourning the hearing, staying proceedings or by giving judgment on the terms agreed by the parties. At the very least, the court will have to make an appropriate order to reflect what has been agreed should happen to the interim application and/or the case. This order may or may not include reference to the other terms agreed by the parties (eg, payment of money or specific acts to be done or not done by the parties).

Where a compromise is made post-issue but not at the court door, the parties have a choice of either not involving the court (see above at **18.2.1**) or seeking an order from the court to enshrine all or part of what has been agreed. The decision as to whether or not to involve the court will depend on what was agreed about how the compromise would be enforced in the event of non-compliance by either party. Whether or not the order can be entered by a purely administrative process or requires the approval of a judge depends on the type of order sought. Where the approval of a judge is required, it may be given with or without a hearing (for further details, see 'Judgments and orders' in the ***Civil Litigation*** manual).

Whether the order is entered purely as an administrative process or is put before a judge either at a hearing or not, the fact that it is made on the basis of agreement by the parties will be made clear by including the words, 'by consent', on the order.

18.2.2.1 Terms of the compromise not forming part of the order

The court order may just set out what will happen to the application (where relevant, for example, dismissing or adjourning it) and/or case (eg, dismissing or staying it). The other terms of the compromise may then be recorded in any of the ways set out above at **18.2.1**. Enforcement of these terms will require the issue of fresh proceedings for breach of the compromise agreement (contract). However, the terms of the compromise can remain confidential, which is more difficult to achieve where the compromise forms part of the order.

EXAMPLES OF INTERIM ORDERS

1. Setting aside a judgment in default on agreed terms.

(Since there has been an application to set aside a judgment in default, the following is a further alternative to the exchange of letters or the memorandum of agreement above.)

IN THE TAUNTON COUNTY COURT Claim No. TA501008

BETWEEN

MEGADELL FOODS LIMITED Claimant

and

ANGUS WARLEY (t/a CHOC FOLIE) Defendant

DRAFT MINUTES OF ORDER

Upon hearing counsel for the claimant and for the defendant

By consent it is ordered:

1. The judgment in default obtained on 11th February 2009 be set aside upon the basis of terms agreed between the parties.

2. Each party to bear their own costs.

Dated

(The precise terms could then be recorded in a separate contract or exchange of letters.)

18.2.2.2 Terms of the compromise are part of the order

Alternatively, the court order may include both what will happen to the application/case and the other terms of the compromise. Enforcement of the terms of the compromise can be done within the existing proceedings by seeking enforcement of the order. There is no need to issue fresh proceedings. An order may include one or more of the methods set out below for recording the terms of the compromise.

Interim orders on conduct of the case

An interim order may specify what happens to the case on the basis of agreed terms specifying the parties' rights on compliance or breach of the agreed terms. For example, the court may order that the case be adjourned generally on terms agreed and specify what further steps the parties are entitled to take on compliance with or breach of the order. The parties then take the appropriate action depending on whether or not the terms are fulfilled or breached.

2. An adjournment upon agreed terms

IN THE WINCHESTER COUNTY COURT — Claim No. 9876

BETWEEN

ALGERNON SMYTHE — Claimant

and

HONEST JOHN MOTORS LIMITED — Defendant

BY CONSENT it is ordered that the claim and Part 20 claim in this action be adjourned generally upon the terms set out below:

1. That the Defendant pays to the Claimant the sum of £5,000 within 28 days of the date of this order.

2. That the Claimant returns to the Defendant the Ford Fiesta motor car registration number M 143 SUE within 28 days of the date of this order.

AND IT IS FURTHER ORDERED that in the event of the terms being carried out by the parties the claim and Part 20 claim be and are hereby dismissed with no order as to costs.

AND IT IS FURTHER ORDERED that in the event of any of the terms not being carried out, either party shall be at liberty to restore the claim for trial.

Consent court order or judgment

Some or all of the promises by the parties which make up the compromise may become orders of the court. The most common types of court orders are:

(a) *Orders for payment of money or delivery of goods/possession of premises.* For example, the claimant may be ordered to pay the defendant £1,000 by a specified date or by specified instalments on specified dates, or the defendant may be ordered to return a specified car by a specified date. Failure to comply with the order will mean that the other party may enforce this order using normal enforcement methods (see the ***Civil Litigation*** manual on 'Enforcement').

(b) *Injunction orders (prohibitory or mandatory).* For example, the claimant may be forbidden from carrying out building works on a specified site before 8am or after 6pm, or the defendant may be required to move his car from a specified site by a specified date. Failure to comply with an injunction order is contempt of court.

Although these orders are usually drafted by counsel, and the wording is agreed as part of the compromise, they are technically made by the court. The court has no power to make an order outside its jurisdiction in the particular case. This is defined by the statements of case and so limited to the causes of action and claims for relief pleaded. Thus, when drafting the terms of the order, you must check the statements of case to ensure that the order is within the court's jurisdiction. Thus, where a landlord's claim against a tenant is for a money judgment for rent arrears and the compromise is that the tenant will move out of the premises, the court has no power to order the tenant to give the landlord possession as it is not part of the landlord's pleaded case. In this case, you may seek permission to amend the statements of case to include a claim for possession to bring the order within the court's jurisdiction. Whether or not the court will be willing to allow the amendment will depend on the circumstances and the degree to which the amendment alters the case. Where the compromise does include matters outside the court's jurisdiction, it may be better to choose one of the other forms of recording the compromise or that part of the compromise.

Undertakings

Some or all of the promises made by the parties which form part of the compromise may become undertakings by the parties to the court. Failure to comply with an undertaking is contempt of court (ie, the same as failure to comply with an order).

The main practical difference between enshrining promises by the parties in an order or an undertaking is that the court has the power to accept undertakings by the parties which go beyond matters contained in the statements of case. Thus, in the example above of a landlord's action against a tenant, the court could accept an undertaking by the tenant to give up possession by a specified date. The judge will ensure that any party giving an undertaking understands both what it involves and the consequences of not abiding by it. Generally, the judge will check with the party directly rather than accepting assurances from counsel.

EXAMPLE COURT ORDER

This order includes both (b) court orders and (c) undertakings.

IN THE HIGH COURT OF JUSTICE 2008 T No. 7564

QUEEN'S BENCH DIVISION

BETWEEN

TOP WOMEN (a firm) Claimant

and

MANAGEMENT CONSULTANTS PLC Defendant

DRAFT MINUTES OF ORDER

Upon hearing counsel for the claimant and for the defendant.

And upon the defendant undertaking:

1. Not to take any action to exclude the Claimant's clients from the Defendant's offices.

2. To continue to pay the Claimant's clients as specified in the agreement dated 4th March 2004.

By consent it is ordered:

1. The Defendant to pay to the Claimant damages of £40,000 within 4 weeks of the date of this order.

2. The defendant to pay the costs of this action.

Dated

Tomlin order

Under a Tomlin order (named after the judge who set out the method in a Practice Direction), the court orders that further proceedings in the action be stayed except for the purpose of carrying the terms of the compromise into effect, the terms of which are set out in a schedule to the order. The order will also contain a provision giving the parties liberty to apply to the court if necessary to compel compliance with the terms. As with an undertaking by the parties, the terms set out in the schedule can go beyond matters covered by the statements of case in the action. They can even go beyond the ambit of the original dispute between the parties.

A Tomlin order differs from enshrining the parties' promises either in an order by the court or by an undertaking to the court in that, if the terms set out in the schedule are broken, enforcement requires two stages:

(a) the party seeking to enforce the terms must apply to court to have the matter restored (ie, brought back before the court) and seek an order requiring the guilty party to comply with the terms in the schedule which have been breached;

(b) failure to comply with this order is contempt of court.

Using a Tomlin order also enables the parties to keep the terms of the agreement confidential. Orders and undertakings will be repeated in court, which will be in public unless there is a reason for the proceedings to be in private. In addition, a consent order forms part of the court record, which is also available for scrutiny. The court may, however, direct that the schedule to a Tomlin order not be released to anyone other than the parties or their advisers.

EXAMPLE TOMLIN ORDER

IN THE HIGH COURT OF JUSTICE 2008 C No. 666

QUEEN'S BENCH DIVISION

BETWEEN

COMPUTER PRODUCTS PLC Claimant

and

UNITED DISCS PLC Defendant

Upon the parties having agreed to the terms of settlement set out below.

By consent it is ordered that all further proceedings in this action be stayed upon the terms set out in the attached Schedule, save for the purpose of enforcing the terms, with liberty to apply for such purpose.

And it is further ordered that there be no order as to costs.

SCHEDULE

1. The warehouse at Lot 9, Molesworth Industrial Estate, Polehurst, Hampshire be sold within six months of the date of this order for the best price obtainable, and the net proceeds be divided as to 60% to the Claimant and 40% to the Defendant.

2. A valuation of the computer software remaining in the warehouse will be obtained by each party within 14 days of the date of this order, the Defendant to pay to the Claimant a sum half way between the two valuations obtained within three months of the date of this order. Should the sum not be paid within this time it will carry interest at the rate of 10% per annum.

3. The Defendant will destroy all copies of the 'Drawpro' program remaining in their possession forthwith.

18.3 Advising the client and seeking approval

The importance of making any compromise you reach with your opponent 'subject to your client's approval' is set out at **16.2.1**. This means that any compromise you reach is not binding until your client approves it. Once you have reached a compromise with your opponent, you must then present what was agreed to your client:

(a) Explain the terms of the compromise fully and clearly so that the client understands what he or she must do or not do and what the other side must do or not do. The client will have to understand precisely what is required to comply with the terms to avoid breaching them. In addition, he or she must make an informed decision as to whether or not to approve the compromise, including considering whether or not the terms are too onerous.

(b) Explain the consequences of non-compliance with the compromise by either party. This includes explaining to the client how the compromise will be enforced, eg, if in a court order, failure to comply could lead to contempt proceedings.

(c) Where you are acting under a conditional fee agreement, you must follow the guidance given by the Bar Council (see the ***Professional Conduct*** manual for further details).

(d) Your client may be reluctant to approve the compromise because he or she feels that you should have obtained an agreement which was more favourable to him or her. Frequently, a client will not understand the weaknesses of his or her case or the difficulties of obtaining certain concessions from the other side or orders from the court. In such a case, you must use all your persuasive powers to make your client understand why you consider the compromise is good or the best that can be achieved in the circumstances.

(e) If your client does not approve the compromise, then you must tell your opponent. It is the client's decision, not yours. Where you are acting for a publicly-funded client who has declined an offer, the client will have to be told if this may result in a report to the Community Legal Service with the consequence that funding is withdrawn (see the ***Professional Conduct*** manual for further details).

18.4 Informing/seeking permission of the court

Once proceedings have been issued, there is a duty to inform the court if settlement is reached, whether or not this occurs at the court door. Where settlement is not at the court door, the solicitor will usually inform the court or seek the required permission for a consent order.

Where the settlement is at the court door, it will be your duty as advocate to inform the court and seek any necessary permission. In doing this, you must be conscious of both the concerns of the court (eg, whether or not the order comes within the court's jurisdiction) and the client (eg, the client's wish for confidentiality) and formulate what you say accordingly.

19 Assessing negotiation skills

19.1 Learning lawyers' negotiation skills

19.1.1 Negotiation skills for barristers

Learning how to adapt and expand existing negotiation skills for use as a lawyer entails performing and observing the skills in appropriate contexts and being reflective about what you do, see and hear. Most barristers will use their negotiation skills, at least in the early years of practice, primarily in the context of resolving disputes within the litigation process, generally at the court door.

The BVC negotiation course covers a range of cases and types of negotiation (see **2.2**) but concentrates on situations in which settlement is sought at some stage in the litigation process, generally using scenarios where negotiations are done at the court door. The course focuses on teaching the skills necessary to conduct such negotiations within the limitations imposed (see **Chapter 4**, in particular **4.3**). It includes the theoretical and behavioural aspects of negotiation and you are expected to understand and recognise the different strategies and tactics and use those that are appropriate in the circumstances. The main thrust of the course, however, is ensuring that you understand and can control the content of the discussion in a negotiation.

19.1.2 Learning skills using performance criteria

Negotiation is a complex skill. It requires intellectual and presentation skills. It also involves emotional and behavioural aspects, some of which operate on an unconscious or semi-conscious level. Although recognising a good settlement is relatively straightforward, it takes a solid understanding of negotiation to analyse a performance and identify precisely how this particular settlement was achieved and what was and was not effective. To be able to analyse a performance and use that analysis to improve your own skills, you must be able to identify those aspects of the negotiation that were well done and those that were badly done. You must also be able to understand how you can reinforce those aspects of the skill that you already do well and recognise those aspects of the skill that you need to and can improve. Although you cannot change your personality and it is very difficult to alter long-standing behaviour patterns, you can develop the ability to control the substance of the negotiation discussion and to present and respond effectively. However, there is a limit to the number of factors to which you can attend in observing or critiquing a negotiation performance. The performance criteria highlight those aspects that will influence the content and outcome of the negotiation and which you can change or reinforce as appropriate. They identify the aspects of negotiation on which you should be concentrating in learning the skill.

The criteria are used throughout the course. The tutor relates his or her feedback on performances to the criteria. You are also expected to assess and give criteria-based feedback on your own and colleagues' performances.

19.1.3 Reflecting on your preparation, planning and conduct

Reflecting on your own preparation and performance is probably the most effective way of improving your negotiation skills. In the final sections of this chapter we set out three guidance notes to assist you to do this. The first one is a checklist for preparation. This should assist you to check that your preparation is well focused and thorough. The second one is a checklist for a plan. Again, this should assist you to write a plan which is useful to you in the negotiation. Finally, there is a questionnaire which you can use with your colleague following a negotiation to review your performance.

19.2 The negotiation course

19.2.1 The tasks

During the negotiation course and in the assessment you will be required to undertake the following tasks:

(a) prepare to negotiate by carrying out the appropriate analysis, evaluation and planning;

(b) write a plan setting out your analysis, evaluation and proposals for the conduct and structure of the negotiation;

(c) conduct a negotiation involving one or more items on which agreement is required to reach an overall settlement, including determining the appropriate method of recording the settlement to ensure that it is enforceable and effective;

(d) draft an agreement which accurately reflects the settlement reached ensuring that all matters are included in sufficient detail and in an appropriate form.

19.2.2 The aspects being assessed

The course has a very practical focus. Although it requires an understanding of some theoretical aspects, the course is designed to teach you how to prepare for and conduct a negotiation effectively by being able to control the content of the discussion in the negotiation and focus the discussion on seeking a good settlement. The performance criteria are therefore focused on assessing these practical skills, ie, how well you have identified and evaluated the matters which will form the content of the discussion and how effectively you use this analysis and evaluation in presenting your case and responding to your opponent in the negotiation to reach a good settlement for your client. Thus, the criteria are used to assess ability in two distinct areas. First, they assess the intellectual skills of analysis and judgement which you will use both preparing for and conducting the negotiation. Secondly, they assess presentation skills used in controlling what you say and how you say it in the negotiation.

Some skills can be broken down into identifiable aspects that can be considered discretely, eg, questioning and advising in conference skills. However, a negotiation is a dynamic interactive process without identifiable discrete phases. The behaviour patterns that have been identified are very general and involve a multiplicity of aspects with overlapping phases which are frequently repeated. Not all negotiations exhibit the same phases and, in any one negotiation, neither negotiator has more control than the other over how it is conducted. It is therefore not possible to break a negotiation performance into identifiable stages and assess the effectiveness of each stage.

The performance criteria therefore focus on the following aspects:

- identifying and pursuing objectives and using concessions to move to settlement;
- doing relevant analysis and evaluation and using that appropriately in the negotiation;
- presenting your client's case;
- responding to your opponent;
- observing the rules of professional conduct.

19.2.3 The performance and role of the plan

Negotiation is a skill that involves moving to a compromise that reflects both what the parties want and what can be argued on their behalf. Although your preparation should identify the strengths and weaknesses of your case and the arguments that can be used for and against you, what you actually say in the negotiation will be circumscribed. Getting the best for your client means revealing information that assists in reaching a good settlement and using arguments that will persuade your opponent to move towards you. Although much of your analysis will inform what you say in the negotiation, much of it will not be expressly stated or revealed to your opponent. Thus, for example, you may have an opponent who has not seen some of the weaknesses of your case or arguments that could be put on his or her client's behalf. It would be counter-productive to set them out in the negotiation. Alternatively, your opponent may offer something by way of compromise that is a very good deal. It would be fruitless and counter-productive to respond by explaining why you are accepting the offer. You just accept it.

The plan therefore serves two purposes. First, it is an 'aide-memoire' for you to assist you to be 'on top of the case' in the negotiation and to be clear about the arguments and compromises that can or should be made in the negotiation. Secondly, it assists anyone watching the performance to understand your rationale for what you say in the negotiation and the proposals you put to or accept from your opponent.

19.3 The negotiation criteria

19.3.1 Objectives and concessions and moving to settlement

This criterion assesses how well you have identified what you wish to achieve in the negotiation and planned how you are going to move from what your client ideally wants to something which is acceptable to the other side without sacrificing more than is necessary of what your client wants. It also covers how effectively you then pursue this in the performance. Thus it assesses your ability both to analyse the case and to put that analysis into practice in the negotiation. It breaks down into a number of overlapping aspects.

19.3.1.1 Identifying the objectives of both parties

Consideration of this aspect includes looking at how thoroughly and precisely you have identified what your client wants. Have you identified all of the client's relevant wishes, extending your analysis to both legal and non-legal objectives? Have you looked beyond the client's stated goals at the underlying needs, interests and reasons which may influence those goals and considered the context of negotiation, for example, whether or not the parties have/wish to have an ongoing relationship? It also includes consideration of how effectively you have prioritised the objectives by reference to the value placed on them by the client. Have you clearly identified and differentiated between what the client must have (the point beyond which the client will not settle), what the client would like to have and what he or she is prepared to forgo to get the more valued items? Full consideration of what the other side might be seeking from the negotiation is another aspect of this criterion. How well have you identified what the other side may want and the reasons why they may have to settle? It also includes assessing the extent to which you have differentiated between those objectives on which the parties are in direct conflict, ie, satisfying one party will be at the expense of what the other party wants, and those on which the parties' objectives may be more compatible and where there may be scope for creating solutions which partially or wholly satisfy both sides.

19.3.1.2 Identifying the 'items' to be negotiated

Not all of the parties' objectives or areas of disagreement between them are matters that will be negotiated, and identifying the items which are likely to be negotiated is an essential aspect of this criterion. This includes consideration of whether you have differentiated between matters which must be negotiated to reach settlement, eg, precisely how much money changes hands or whether a boundary line will or will not be moved, and other matters which will not necessarily be negotiated because they are about the parties' positions (eg, determining whether or not a contract was breached) or matters which are not really negotiable (eg, maintaining a friendship). Thus the 'items' to be negotiated should include all those matters on which reaching settlement is both necessary and realistic in the circumstances. In addition to the specific negotiable objectives of the parties, this should include the method by which any settlement is recorded, ensuring that it is the most appropriate method given the terms of the settlement, any procedural requirements and the wishes of the parties.

19.3.1.3 Planning the concessions

This criterion also assesses how well you have planned the concessions you will seek and make. Concessions are proposals for moving to settlement on items which are subject to negotiation and must be distinguished from matters which are not concessions, eg, admissions of fact or agreement on the law (see **11.4**). Effective concession planning involves identifying both what concessions you will seek from your opponent and what concessions you will offer. These should be based on a combination of your client's wishes and priorities, your evaluation of the case and the best overall settlement achievable for your client. You should identify the most achievable settlement for your client and plan so that the offers you make are staged, starting with the most achievable and working towards compromise gradually, each proposal sacrificing as little of what your client wishes as possible. Concessions should also be planned so that you are trading items of lower value to your client to get those that are more valued. Finally, concessions should build on what the other party appears to be seeking.

19.3.1.4 Planning how to conduct the negotiation

One of the objectives of a court-door negotiation is to attempt to reach settlement in the time available. That means using the time efficiently. This includes identifying the areas on which discussion would be useful and those on which it would not; identifying what information exchange would assist and how much testing of the case would assist to determine an appropriate settlement standard. It also includes consideration of how to structure the negotiation to ensure that all relevant matters are covered as efficiently as possible and in an order that will enable you to obtain the best for your client. Finally, it covers consideration of how to start the negotiation in a way which is conducive to the structure you would like to adopt.

19.3.1.5 Pursuing a good settlement

This aspect of the criterion assesses how well you put your analysis into practice in the negotiation. It includes assessing your ability to conduct the negotiation in a way which gives your client the best possible overall outcome given the wishes of both parties, the arguments advanced on both sides and the approach taken by the opponent. It assesses your ability to reappraise issues in light of information exchanged, arguments put by the opponent and assessment of what the opponent is likely to be prepared to do to move to settlement. It also assesses your ability to make rational judgements on what is a reasonable compromise based on the client's priorities, the merits of the case and the practicalities of what is suggested and to resist succumbing to behavioural strategy and tactics and either becoming too positional or giving away too much. This is judged on the basis of the concessions sought and made, eg, not making any unnecessary concessions or not refusing to make reasonable ones, and the reasoning for what is proposed and agreed.

19.3.1.6 The settlement

Finally, under this criterion, any settlement reached is considered to see whether it is as close to your client's objectives as possible, covers all the relevant matters in sufficient detail and is recorded in an appropriate form given the context in which the negotiation took place. This includes consideration of both the overall agreement and the individual terms agreed to see whether they are within the client's objectives and are clear, practical and enforceable.

19.3.2 Analysis and evaluation

This criterion assesses your ability to analyse the case, evaluate it on the basis of that analysis and then use that analysis and evaluation in preparing for and conducting the negotiation. It also breaks down into a number of overlapping aspects that divide into two main categories of analysis and evaluation.

19.3.2.1 Analysis

This includes identifying the issues underlying the dispute, using the law and facts to formulate arguments that can be used for and against you in the negotiation and identifying the information which is likely to be exchanged in the negotiation. The main component parts of analysis are:

(a) The issues in dispute. It is important to understand the issues that will form the negotiation. This involves clearly identifying the underlying legal and factual issues and differentiating between those that are disputed and those that are not.

Thus a claim may be based on a breach of contract in which breach is admitted but loss is denied.

(b) The facts. A fluent grasp of the facts is essential for effective negotiation. This includes clear identification of the relevant facts and any gaps or ambiguities and differentiation between those facts that are agreed and those that are disputed. Being on top of the figures is also important as is being able to do the necessary calculations in the negotiation.

(c) The law. A solid understanding of the relevant substantive, procedural and evidential law is essential as is a sound application of the law to the facts of the case to reach a well-reasoned view of the merits of the arguments on both sides.

(d) Evidence and information. Identifying the evidential basis of the parties' allegations is important as is distinguishing between solid and weak evidence and determining how this can be used in the negotiation. Equally important is identifying the information you should seek from your opponent and the information that might be sought by your opponent and planning how you will deal with this in the negotiation.

(e) Argument formulation. This involves putting all of the above analysis together to construct legal, factual and practical arguments that you can use to support your case. Equally it includes identifying those arguments that your opponent might use against you in the negotiation so that you are prepared to deal with points raised by him or her. It also involves relating these arguments to the issues in dispute and the items to be negotiated so that you are clear how the arguments can be used in seeking settlement.

19.3.2.2 Evaluation

On the basis of the analysis done, you must evaluate the case considering your client's claims and your opponent's claims both overall and on individual items. This involves being clear where your strengths and your opponent's weaknesses lie and planning how you can use them effectively in the negotiation. Equally it involves being clear where your weaknesses and your opponent's strengths lie and planning how to counter them. Evaluation of the arguments available to both parties and how these arguments would influence a court judgment is clearly an important aspect. However, strengths and weaknesses may also stem from the availability of information to the parties, the evidential basis of allegations or interpretation of legal principles. Identifying how the merits of the case may influence the negotiation, in particular in determining any standard against which to judge whether or not any offer made or settlement suggested is reasonable and/or fair, is also an important part of evaluation. It is also essential to relate this evaluation and assessment of an appropriate settlement standard to your analysis of the client's objectives and concession planning to determine what is achievable and how best to use it to seek settlement. Finally, consideration of what strategy is appropriate given the context of the negotiation and the client's objectives should be based on the analysis and evaluation.

19.3.3 Presenting your client's case effectively

This criterion assesses your ability to present your client's case in a way that enables you to achieve the best settlement, and your ability to use persuasive argument and proposals for compromise to move to a settlement which is the most favourable one achievable for your client in the circumstances. Aspects considered under this criterion include the following.

19.3.3.1 Clear, concise and coherent presentation at an appropriate pace

As with good advocacy, speaking clearly and concisely is important as is having a coherent approach, in particular in respect to what you are seeking and the arguments you use. Your presentation should take into account that you are negotiating with a fellow lawyer and terminology and explanations of concepts should be tailored accordingly. In addition, your presentation should take on board the time frame in which you are working and the need to deal with the matters at an appropriate pace.

19.3.3.2 Presenting your client's case in the best light

This includes setting out what your client is seeking from the negotiation clearly and precisely. It also includes presenting your client's case in the best possible light, where appropriate, using the strengths and marginalising weaknesses or not unnecessarily revealing those that may not be known to the opponent.

19.3.3.3 Persuasion through argument and proposals

Your ability to persuade your opponent to move towards you in reaching settlement is an important aspect of this criterion. This involves presenting cogent, relevant argument clearly, confidently and concisely. This involves more than just repeating what is in your brief or asserting facts or law. It means giving your opponent justifiable reasons why your client's point of view should prevail. It also involves using argument appropriately, ie, in a way that is likely to achieve the desired settlement. Thus, argument can be used to test the opponent and the case where such testing is useful. Alternatively it can be used to justify or explain a proposal or concession being sought from your opponent. Persuasive techniques also include initiating proposals for settlement. In presenting your client's case, you also need to be able to make or seek concessions appropriately. Deciding exactly when and how to do this is one of the most difficult aspects of negotiation. You need to be flexible and 'make the running' where it would assist in moving the negotiation on. You also need to make judgements 'on the hoof' taking into account what you are seeking to achieve, your view of the case given the discussion which has taken place, the time available to reach settlement and how far the negotiation discussion has progressed.

19.3.3.4 Seeking or offering information appropriately

Seeking and offering information is part of negotiation. In presenting your client's case, you need to ensure that you seek information from your opponent or offer it when this would be beneficial to the negotiation or to you in assessing how you will work towards compromise. However, just seeking information for the sake of it can be counter-productive and a waste of time.

19.3.3.5 Using appropriate strategy/language/manner

The strategy, language and manner you adopt in presenting your client's case will have an effect on the negotiation. Being too adversarial is counter-productive where it increases the confrontational nature of the negotiation unnecessarily and pushes both negotiators away from seeking settlement and into purely justifying their client's positions and not seeking ways to move to settlement. Being too conciliatory and cooperative can also be counter-productive where there is a failure to recognise that the negotiators, while attempting to seek settlement, are also representing parties with potentially opposing interests. The result may be that the client's objectives are not properly pursued and the settlement reached is less good than it might have been.

19.3.3.6 Being flexible/taking control where appropriate

A negotiation will rarely go exactly as you planned, and you will have to adapt to the approach and style of your opponent. There are no rules about the order in which the negotiators should conduct the negotiation, nor how the time should be divided between the negotiators in discussion. Sometimes, both negotiators have a similar and compatible approach to the negotiation. However, sometimes, the two negotiators have different approaches or styles which mean that one does more of the talking than the other. There is nothing wrong with this, provided the discussion is productive and moving the negotiation towards a settlement which will be a good one for your client. However, when this is not the case, you must be prepared to step in and steer the negotiation back to a more productive discussion.

19.3.4 Responding to your opponent

This criterion assesses your ability to listen to what your opponent says and respond to it in a way which progresses the negotiation, protects your client's position as far as possible and increases the prospects of reaching a good settlement for your client. This means being flexible, maintaining your cool and ensuring that you have your eye on the ball (ie, seeking settlement) and do not get side-tracked into discussions that are counter-productive or irrelevant. It also means responding confidently, clearly and persuasively. Aspects considered under this criterion include the following.

19.3.4.1 Listening carefully

A very important aspect of responding to your opponent is listening carefully to what is said, ensuring that you do understand the points he or she is making. You need to ensure that thinking about your response or the points you want to make does not interfere and result in you not hearing what is said, hearing inaccurately or misunderstanding what is being said. Even when you do listen carefully, you may not understand what your opponent means and may need to check the meaning of what was said.

19.3.4.2 Responding quickly, accurately, coherently and moving to settlement

Responding to your opponent effectively includes responding efficiently, replying quickly and being very clear and accurate in what you say. It also includes ensuring that you keep a clear focus on your client's objectives and your view of the case and that this is reflected in your responses. You also need to ensure that your response is one that will assist in moving to settlement and is not taking the discussion off course into irrelevant or peripheral matters.

19.3.4.3 Responding to argument

Your ability to respond appropriately to arguments put by your opponent includes consideration of whether or not your response assists in reaching a good settlement for your client. Arguing for the sake of it is counter-productive as it can make the negotiation more confrontational than necessary and wastes valuable time. Your responses need to be reasoned ones which have a purpose, eg, useful testing of the case or your opponent to assist you to gauge what compromise would be reasonable in the circumstances. Continuing to respond to an opponent's argument with further argument long after the merits of the case or issue under discussion are clear is inappropriate where it serves no useful purpose. You must use your judgement and be ready to respond in some way other than just continuing the arguments on the merits. Thus, for example, you could, on the basis of the testing already done, put a proposal for settlement to your opponent, either seeking a concession from him or her or offering a concession.

19.3.4.4 Responding to weaknesses revealed by your opponent

In court-door negotiations, particularly those at interim stages, neither negotiator will have full information about the case. Your opponent may have information that you do not which weakens your case and reveals this at some point in the negotiation. Although you may absorb the information and readjust your assessment of the case and the settlement which is achievable on behalf of your client, your response to your opponent should be measured and protect your client's position as far as possible. Conversely, your opponent may reveal a weakness in his or her case of which you were unaware. You need to be able to factor this information in to your assessment of the case in much the same way. You also need to gauge how this information can be used appropriately in the negotiation discussion to reinforce its impact on any settlement standard.

19.3.4.5 Information exchange

Your opponent may seek information from you. You need to be able to gauge whether or not the revealing of the information sought weakens or strengthens your client's case or is neutral. You also need to be able to gauge whether or not you should reveal it and, if so, how best to frame your response. In providing information, you also need to ensure that you do not mislead your opponent as this is unprofessional behaviour (see **19.3.5** below). Your opponent may also present you with information which is not contained in your brief (eg, expert evidence of the value of an item) and you need to respond appropriately, eg, asking for the source or validity of this and/or asking to see any documents held by your opponent.

19.3.4.6 Concessions

If and when your opponent makes proposals to you, either on individual items or as to overall settlement, you need to respond appropriately, ensuring that your response is based on rational judgement and not just a reaction to any offer having been made or to your opponent. Your response should take into account your analysis and evaluation of the case and any changes to that evaluation as a result of what has been revealed or discussed in the negotiation. If you require time to consider proposals, take it, but bearing in mind the need to use time efficiently. Similarly, you may be tempted to respond to an opponent's argument by making concessions yourself. If so, ensure that this response is appropriate and based on proper evaluation of the case and that you are not just reacting to your opponent and succumbing unnecessarily.

19.3.5 Professional conduct

As a barrister you are bound by the Code of Conduct and must act within it at all times. The principles in the Code apply equally to conducting a negotiation at the court door as they do to conducting a case in the courtroom. This criterion assesses your observance of the Code of Conduct and ethical behaviour. It includes consideration of your ability to identify ethical issues in your preparation and to act appropriately both in presenting and responding in the negotiation. Matters that fall within this criterion include ensuring that you are acting within instructions, seeking settlement in accordance with your client's wishes and not misleading your opponent. It also includes acting professionally towards your opponent, being polite and courteous at all times.

19.3.5.1 Acting within your instructions

This covers several aspects. You must ensure that you do not exceed the authority given to you by your client. This means ensuring that you are clear about the extent of your authority and any specific limits that have been put on it. You must also ensure that you do not actively mislead or deceive your opponent (eg, by not inventing facts, overstating your case, or stating that you have evidence to support a particular allegation which you do not have). In addition, you must not knowingly conceal matters that ought properly to have been disclosed (eg, a document which should be included in the disclosure process), and you must give full and frank disclosure where appropriate.

19.3.5.2 Acting professionally towards your opponent

As a barrister you must always act professionally, treating all those with whom you deal with courtesy. This includes your opponent in a negotiation. You must be polite and avoid bullying or unseemly aggressive behaviour. Adopting a competitive strategy or style does not give you a licence to be rude. You can state your case assertively but politely. When negotiating against an opponent who has overstepped the boundary of professional behaviour, you must resist the temptation to respond in kind. You must remain professional and polite. In addition, if you have said something you regret having said (eg, you have made a mistake or accepted a proposal that you should not have), you must not pretend that the words were not spoken. You must accept that they were spoken and deal with the result ethically.

19.4 Checklist for preparation

This checklist sets out the matters which you should consider when preparing to negotiate. As all negotiations are different, no one checklist will suffice for all. However, this does cover the main areas relevant to most legal dispute negotiations which we have dealt with in the chapters on preparation.

Context

- The case: basics of claim: cause of action and remedies.
- Stage of proceedings.

Parties' objectives

Client:

- items wanted;
- priorities;
- potential trade-offs.

Opponent:

- items wanted;

- priorities;
- potential trade-offs.

Issues, argument and information exchange

- Issues in the case.
- The law:
  - causes of action; elements;
  - necessary legal research done;
  - cases, etc obtained where necessary.
- The facts:
  - allegations by both sides;
  - gaps/ambiguities—information to seek and which may be sought;
  - evidence to support the allegations;
  - figures understood, calculated, accessible.
- Arguments for and against you on each issue:
  - formulated;
  - evaluated;
  - settlement standard considered.
- Information exchange:
  - identified;
  - risks of giving information considered;
  - how to deal with lack of information where essential.

Concessions

- Overview of case of what client wants:
  - any things client must have;
  - best overall outcome;
  - least acceptable overall outcome;
  - items to trade.
- Individual items (where appropriate):
  - opening offer and justification;
  - best possible outcome;
  - least acceptable outcome;
  - staging of concessions.

Structure

- Opening.
- Structure—including order with which to deal with items.

Agreement

- Form of agreement.
- Matters which must be covered.

19.5 Your written plan

A written plan for a negotiation means having notes which are useful to you while negotiating. Much of your preparation will be done either in your head or by making your brief and the documents in it. To be effective, your plan or notes should be short and concise and contain the relevant material.

19.5.1 Short and concise

Your notes should:

- be in note form;
- use lists where appropriate;
- use headings and sub-headings;
- be useful in the negotiation—a checklist/an 'aide-memoire';
- focus on the matters to be discussed.

19.5.2 Contents

The contents will depend on the case in question. For example, a chronology of events may be useful if the history of the case is complicated and important to the negotiation, but pointless if it is straightforward. A long section on the law may be useful if there are several legal issues, but not if there are few legal issues or the case depends on basic law. Having said that, it is useful to include the following:

- The items to be negotiated—prioritised and particularised to act as a checklist:
  - your client's wants/needs;
  - the opponent's wants/needs.
- The issues in dispute—there may be only one or several; for each one:
  - legal principles (where you are not au fait with them);
  - the arguments for and against you (including allegations of fact/evidence);
  - information you will seek from your opponent.
- Concessions:
  - any limitations by your client on what you can accept;
  - overall settlement: best and worst;
  - on individual items: opening offer, least acceptable, staging of offers.
- Structure:
  - how you will open;
  - the structure you want to adopt.

19.6 Reviewing your conduct of a negotiation

Every negotiation you perform should assist you in building your skill by providing you with further insights into the negotiation process. It is therefore worth spending at least a few minutes reviewing what happened. While you are learning to negotiate, it is well worth discussing what happened with your opponent. The following checklist suggests the sort of things you might usefully consider:

- Did you reach settlement? If not, why not?
- How closely did your settlement reflect:
  - your client's objectives?
  - your planned optimum outcome?
  - your worst realistic outcome?
- Could you have achieved more for your client:
  - overall?
  - in respect of any particular item?
- What order did you deal with the items? With hindsight, would it have been more beneficial to adopt a different order?
- Use of argument:
  - What was your most effective argument and your least effective argument?
  - What was your opponent's most effective argument and least effective argument?
  - Did you link your argument to concessions?
  - Did you seek justification from your opponent for his/her proposals?
- Concessions:
  - What was the first one you made? Was it too generous? Did you make it too early?
  - What was the first one your opponent made? Did you accept it? If yes, why? If no, how did you respond?
- Strategy:
  - Were you competitive or cooperative?
  - Was your opponent competitive or cooperative?
  - Did you or your opponent modify your behaviour during the negotiation?
- Future negotiations:
  - What did you find most difficult in this one? Why? How might you deal with this in future?
  - With hindsight, how could you have planned more effectively?

20

Adapting skills for Alternative Dispute Resolution

20.1 Alternatives in civil dispute resolution

Training for the Bar is quite rightly focused on learning those skills necessary to undertake criminal cases or to resolve civil cases within the context of litigation, either in a court or tribunal. Learning the skills necessary to deal with civil disputes is very much focused on how to prepare for and present cases in the formalised structure dictated by courts and increasingly, by tribunals.

However, over the last 20 years, a wider range of options for resolving civil disputes has been developing and various alternatives to courts are now available. These alternatives are generally lumped together under the title of Alternative Dispute Resolution methods (ADR).

The courts now actively encourage the use of ADR where appropriate. CPR r26.4(1) enables a party when filing the allocation questionnaire to request that proceedings be stayed while parties try to settle the case by ADR. The judge at case management conferences may invite parties to try ADR. There may be costs consequences if a party does not take its duty to consider ADR seriously. The court may consider this when looking at the manner in which a party pursued or defended the case or a particular allegation or issue (CPR r44.3(5)(c) See *Halsey v Milton Keynes General NHS Trust* [2004] EWCA Civ 576 [2004] 1 WLR 3002).

The development of these alternatives has two main consequences. Firstly, some changes are being made to the civil justice system. Thus the Woolf reforms set out to bring more openness to the process through the use of pre-action protocols, exchange of witness statements prior to hearing etc. Secondly, the 'alternative' methods available are becoming better known and used more to resolve disputes. Arbitration as an alternative to court has been available for some time. Although it is different from court proceedings (eg, the parties often select the arbitrator who fulfils the same role as the judge in court) the proceedings are generally in private and the jurisdiction and powers are more circumscribed than courts, the principal method of determining the result of the dispute is still the same as court (ie, the arbitrator or judge listens to the parties and then decides who wins). Indeed many would say that arbitration has developed rules almost as complex as those used in litigation. The newer forms of dispute resolution, of which mediation is the best known and most used, are very different in that the parties no longer look to an objective third party to make the decision as to how the matter will be resolved, but seek to make the decision jointly.

The purpose of this chapter is to explain briefly how mediation works, how it differs from determination by courts and how it is likely to influence and change the skills you may be required to learn to practise successfully as a lawyer. The focus of the chapter is therefore on how the skills required of a litigation lawyer and courtroom advocate, a negotiator and a mediator differ. It is not intended to be a comprehensive review of the different forms of alternative dispute resolution or mediation.

20.2 Mediation

20.2.1 The process

Mediation is a form of voluntary, non-binding, 'without prejudice' negotiation assisted by a neutral third party. The third party, the 'mediator', does not have power to make a decision nor to give individuals legal advice. The mediator's role is to attempt to bring the two parties in dispute closer together to assist them in reaching agreement. Agreement by both parties that they will use mediation to attempt to resolve the dispute is essential (without agreement of BOTH parties it will not proceed).

There is no set procedure for the conduct of a mediation. Different organisations have developed their own procedures which may vary depending on the type of dispute. Most, however, will ensure that before the date of the mediation meeting, the mediator has met with or spoken to each of the parties separately to ensure that they do understand the purpose and ethos of mediation and are happy to proceed with the process. On the day of the mediation meeting, there will be an opening session with the mediator and both parties. The mediator will set out the purpose of the mediation and his or her role, emphasising that it is for the parties to reach agreement, not for him or her to impose one. The mediator will also either set out or ask the parties themselves to establish 'ground rules' for the conduct of the mediation. These are generally about how the parties will treat each other (eg, not talk over each other, not be rude, etc). Each party may then be given an opportunity to explain how he or she sees the case. This enables the parties and the mediator to get some idea of the extent of the dispute and the positions of each party.

The mediation will then focus on the parties attempting to reach agreement with the mediator facilitating this. This part of the mediation can take place with the parties present in the same room or with the parties in different rooms with the mediator moving back and forth (or shuttling) between them.

Some mediations (face-to-face mediations) take place with the parties present in the same room for the whole or at least the bulk of the mediation. The focus of the mediation is on the parties speaking to each other and resolving the issues with assistance where necessary from the mediator to move it along or suggest breaks if they are needed. In such face-to-face mediations, the mediator may consider that a short break may be useful (eg, if tension is too high or tempers too short). The mediation will end when either the parties reach agreement, or it is clear that full agreement is not going to be an outcome of the mediation, in which case there will be a conclusion summarising those points which may be helpful to the parties.

Some mediations (shuttle mediations) take place almost completely with the parties located in separate rooms and the mediator seeing them separately to discuss the dispute from their individual points of view (Americans call this part of the process 'caucusing'). Having discussed the case with the individual parties, the mediator can take information, which each party permits the mediator to take, to the other side. The mediator 'shuttles' back and forth between the parties trying to get them to reach agreement. In the sessions with the individual parties, the mediator will be doing two things, principally: first, giving information that he or she is permitted to give to the other side, and secondly, getting the party with whom he or she is discussing the case to really think about realistic possibilities for settlement. A concluding session will be held jointly, to confirm what has been agreed between the parties or that there has not been agreement, if this is the case.

20.2.2 Different styles

In all forms of mediation the principle is that the parties make the ultimate decision as to how to settle the dispute. However, the style and range of techniques used by the mediator will vary depending on the type of dispute and the philosophy of the mediator or the organisation to which the mediator belongs. Three main styles of mediation are described below.

20.2.2.1 Facilitative

In facilitative mediation, the mediator controls the process (ie, sets out 'ground rules'), explains how the procedure works, and through questioning of the parties and encouraging them to talk to each other, facilitates their working together to find and consider options for resolving the dispute. The parties are completely in charge of what possible options are discussed as well as the outcome. The mediator does not make suggestions about possible options, give advice about the strengths of the case (eg, what might happen if it went to court) or state his or her own view or opinion on the possible outcomes or options. The mediation focuses very much on the parties working through the process to ensure that their underlying needs and interests are being addressed in the final settlement. It is less concerned with an external view of whether or not the settlement was fair in terms of strict legal rights.

Facilitative mediation was the style used when mediation was first developed as a way of resolving disputes. It was often used for matters which would not reach court (eg, neighbour disputes about noise where neither party had the money to pursue it through the courts). Developed largely in the voluntary sector, mediators came from a variety of backgrounds. They were more likely to be community workers or social workers (ie, those working in the caring professions) than lawyers.

20.2.2.2 Evaluative

In evaluative mediations, the mediator does make suggestions and state his or her view on the strengths of the case from an objective or legal point of view. There is much more emphasis on the parties' legal rights. The mediator's role is more interventionist. He or she takes an active part in seeking settlement both by suggesting and commenting on solutions and evaluating the outcome based on legal concepts of fairness.

Evaluative mediation developed as mediation came to be used to settle disputes which would normally go to court. The mediators in this type of mediation tend to be lawyers.

20.2.2.3 Transformative

Transformative mediation is much newer and not as well known or widely used as the other two styles. It attempts to 'transform' the parties' lives by assisting them to genuinely understand the other parties' needs, values and points of view. The parties take responsibility for the mediation. They are in charge of both the process and the outcome with the mediator merely 'reflecting back' statements or views the parties have expressed. Transformative mediators are less concerned with the parties reaching a settlement than with the parties feeling 'empowered' and determining whether they will reach a settlement and what the settlement will be.

Most mediators will use techniques ranging from those which are quite interventionist and/or 'evaluative' to those which are purely 'facilitative'. On the very strongly interventionist/evaluative end of the range, the mediator is likely to have substantial expertise in the area of the dispute and have a very direct effect on the outcome. At the truly facilitative end of the range, mediators see their role as enabling the parties to find and agree their own solutions. There are therefore, strong prohibitions on the mediator either suggesting or commenting on solutions. Which end of the range is used will depend to an extent on the type of mediation.

20.2.3 Different uses

Mediation is a rapidly developing field of work and therefore changing. It is difficult to set out all the areas in which it is being used as a method of resolving disputes. There is no specific professional body for all mediators. However, the Legal Services Commission has introduced a Mediation Quality Mark for Family and Community Mediation. One could differentiate between three basic types of mediation:

20.2.3.1 Family mediation

Mediation is used increasingly in family matters, in particular, by separating and divorcing couples. The main aim is to reduce the conflict and encourage cooperation between parents, which may have an impact on the children, or which may involve the children directly (eg, where the dispute is about who has parental responsibility and what contact the parents may have with the children). The UK College of Family Mediators, an independent, non-government umbrella body has a Code of Practice and provides training in family mediation. Solicitors who wish to practise in family mediation must be members of the Law Society's Family Mediation Panel. Barristers who practise as mediators are accountable to the General Council of the Bar. To be recognised by the Legal Services Commission, family mediators must have taken training recognised by the UK College of Family Mediators or the Law Society's Family Mediation Panel.

20.2.3.2 Commercial mediation

Commercial concerns are turning to mediation to resolve disputes which might otherwise take a lot of time and money to resolve through the courts. The Rules of the Supreme Court require a statement setting out what alternative methods have been considered to resolve the matter prior to setting down in High Court. The Centre for Dispute Resolution (CEDR) is the biggest provider of this type of mediation in the UK. It was launched in November 1990 and has as its members over 150 of Europe's leading companies and professional firms.

20.2.3.3 Community mediation

This type of mediation covers a fairly broad range of disputes which are matters of concern to an individual or possibly the community at large. Thus it could cover neighbour disputes, problems in school, environmental issues, etc. These types of disputes could be the subject of litigation, eg, seeking an injunction against a neighbour in respect of noise or an anti-social behaviour order against a person who is causing a disturbance on a housing estate. Mediation UK acts as an umbrella organization for community mediation. It fulfils much the same function as the UK College of Family Mediators in family mediation.

Family and community mediations are more likely to involve face-to-face mediation and a truly facilitative mediation style. Some community mediations now use only the transformative mediation style. Family mediations have non-binding outcomes; proposals for settlement in the mediation are subject to independent legal advice. Similarly, community mediation processes also emphasise that any agreement reached is not legally binding.

Commercial mediations are more likely to involve shuttle mediation and include evaluative mediation styles. They are extremely unlikely to use a transformative mediation style. Commercial mediations may also include a step whereby the settlement reached by the parties is formalised in an agreement drawn up by lawyers which, when signed, does become binding on the parties.

20.3 How the different processes influence the skills used

As lawyers you will need to know when to advise your client to consider mediation as an alternative to litigation. You may also be instructed to represent clients in commercial or family mediations. Legal representation in community mediations is rare and not really considered appropriate by many community mediation organisations. Finally, some barristers are themselves acting as mediators as part of their practice.

The development and underlying ethos of the different forms of dispute resolution (court adjudication, mediation and negotiation) mean that different skills are required.

20.3.1 Court adjudication

20.3.1.1 The process

Courtroom trials are conducted in a public forum with a public official (judge) randomly appointed to supervise the process and decide the outcome. Litigation is highly complex, with a large number of procedural steps and devices which take time to explain and which parties do not understand. Trial dates are not fixed for the benefit of the parties but to fit in with the court diary and, possibly, the lawyers. The underlying ethos is adversarial whereby the two parties in dispute put their cases, usually through lawyers, to the judge to decide. The judge relies on the two disputing parties to put forward all the relevant evidence and arguments, usually in the form of an oral hearing. The decision is then made on the basis that one side wins and one loses (ie, the judge 'finds' for one side only).

20.3.1.2 Litigation and courtroom skills

When a person with a problem or dispute instructs a lawyer to assist in resolving it, the lawyer will approach the problem by determining what legal right has been infringed or what legal wrong has been done. The problem or dispute is reshaped by the lawyer into a form suitable for the legal system. This means the lawyer will identify the particular rules which have been breached or infringed and will then put together a case to demonstrate the strengths of their client's case and hide or disguise the weaknesses. The lawyer will then 'fight' the case using the procedural and evidential rules of the litigation process to put the best case forward.

The lawyer uses analysis, knowledge and logic to identify the issues, formulate arguments and ensure that the matters which must be decided by the courts are addressed as persuasively as possible. While the lawyer is also likely to be aware of the impact of the court case on the client's life and feelings, these considerations are not relevant to the formulation of the case being put to the court. The lawyer, while being sympathetic to the client, will focus on ensuring the case is properly prepared for trial which means focusing on the issues which must be determined by the court. The lawyer also 'has charge' of the case because of his or her expertise in the substantive law and the rules used in determining the outcome. The client will often defer to the lawyer's views both about the information which is important for the lawyer and court to know and about the outcome which should be expected.

Lawyers therefore develop the rational or 'left brain' skills of analysis and logic. They learn to focus on the issues which have been identified, to be decisive and to present confidently and persuasively in front of a judge.

20.3.2 Mediation

20.3.2.1 The process

Mediations are conducted in private with the parties deciding both what the issues are and how they will be resolved. The possible outcomes are infinite. Theoretically both parties will win in that they will only agree to an outcome which they feel is satisfactory for them. This may be according to some norm of fairness or it may not. There is no obligation to consider, and no particular emphasis given to, the strengths of the competing legal rights of the parties. The mediator controls the process by setting out how the mediation will be conducted (eg, face-to-face or shuttle mediation) and ensuring that ground rules are established. The mediator may also attempt to move the parties forward by asking questions. However, the parties determine the issues to be resolved, discuss how this might happen, and work together to reach an outcome which is sufficiently satisfactory to both parties. It is the parties' needs, interests and understanding of the problem which is paramount.

20.3.2.2 Mediation skills

Where a lawyer accompanies a client to a mediation, his or her role is more akin to the usual role of the lawyer in litigation, ie, to assist his or her client. Lawyers acting in mediations will have to learn not to be wedded to the legal issues and merits in considering the settlement.

Where the lawyer acts as mediator, he or she must adopt the ethos of mediation and shake off both the adversarial mindset of the litigation lawyer and the decision-maker mindset of the judge. The mediator is not arguing for either party, nor does he or she determine the outcome.

A mediator's skills are in assisting the parties to identify their underlying needs and interests and to express their concerns and priorities to ensure they are addressed in any settlement. The mediator is therefore much more concerned with how the problem presented impacts on the lives of the parties as well as how they feel about the problem and possible solution. Although they do apply logic and rational thinking in the process, they will also rely on their sensitivity to subtle psychological and behavioural indicators, their intuition and instinctive reactions.

Lawyers who wish to be mediators will therefore also need to develop their creative or 'right brain' mental processes. They will also need to learn to give over control of the discussion to the parties and resist making suggestions or commenting on the viability of solutions.

Evaluative mediations require less adjustment by lawyers as they involve a greater degree of merit-based considerations and comment by the mediator on solutions proposed.

20.3.3 Negotiation

20.3.3.1 The process

Negotiations done in the context of the litigation process have some of the characteristics of courtroom adjudication and some of mediation. They are done 'in the shadow of the law' so the merits of the case will matter. However, they are also done with a view to a more flexible outcome than the win/lose outcome of a court decision. They also enable the negotiators to take into account the client's needs, interests and feelings.

20.3.3.2 Dispute resolving negotiation skills

The development of skills training in negotiation has been heavily influenced by concepts from mediation. This manual sets out in great detail the skills required for legal dispute negotiations and how this differs from more standard concepts of negotiation used by salespeople. The aspect of negotiation which most lawyers find most difficult is determining a reasonable settlement standard. This may be because they are trying to find a solution which reflects both the decision a court would reach on the basis of the legal rules and the outcome the parties would reach in a mediation.

APPENDIX
CASE STUDIES

Case Study A

MEGADELL FOODS LIMITED

and

ANGUS WARLEY (t/a CHOC FOLIE)

INSTRUCTIONS TO COUNSEL FOR THE CLAIMANT

Counsel is instructed on behalf of the Claimant in this matter, Megadell Foods Limited, which is resisting the application to set aside the judgment in default obtained on 11th February 2009.

This firm was instructed to commence proceedings at the beginning of December 2008. Counsel will note the nature of the claim from the Particulars of Claim enclosed with these papers. Judgment was regularly obtained. On 26th February 2009 the Defendant applied to have the judgment set aside and Counsel will see from the witness statement in support enclosed with these papers that Mr Warley is claiming that he was in hospital and he did not know of proceedings. He is attempting to set aside the judgment on the merits.

The view of the Claimant company is a commercial one in that if the judgment is to be set aside they are interested in a settlement that disposes of the entire matter without recourse to further delay and costs. The chocolate retained has not yet been sold on and the company is keen to get the Defendant to buy this from them provided the original terms as to payment can be met. Counsel is directed to the enclosed statement of Rupert Bryson for full details of the company's position and the full background to this action. The company is not however willing to settle at any cost as it is of the view that the Defendant has been the author of the problems.

This firm contacted solicitors for the Defendant upon being served with the application. They are instructing Counsel and we have suggested a meeting prior to the hearing to see whether this matter can be resolved to the interest of both sides. They are agreeable and Counsel is therefore instructed to attend early and speak to the other side with the purpose of coming to terms if possible. Counsel is entrusted to examine the issues fully and reach the best acceptable settlement for the Claimant. Failing acceptable compromise Counsel is instructed to resist the setting aside of the judgment obtained.

Costs to date excluding Counsel's fee are approximately £400. (Counsel's fees for today are £180.)

(Note: Counsel for the claimant would also have the particulars of claim and both witness statements; see **5.4.1**, Case Study A.)

STATEMENT OF RUPERT BRYSON

I am the managing director of Megadell Foods Limited. We are a company importing various foodstuffs from the continent. One of our lines is premium grade chocolate which is the subject of this dispute.

The company employs various representatives who visit retail outlets and set up deals with them and supply aftercare. One of our representatives was a Mr Leon Haalen who left us in September last year. He appears to have set up the contract with Choc Folie. As is usual he set up a deal whereby we contracted to provide a year's supply of the product. The other terms were our standard ones, to supply the product to the customer's premises, and payment to be made 30 days after invoice (which was on delivery) with an interest clause for late payment. I see that Mr Haalen arranged for delivery to be in the first half of the month.

Of course it is our policy to provide foodstuffs of high quality and to keep the customer happy at all times. It is correct to say that we train our representatives to keep in touch with the customer and tell the customer to address any queries to the representative. Unfortunately in this case, due to Mr Haalen's departure, there was a slight hiatus with customer care in the West Country as we were unable to replace Mr Haalen until the end of November.

To fulfil our side of the contract, we contracted with Luglian Chocolate of Ghent, Belgium to supply us with the chocolate at a total cost of £9,000. Our storage, delivery and operating costs can be assessed at £200 per month (I can get full details from our accounts department if necessary). They contracted to deliver to us in two cargoes, the first six months' supply in August and the second six months' supply in January. The profit we were due to make on the deal was £14,920 in total.

The first record I have of any complaint from Choc Folie is a fax sent on 20th October 2008 (the one exhibited to Mr Warley's affidavit). That seems very late in the day if the product was not up to standard when delivered on 6th October. I note that the fax does not say what the problem is. I have to accept however that we did have a West Country customer care problem at the time. I am suspicious when Mr Warley says in his witness statement that he telephoned us many times as we have an efficient system and *all* telephone messages are recorded. I have investigated and not found any messages recorded from him at that time. I cannot say whether messages were left on Mr Haalen's mobile.

When the fax was brought to my attention I took personal action and telephoned the customer. My records show that this was on 22nd October 2008. I pride myself in being of an equable disposition but found the customer most unreasonable. I said that the foodstuffs would be examined when delivery of the November order was made. I said this could take place a little early on 30th October just a few days after the conversation. This seemed to me the most sensible course to take. As I recall it was very difficult to make sensible headway with the customer who kept complaining about our poor service. The conversation was lengthy but not very productive.

I had checked the customer records before telephoning and noted that the customer had not made any payment for the September delivery and enquired of the customer what the position regarding this was. Again the response was confusing and negative. I pointed out the customer's obligations and the customer reacted in an almost hysterical fashion.

After about twenty minutes of conversation when little I was saying was accepted, the customer told me that as far as he was concerned he was not interested in our product and would not be paying for anything else delivered. He told us not to bother coming to look at the October chocolate delivery as he was going to bin it. I find it hard to believe that he would have said that if there had been anything wrong with the chocolate and I then took the view that he was just trying to avoid payment for the goods already received.

After the conversation I made a note for the orders department to hold back the November delivery to the customer. I have checked with the department and there is no record of further contact from Mr Warley or from Choc Folie. In November the accounts department referred the matter to our action department and a warning letter was sent (copy attached). No communication or payment was received from the customer. The matter was put in the hands of our solicitor.

The company was able to sell on the remaining product from the first cargo delivered in August 2007 (2,000 kilogrammes). However, although we did try to cancel the January cargo, the terms of the Luglian contract made this impossible. We therefore have six months' supply left, ie, 3,000 kilogrammes. It is a specialised product which has proved difficult to sell on. The chocolate is still in good condition having an 18 month shelf life from the date of the delivery to us.

I see from Mr Warley's affidavit that he is claiming half the October delivery was defective. I can only say that it is a great shame that he did not let us investigate the position thoroughly at the time. I am still rather suspicious about the whole thing. However, I can concede that our after sales service in the West Country was not up to scratch during the relevant period last year. We now have a thoroughly efficient West Country representative, Mr Knox, whom I have been personally overseeing since he started with us. We have received good reports about him from our West Country customers.

I cannot really comment about Mr Warley being in hospital at the time although again it seems rather dubious. It is just raised as if that decides the whole thing. If there had been some proper communication at the time then this contract might have continued without a hitch. Indeed we still have the product and would be willing to resupply if the customer is absolutely clear that the full contract terms regarding payment must be complied with. Of course payment for the chocolate already supplied must be made at once. Having said that, Choc Folie clearly could be a good continuing customer for us and if this matter can be resolved so that relations might continue in the future then we would be satisfied. I am willing to be advised on what would be a satisfactory settlement as continuing this matter is not commercially attractive to us.

MEGADELL FOODS LIMITED

15, THE ESTATE, CHEAM HILL, SOUTHAMPTON, SO33 7JM

our ref 00/GHCF0007

14th November 2008

Choc Folie Angus Warley,
17, Lebbell Spring Way,
Bridgwater,
Somerset.

OUTSTANDING AMOUNT £2,520

Our records show that the above amount remains outstanding on the following invoices:

1. ch99/0001 date 6.09.2008
2. ch99/0002 date 4.10.2008

UNLESS PAYMENT IS MADE IN FULL WITHIN THE NEXT 14 DAYS WE WILL HAVE NO ALTERNATIVE BUT TO SEEK THE FULL SUM BY LEGAL ACTION

If payment has been made already please accept our apologies for this demand for payment.

ACCOUNTS DEPARTMENT,
MEGADELL FOODS LIMITED

Case Study A: Plans and Notes of the Law

The notes setting out the preparation for negotiating Case A from the point of view of counsel representing the defendant which show the thought processes at each stage of preparation are set out at:

Chapter 6—understanding the context

Chapter 7—determining the objectives

Chapter 9—formulating argument

Chapter 10—assessing information to exchange

Chapter 11—planning concessions

Chapter 13—planning the structure

Set out here are examples of plans, one for the claimant and one for the defendant which could be written for use in the negotiation. Attached to the plan would be the Notes of the Law on which you would rely. These Notes would be the same for claimant and defendant.

C = claimant; D = defendant

PLAN FOR DEFENDANT

OBJECTIVES

Defendant's objectives

General overview

No specific limits by client—so get as much money as possible

Would like to continue trading with C

Try to use future custom (purchases as trades on C's losses)

Specific objectives

- judgment set aside & have whole case dropped
- pay as little as possible on C's claims
- get as much as possible on D's own claims
- have D's costs paid to date & not pay C's costs
- continue trading with Megadell: 500 Kilo a month; assurances re service

Claimant's likely objectives

- resist having judgment set aside & continue with claim unless happy with settlement
- receive as much as possible on C's own claims
- give as little as possible on D's claims
- have C's costs paid & not pay D's costs
- possibly? continue trading with D

ITEMS TO BE NEGOTIATED (in order of preference)

1. Open by getting assurance that if settle > judgment set aside & C discontinue claim
2. C's claim for instalments 1 & 2 & D's claim for losses re weekend
   - try to link them
   - deal with instalments 1 & 2 together
   - show how D's claim (£3,500) larger than C's claim for price (£2,520)
3. C's claim for loss on remainder of contract
   - link to offers to buy chocolate
   - consider future trading
4. Costs

Individual Items—arguments & possible concessions

a. the case

Not subject to bargaining—assuming above items agreed; ensure get agreement that C will discontinue case

b. C's claim for the price £2,520 (£1,260 each instalment) plus interest (c£50)

Instalment 1—no legal argument; but if judgment set aside—C must wait

Instalment 2—poor quality; representations by Mr H; difficulty contact company; still has chocolate so has proof that bad. (C argue—delay in notice of defect; D accepted; D no evidence to C of fault; inspection now too late; only 1/2 not useable)

Query deal with 2 instalments together:

Opening offer: £1,260—agree to pay 1/2 the claim; chocolate clearly faulty

Best outcome: as above (cannot resist paying 1st instalment)

Least outcome: pay instalment 1 and 3/4 instalment 2 = £1,260 + £945 = £2,205

Staging: in £200/£250 steps—likely goods will be found to be faulty

c. D's loss of profit on Chocaganza Weekend (£2,000—got 2/3 contract price)

D's reasonable case on causation (see above) less good on remoteness (no info in phone call/fax); reasonable on mitigation;

Opening Offer: dependent on arguments on faulty goods; seek all (emphasise causation and proof of loss)

Most get: 3/4 = £1,500

Least get: 1/4 = £500

Staging: reduce in small steps of £200

d. D's loss of profit on shops

D reasonably strong claim

Opening: all = £1,500—clear causation, contemplation & proof of loss

Most get: all = £1,500

Least get: 1/2 = £750

Staging: £150 steps

e. C's loss benefit of remainder of contract £4,100 (5,000 Kilo @ 82p kilo)

C must prove D repudiated (burden on him) but D weak on repudiation (given phone call PLUS failure to pay or respond)

C must prove loss—potential weaknesses for C (no loss if sold or still have & D buy)

Get information about what happened to chocolate before offer (provided still has it and in good condition—use offers to buy it to offset claim). If not available—must get information about whether sold/steps to sell etc before offer; outcome VERY dependent on this (ie, mitigation)

Opening offer: buy remainder at 500 Kilo per month at contract price—solves both parties problems

Best outcome: the above

Least acceptable outcome and staging:

If buy any chocolate resist paying further money; if essential offer small % of loss claimed (notional sum 'goodwill'—start £200 work up to £1,000; ALTERNATIVELY: offer increased price per month eg £20 per month (ie, 4p kilo) to 6p kilo (£30 per month) (£30 per month = £300 for whole contract) (query get client permanently into higher price range)

If no purchase of chocolate: dependent on whether chocolate sold or not/steps to mitigate; start small £200 (C produce problem; failure to mitigate); if sold—work through to 1/2 of remaining loss; if not sold—pay up to a maximum of 1/2 the claim = £2,000)

f. costs - D's are £425 (£175 for today & £250 generally)

Normal order—D pay today; Get information re C's costs to date—today & generally

Open: C pay some of D's costs—C jumped the gun; no further investigation of difficulties; C cause legal cost

Least get: D pay C's costs of today; otherwise each pay own

OVERALL OUTCOME

This is dependent on whether or not chocolate still available to buy and/or been sold as this affects C's claim substantially

Best possible outcome

- D buy chocolate at 500 Kilo a month at normal price/C drop claim for £4,100
- C pays D money—D offset payment on 1st instalment for payment on his claims—most D likely to get is payment in region of £500 – £1,000

Least acceptable outcome

- chocolate not available to buy—
- C and D's money claims therefore offset—but need to deduct price received for remaining chocolate/sum for mitigation and see concession planning above
- D pay C—a maximum in the region of £2,500

PLAN FOR CLAIMANT

OBJECTIVES

Claimant's objectives

General overview

Want money due but also wish to settlement—commercial view—dispose of matter

Still have chocolate from January delivery 3,000 Kilos—difficult to sell

D could be good continuing customer

Specific objectives

- resist having judgment set aside & continue with claim unless happy with settlement
- receive as much as possible on C's own claims
- give as little as possible on D's claims
- have C's costs paid & not pay D's costs
- sell the 3,000 Kilos of chocolate to D
- continue trading with D possibly

Defendant's likely objectives

- judgment set aside & have whole case dropped
- pay as little as possible on C's claims
- get as much as possible on D's own claims
- have D's costs paid to date & not pay C's costs
- continue trading with Megadell?

ITEMS TO BE NEGOTIATED (in order of preference)

1. If settle >—judgment set aside & C discontinue claim IF D drop all claims too
2. Deal with C's claim for 1st instalment first—can't be resisted
3. Deal with C's claim for 2nd instalment with D's counterclaim
4. C's claim for loss on remainder of contract
5. Possibility of future trading
6. Costs

Individual items—arguments & possible concessions

a. The case & D's general position

Start conciliatory—set aside & discontinue & seek D drop all claims if settle

Get information re D's views on continue trading—agree possible if reasonable settlement

b. C's claim for price £1,260 on first instalment plus interest

Instalment 1—confirm no complaints on this—so confirm payment due

NOT an item for negotiation (separate out from other items) seek full £1,260

c. C's claim for price £1,260 on second instalment

C good case: no reasons given by D; C's offer to replace; D say bin it; C no chance to inspect

Opening offer: want all

Best possible outcome: get 3/4

Least outcome: only get 1/2 = £820

Staging: come down in £200/£250 steps

d. D's loss of profit on Chocaganza Weekend (£2,000—got 2/3 contract price)

D prove faulty (If have chocolate still may); but C has arguments (see above pt c) also D difficulty on remoteness (C's knowledge) check steps on mitigation

Opening offer: dependent on arguments on faulty goods; offer nothing

Best possible outcome: pay nominal figure

Least possible outcome: pay 3/4

Staging: increase in steps of £500

e. D's loss of profit on shops

Arguments as above; Remoteness possibly less of issue for D here

Opening: pay nothing

Best possible outcome: pay nothing

Least possible outcome: pay all £1,500

Staging: increase in £300 – £1,500 stages

f. C's loss benefit of remainder of contract £4,100 (5,000 Kilo @ 82p kilo)

C must prove D repudiated (burden on him) but D weak on repudiation (given phone call PLUS failure to pay or respond)

C must prove loss—potential weaknesses here for C

Get information re D's wish to continue trading; if does offer accept £2,000 & continue sell for 2 more months on same terms

Best outcome: the above

Least acceptable outcome: sell chocolate at same price

Staging: Dependent on other items as well—trade off with costs as well

g. Costs—C's costs are about £400 (£180 for today & £220 generally)

Normal order—D pay today

Open: D pay all > D pay today & 1/2 other costs of C

Least should get: D pay today (but could trade for other items above)

OVERALL OUTCOME

This is dependent on whether or not D wish to continue trading

Best possible outcome

C get 1st & 2nd instalment; pay some of D's claim eg, £1,000 & get some on C's loss of benefit eg, £1,000—so trade off of these two claims & continue trading with D at slightly increased price

Least acceptable outcome

C get 1st & 1/2 2nd instalment; C pay 2/3 D's claim c£2,500 & continue trading at same price

NOTES OF THE LAW—same for Claimant and Defendant

Setting judgment aside—CPR, r 13.2

Apply by notice of application and witness statement.

- If wrongly entered: varied as of right.
- Otherwise: only if D has real prospect of successfully defending the claim/some other reason; court also take into account D's explanation for allowing judgment to be entered/delay in applying to have set aside.
- May set aside on terms: D pay sum into court.
- Costs incurred usually awarded against D.

Contract for supply of goods

Sale of Goods Act 1979 and Sale of Goods and Supply of Services Act 1994 (contracts MADE after 3.1.95). NOTE: no exclusion clause pleaded. Non-consumer contract.

Instalment contract (Legal Test: where instalments delivered and paid for separately > severable (instalment) contract, not entire contract). For delivery and acceptance each instalment regarded as a separate contract which can be sued on (*Jackson* v *Rotax Cycle Co* [1910] 2 KB 937, CA).

Failure to pay breach? Seller sue for price

- *B duty to accept/pay*: s 27
- *B 'accept'*: s 35 if intimate to S; B does act inconsistent with S ownership; B retain without intimate to S rejected; not deemed until B reasonable opportunity to examine goods.
- *B right to reject*:
  - failure to comply with implied terms (breach of condition)
  - implied condition includes s 14(2) of satisfactory quality, ie: s 14(2A) meet standard reasonable person regard as such taking account of description, price, relevant circumstances; s 14(2B) state and condition (including fitness for purpose, appearance and finish, freedom from minor defects, safety, durability). And s 15A if breach so slight to be unreasonable to reject > breach of warranty (not condition but burden on S to show)
  - right to reject can be lost by deemed acceptance (see above s 35) > breach of condition become breach of warranty
  - if reject, B no duty to return (s 36) but must make available for collection at place of examination
  - lawful reject > property revest in S; B sue for non-delivery BUT no lien.
- *S sue for price*: s 49
  - s 49(1) if property passed to B and B wrongfully rejected or refused to pay
  - s 49(2) even if property not passed to B: where date fixed for payment irrespective of delivery and wrongful failure to pay
- property pass (specific v unascertained goods, s 61—here unascertained becomes ascertained when separated and irrevocably attached to contract; s 18, Rule 5: property pass when unconditionally appropriated to contract by S with consent of B or by B with assent of S).

Set off?

- Section 53 (1) (a) B may set off counterclaim for breach of warrants or where B elects/compelled to treat breach of condition as breach of warranty against S claim for price.
- Breach of warranty: normal *Hadley* v *Baxendale* measures (1. directly and naturally resulting and 2. unusual in contemplation of parties) (s 53 (2)).
- Section 51 (damage for non-delivery) goods rejected where there is a market: *prima facie* measure difference between contract and market price.
- Loss of profit recoverable where at time of contract S knew/ought to have known the use to which goods were to be put and that B intended to produce a profit and breach likely to reduce/extinguish that profit.
- Damages may also be available for loss of repeat orders from customers (*GKN Centrax Gears Ltd* v *Matbro Ltd* [1976] 2 Lloyd's Rep 555).

Repudiation?

Sale of goods Section 31 (2): instalment contract for sale of goods, where S make defective delivery/B fail to pay for 1/more instalments > terms of contract and circumstances of case > whether breach = repudiation of whole contract or severable breach of one instalment.

- Failure to perform must go to root of contract (*Mersey Steel and Iron Co* v *Naylor Benson & Co* (1884) 9 CA 434).
- Main tests are:
  - the quantitative ratio of the faulty instalment to the whole contract
  - the degree of probability that breach will be repeated (*Maple Flock Co Ltd* v *Universal Furniture Products (Wembley) Ltd* [1934] 1 KB 148, CA).
- The further the parties have proceeded with performance of the contract the less likely it is that one party is entitled to claim contract repudiated by one breach (*Cornwall* v *Henson* [1900] 2 Ch 298).

General contract By renunciation: where one party evinces unconditional intention not to perform or be bound by contract or essential term (*Freeth* v *Burr* (1874) LR 9 CP 208).

Anticipatory breach: where party renounces before time to perform > innocent party may elect to accept repudiation and sue OR wait for time for performance.

Seller's claim for damages

Section 50 B refuse to accept/pay > S can sue for damages for non-acceptance

- Section 50(2) measure is estimated loss directly and naturally resulting in the ordinary course of events from B's breach.
- Section 50(3) available market > difference between contract and market price at time ought to have been accepted (*prima facie* rule which may be displaced if unjust/inappropriate (*WL Thompson Ltd* v *Robinson (Gunmakers) Ltd* [1955] Ch 177)).
- Section 50(3) no available market (eg, unique, manufactured to B specification) > usually contract price and price at which sold *(Gebruder Metelmann GmbH & Co KG* v *NBR (London) Ltd* [1984] 1 Lloyd's Rep 614).
- 'Lost volume' S can recover loss of profit (eg, B throw back onto S's hands good of same type as in stock, difficulty shifting because supply exceed demand) > prevented opportunity to sell to same B the S's remaining stock. Profit on 2nd sale recoverable, presumed to be same as profit on sale to B (*WL Thompson* above).

Case Study B

PRISTINE CONSERVATORIES AND SUMMER HOUSES LIMITED

and

THE HARROGATE ENCHANTED CONSERVATORY LIMITED

INSTRUCTIONS TO COUNSEL ON BEHALF OF PROPOSED CLAIMANT

Counsel has herewith:

(1) Statement of Felicity Parker.

(2) Receipt dated 3.6.09.

(3) Estimate dated 6.6.09.

Instructing Solicitors act on behalf of Felicity Parker, proprietor of The Harrogate Enchanted Conservatory Ltd. We understand that proceedings are about to be commenced by Pristine Conservatories and Summer Houses Ltd for a final payment due under a building contract drafted and approved by ourselves and dated 10th March 2008. The amount outstanding is £30,000 which Miss Parker has withheld.

The contract was to build a rather unusual structure comprising six linked conservatories for the retail sale of exotic house plants. The areas of dispute are, first, concerning a teak floor which, under clause 15.1.5 of the contract, was to be fitted to the Japanese conservatory. Miss Parker insists that this term was breached without her instructions since a birch floor was installed by the contractor. Miss Parker paid a local joiner £4,000 to rectify the breach.

Secondly, and perhaps more importantly, Miss Parker alleges that the door 'air lock' system to preserve the various microclimates within the individual conservatories is inadequate. She alleges that she has lost valuable plants through the deficiency and has obtained an estimate of £10,000 to rectify the defects.

Miss Parker would however like to settle the dispute if possible. As Counsel will see from instructions this is a delicate family matter and Miss Parker is concerned that details of her financing of the operation may be publicised. She wishes to restore relationships if at all possible but feels that this must be done carefully.

Instructing Solicitors have agreed with solicitors for Pristine Conservatories to see whether settlement is possible. Accordingly, Counsel is instructed to meet with Counsel for the other side to see if any settlement can be found.

ASSUME YOUR INSTRUCTIONS ARE RECEIVED IN THE 2ND WEEK OF JUNE 2009

AND EASTER WAS APRIL 20TH 2009

Your fee is £70.

STATEMENT OF FELICITY PARKER

I own The Harrogate Enchanted Conservatory Ltd, a company which I started in January 2007 so as to open for business in April 2009. The business is a retail unit which was purpose-built to house a wide variety of exotic plants. I felt that since the home conservatory market was booming it would be a good idea to offer plants to the public, housed in similar conditions to their own properties.

When I had the idea for 'The Enchanted Conservatory' I discussed it with my brother-in-law Patrick Batchelor. Paddy owns Pristine Conservatories and Summer Houses Ltd. I told him that I would like a unit which featured six themed conservatories and summer houses of slightly larger than domestic proportions. I wanted the customer to be able to see how their garden rooms would look with, for example, a Mediterranean theme, with Oleander, Bougainvillea, etc, set in terracotta pots, or a desert theme with various cacti and succulent plants.

Since these areas would have different humidity and temperature requirements it was necessary to have an 'air lock' type system to maintain stability. Paddy assured me that although my idea was a novel concept it should be possible to put into action.

I already owned a suitable site so, once plans were drawn up, we were able to proceed quite quickly. Paddy quoted £180,000 'cash in hand' to be paid in six instalments. I knew that it was an excellent price. I didn't have the full amount but I presented my business plan to Mr Brown, manager of my bank, Midshires, and he agreed to extend my overdraft facility on the existing business and to refinance the land. To be absolutely honest I massaged the figures slightly to include an amount which I needed to pay for some antiques which I'd wanted for some time. I don't want that to get out.

Everything went ahead as planned and I was really excited about the grand opening ceremony which was to be held over the Easter weekend (April 20th). Things started to go wrong in the two weeks prior to opening when I started to stock the conservatories with plants. I noticed immediately that the wooden floor in the Japanese conservatory was not teak as we agreed in the contract but birch. Birch does not fit in with the design because it is not a traditional wood. It's also much cheaper than teak and made the display look tacky. I told Paddy to rip it out and put a teak one in. We had a terrible row and he said what did I expect if I wanted everything on the cheap. He also said that I'd agreed to a birch floor which is just untrue. In the end I paid Peter Bugg, a local joiner, £4,000 to fit a new floor. We managed to open in the week before Easter by the skin of our teeth.

The next problem to become apparent was that it was impossible to maintain stability of temperature and humidity in the six areas. The doors between them were ill-fitting and the rubber seals soon perished. I lost £1,800 worth of specimen citrus trees overnight when moisture from the Tropical Rain Forest Area seeped in and killed them. I kept ringing Paddy but he refused to talk to me. Relations got worse, my sister took his side and now we're not speaking either.

I didn't pay the final £30,000 to Paddy. I know he needs it for his business but I feel I've really been messed about. I think he should pay for the new teak floor, my lost plants and to put the air locks right. I've had a quote from 'Sunny Garden Rooms Ltd' of £10,000 to rectify the system.

I really would like to settle this thing amicably if possible if only for the sake of my parents who are worried sick about the split between me and my sister. If I have to go to court though, I will, because my livelihood is at stake. I can't afford to lose any more plants and I need to get The Harrogate Enchanted Conservatory Ltd into shape as quickly as possible.

I'll learn by my mistakes and won't allow family to become involved in my business again.

Sunny Garden Rooms Ltd
15 Smith Road
Knaresborough
North Yorkshire

6th June 2009

Dear Felicity

ESTIMATE

Further to our site visit and conversation earlier today I can confirm our estimate of £10,000 inclusive of V.A.T. to repair and make sound six door air lock systems at the Harrogate Enchanted Conservatory Ltd.

I must say you've got a super business and I do hope you'll be a client in the near future.

Yours sincerely

Ted Moldings
M.D.

Greens
12 High Road
Knaresborough
North Yorkshire

4th June 08

Peter Bugg Joinery
14 Cornwall Street
Harrogate

Received with thanks, £4,000 from 'The Harrogate Enchanted Conservatory Ltd'.

Peter Bugg

Case Study B Preparation Notes

These notes set out the analysis, legal research, argument formulation and evaluation and concession planning which you would do in preparation for the negotiation. This analysis would form the basis for the plan which you would use in the negotiation. The plan would be much shorter and is set out separately.

This section contains the preparation notes for the claimant and then for the defendant.

C = claimant; D = defendant; NB = important

PREPARATION NOTES FOR THE CLAIMANT

Claimant's position

Under building contract 10.3.08 with D: erected novel retail sales unit comprising six linked conservatories with themed areas for sale of exotic plants.

Started: ?

Hitch in March 05 when teak supply disrupted.

Finished on time Easter 2009—20.4.09 and to specifications. Charge £180,000 (not much more than cost). Payment to be in six instalments. Last instalment not paid—£30,000.

Before issue of proceedings.

Possible objectives

What claimant wants from negotiation:

- payment of as much of £30,000 outstanding as possible;
- willing to remedy defects in air lock system (rather than pay someone else);
- avoid publicity;
- repair family relationship;
- costs (brief fee £70 but not know other costs to date).

What defendant might want from negotiation:

- teak floor *or* reduction of £30,000 because of birch floor;
- air locks fixed;
- query what effect this has (themed areas/exotic plants);
- her costs?;
- her business to work (new still and query effect of air lock and floor on it?);
- resume family relations (is C's wife's sister).

Items to be negotiated

The items are:

- the floor;
- the air lock;

- any damage from either of the above (particularly air lock);
- payment of £30,000 to C;
- both parties' costs;
- publicity re work/flower business?
- resume family relations?

Underlying issues to items

1. The floor:

- Legal issues:
  - written contract;
  - variation—oral promise suffice?;
  - consideration for variation?;
- Factual issues: what actually said by PB for C and FP for D

2. The air lock:

- Legal issues: contract for Supply of Goods and Services Act 1982.
  - *the air lock*: contract for transfer of goods (ie, one under which person transfers goods to another whether or not services are also provided):
  - s 4(2) implied term where transferor transfers property in goods in course of business that goods supplied are of satisfactory quality (defined in s 4(2A) as meet the standard that a reasonable person would regard as satisfactory, taking account of any description of the goods, the price (if relevant) and all the other relevant circumstances);
  - s 4(3) condition implied not extend to any matter: (a) specifically drawn to transferee's attention before contract made, (b) where transferee examines goods before contract made which examination ought to reveal, (c) where transfered by sample which would have been apparent in sample;
  - s 4(4) where transferee expressly or impliedly makes known to the transferor any particular purpose for which goods are being acquired then by s 4(5) implied condition that goods supplied are reasonably fit for purpose whether or not that is the purpose for which such goods are commonly supplied. *But* s 4(5) does not apply where circumstances show that transferee does not rely or unreasonable for him to rely on skill/judgement of transferor.
- *Installation of air lock*:
  - Section 12 1982 Act—where supplier agrees to carry out a service.
  - Section 13 implied term for supply of service where supplier acts in course of business that carry out service with reasonable care and skill.
  - Factual issues: C has difficulty on this one because has little information: What is wrong? When did it go wrong? Why not work? What needs to be done to fix it? Why FP not let PB in to see?

3. Query any damage flow from air lock?

- Legal issues: causation; foreseeability.
- Factual issues: C has difficulty as no information on this.

Arguments to be used; information needed; offers to make/seek on issues/items

1. The air lock

Argument

- He erected a novel retail sales unit comprising six linked conservatories with themed areas for sale of exotic plants; air locks installed to ensure that various temperatures and humidity levels required by different areas remained stable.
- Work finished on time and to specifications stipulated.
- Breakdown of communication over floor but first heard re, air locks presumably about Whitsun (ie, sometime after opening if did open at Easter).
- D not let C in to look at it and see what is wrong.
- D still not let C in to look.
- Not known what fault is; could be anything; may *not* be attributable to original work, eg, could have been tampered with by customers.

Information exchange

Need to find out if she had someone else in to fix?

Evaluation and concession planning

- C on reasonable ground given D's failure to let inspect/unreasonable behaviour.
- *If not fixed yet*: to look and fix (although subject to finding that *not* due to tampering by customers/cause outside C control and rectifiable). Need to get D's undertaking that *will* let in.

Need to establish when inspection will take place and general time limit for any necessary works to be done.

Query agree to offer to do for free (subject to above caveats).

- *If has been fixed*: need some report/inspection to be satisfied that fault was C's before discuss any reduction in price for fault.

2. Loss flowing from air lock not working

(arguments include those on above item too)

Information exchange

- C has no information on this at all, although might be able to guess from papers that there may be a claim as knows that shop was to be of exotic flowers; air lock system to preserve microclimates as plants were very sensitive; some knowledge of themes, eg, Japanese and desert with cacti.
- C needs to get full information about what D claims including what plants damaged, when damaged, why damaged, how much claiming for damage and how this is quantified (note D not able from instructions to provide all this information).

Argument

- C can argue not liable: no proof he in breach (ie, that air locks not working due to his failure to perform contract properly); for D to show breach caused the loss (what damage etc—how know that due to faulty air locks *and* timing of loss—could C have rectified any fault before damage done if D had let C in to do it?); not in contemplation of parties when contract made (although difficult to argue given knowledge as set out above) and for D to prove that it was in contemplation of parties.

Evaluation and concession planning

Depends on strength of arguments put in negotiation by D and amounts claimed. Try to trade D's claim on plants with C making offer on birch floor and fixing the air locks—thus C not make payment on plants or very little.

3. The floor in the Japanese conservatory area

Argument

Says oral variation of contract (*but* because he had difficulty because teak supply disrupted).

Told D and suggested put a birch wood floor in instead.

Information exchange

C later had telephone message that she agreed; D has copy of note of message by 'Anne': (C may not know this) *but* who is she, where is she, what kind of witness would she be? What did D say about variation? Why such reaction to floor when agreed it? Has floor been replaced? Who did it? When? Cost?

Evaluation and concession planning

- Argument for C not very strong; burden on C to show variation.
- *If not done*: could C replace floor himself (? not certain for less money—but presumably as get goods wholesale); query then how much additional charge for this? What state birch floor in? Could he reuse the birch to offset against price of getting teak?
- *If done*: why not come to C? (but told to get lost because done a good job; discovered a couple of weeks before opening *not* a strong argument).

  Get details first re who did it, price etc. Offer to knock something off £30,000 to reflect this cost.
- Start low, build up; did whole job for not much more than cost anyway and agreed to instalment payments (because of family relationship) *so* already had reduction in original price; what finally agree depend on agreement on plants.

4. Costs

Nothing in brief on solicitors' costs; fee today £70.

Owed £30,000—needs to get money; D not pay; no recourse but go to law; D pay something towards C costs.

Concession planning

D pay today's costs; each own on others.

Each own on all.

PREPARATION NOTES FOR THE DEFENDANT

Defendant's position

Pristine seeking outstanding £30,000 on building contract 10.3.07 for six linked conservatories for retail sale of exotic house plants.

D not paying because of wrong floor, air locks do not work and lost valuable plants.

Needs to get Harrogate into shape quickly.

Before issue of proceedings.

Possible objectives

What defendant wants from negotiation:

- defects remedied as soon as possible (has estimate of £10,000 for someone else to do it but feels brother in law should do it);
- £4,000 for birch floor;
- £1,800 to replace lost citrus plants;
- not want financial irregularities exposed;
- restore family relationship;
- costs (£75 today but not know previous costs).

What claimant might want from negotiation:

- payment of as much of £30,000 outstanding as possible;
- to know what defects in system are (would he remedy defects in air-lock system rather than pay the bill for someone else to do it);
- keep 'cash' deal secret (query avoid pay VAT);
- avoid publicity?
- repair family relationship?
- his costs?

Items to be negotiated

The items are:

- the floor;
- the air lock;
- damage from broken air lock;
- payment of £30,000 to C;
- both parties' costs;
- secrecy for both parties' financial irregularities?
- publicity re work/flower business?
- resume family relations?

Underlying issues to items

1. The floor:

- Legal issues:
  - written contract:
  - variation—what required?
  - consideration for variation?
- Factual issues: what actually said by PB for C and FP for D

2. The air lock:

- Legal issues: contract for Supply of Goods and Services Act 1982.
  - *the air lock*: contract for transfer of goods (ie, one under which person transfers goods to another whether or not services are also provided):
  - s 4(2) implied term where transferor transfers property in goods in course of business that goods supplied are of satisfactory quality (defined in s 4(2A) as meet the standard that a reasonable person would regard as satisfactory, taking account of any description of the goods, the price (if relevant) and all the other relevant circumstances);
  - s 4(3) condition implied not extend to any matter: (a) specifically drawn to transferee's attention before contract made, (b) where transferee examines goods before contract made which examination ought to reveal, (c) where transfered by sample which would have been apparent in sample;
  - s 4(4) where transferee expressly or impliedly makes known to the transferor any particular purpose for which goods are being acquired then by s 4(5) implied condition that goods supplied are reasonably fit for purpose whether or not that is the purpose for which such goods are commonly supplied. *But* s 4(5) does not apply where circumstances show that transferee does not rely or unreasonable for him to rely on skill/judgement of transferor.
- *Installation of air lock*:
  - s 12 1982 Act—where supplier agrees to carry out a service.
  - s 13 implied term for supply of service where supplier acts in course of business that carry out service with reasonable care and skill.
  - Factual issues: D has little info on this (just that doors ill-fitting and rubber seals perished). What is wrong? When did it go wrong? Why not work? What needs to be done to fix it?

3. Query any damage flow from air lock?

- Legal issues: causation; foreseeability.
- Factual issues: D alleges certain facts (may be disputed).

Information to seek/arguments to use; offers to make/seek on issues/items

1. The air lock

Argument

- C knew purpose etc of conservatory (ie, that contract for unusual structure comprising six linked conservatories for retail sale of exotic house plants) and that air locks essential to preserve the various microclimates with individual conservatories.
- Air locks are inadequate; not possible to maintain stability of temperature and humidity of six areas.
- Doors are ill-fitting and the rubber seals soon perished.

(No indication of whether ill-fitting from start or when seals perished—no instructions on how much been used/how been used.)

- D says 'kept ringing Paddy but he refused to speak to me. Relations got worse' (and on discovery of birch floor—'we had a terrible row') implication that both lost temper re birch floor but then D try to get C to correct air lock fault (the emotional aspect is irrelevant to settlement—NB *not* just accept that their client the 'emotional one' *nothing* in D's instructions to indicate that D did refuse to let C in).
- Has estimate for £10,000 inclusive of VAT to repair and make sound the air-lock system (Sunny Garden Rooms Ltd)—no indication of when can do it.
- If C not fix, alternative is to pay £10,000 for someone else (knock off £30,000).

Information exchange

NB find out what information C has about faults/what approaches D made C to rectify; what information has she given him about the problem? What chance to put it right?

Evaluation and concession planning

NB D *wants* C to rectify it.

Let C in to inspect *if* C agree to fix air locks and do ASAP.

Agree details needed of when he can visit etc.

2. The plants

Argument

- Contract with C to build six linked conservatories for retail sale of exotic plants.
- Discussed it with C. Different areas would have different humidity and temperature requirements and necessary to have 'air lock' type system to maintain stability. C assured D that although novel idea he could put it into action.
- D discovered (not clear when) impossible to maintain stability of temperature and humidity in areas. Doors ill-fitting and rubber seals perish.
- Lost £1,800 worth of specimen citrus trees overnight when moisture from tropical rain forest seeped in and killed them (not say *when* this happened).

- Says did keep ringing C (but not clear whether before or after the damage done).
- Argue that purpose of contract to house exotic plants and air locks to maintain separate units essential part of contract. Breach caused loss and in contemplation of parties when made contract (irrelevant when it occurred or what specific detail C knew of contents of areas).
- Weakness is that have little proof of what did kill trees.

Information exchange

C likely to ask about trees (do we still have them even? some time ago now—even if have can we show what caused death?).

Evaluation and concession planning

Trade off something on exotic plants if C fix air locks asap and accept some reduction on £30,000 for floor.

3. The floor

Argument

- Clause 15.1.5 in written contract specifies teak floor.
- C says D agreed to birch floor—information—if variation alleged by C, for him to prove it. No instructions that did agree (although also no instructions that did *not* discuss at all—ethics).
- When discovered birch 'we had a terrible row' (ie, implication that both parties lost their tempers).
- Birch cheaper than teak *so* cost less for C to install birch than teak (but note D does admit got whole job for excellent price).
- On current papers, D has strong argument—strength in negotiation dependent on what C has *so* NB to get info from C to find out what arguing.
- Need to have floor done:
  - clear teak needed for Japanese area as traditional wood, birch cheaper not fit decor;
  - found out about change 2 weeks before opening and crucial to open at Easter; needed it fixed before then;
  - got local joiner to do it for £4,000 (has receipt dated 4.6.08 proving payment—but no breakdown of cost of wood versus labour).

Information exchange

NB get details from C re alleged variation—when/how/evidence of agreement to birch floor?

Evaluation and concession planning

D in fairly strong position on this so seek substantial amount of the £4,000 knocked off the £30,000 owing; start with £4,000, work down in hundreds *not* thousands; final position dependent on other two items (go to £2,000 if C fix locks and consider some payment towards plants).

4. Costs

Nothing in brief on solicitors' costs; fee today £70.

Enormous hassle in addition to losses suffered because of floors and air locks; can set off damages for breach against contract price; D pay something towards C costs.

Concession planning

C pay today's costs; each own on others.

Each own on all.

Case Study B: Plans and Notes of the Law

These are examples of plans, one for the claimant and one for the defendant which could be written for use in the negotiation. Attached to the plan would be the Notes of the Law on which you would rely. These Notes would be the same for claimant and defendant.

C = claimant; D = defendant.

PLAN FOR CLAIMANT

OBJECTIVES

Claimant

- payment of as much of £30,000 outstanding as possible
- willing to remedy defects in air-lock system (rather then pay someone else)
- avoid publicity
- repair family relationship
- costs (brief fee £70 but not know other costs to date)

Defendant

- teak floor OR reduction of £30,000 because of birch floor
- air locks fixed
- query what effect this have (themed areas/exotic plants)
- her costs?
- her business to work (new still and query effect of air lock & floor on it?)
- resume family relations (is C's wife's sister)

ITEMS TO BE NEGOTIATED

1. payment of £30,000 to C
2. the air lock
3. any damage from either of the above (particularly air lock)
4. the floor
5. both parties' costs
6. publicity re: work/flower business? (depends on other matters—use to help?)

CONDUCT OF NEGOTIATION—structure, strategy etc

1. ask what D wants (ALL items on table, in particular if any losses from air lock)
2. then get information re claims:
   - the floor—what done? information re replacement if that done
   - the air lock—what wrong, when wrong, etc
     —what done

- any detail on further losses needed
- on business—how vital to get floor/air locks done

3. make offer re: air locks (if not done already)—subject to conditions re: access and cause being clearly down to C, etc
4. argue floor—burden on C to prove variation—check balance of evidence on this
5. argue plants—causation an issue—check evidence on this
6. argue offset rectify faults for no claim re: floor/plants
   - move to reduction on £30,000 depending on amount claimed/evidence by D on both of these
   - move in £100 steps on this
   - least acceptable—dependent on claim by C but probably no more than 1/2 of cost of floor and 1/2 other losses (dependent on evidence re: air locks and damage—but her fault not already done). Also dependent on WHEN D pay (if pay NOW, perhaps reduce a little)
7. use costs & publicity as leverage

PLAN FOR DEFENDANT

OBJECTIVES

Defendant

- defects remedied as soon as possible (has estimate of £10,000 for someone else to do it but feels brother in law should do it)
- £4,000 for birch floor
- £1,800 to replace lost citrus plants
- not want financial irregularities exposed
- wants to restore family relationship
- costs (£75 today but not know previous costs)

Claimant

- payment of as much of £30,000 outstanding as possible
- to know what defects in system are (would he remedy defects in air-lock system rather than pay the bill for someone else to do it)
- keep 'cash' deal secret (query avoid pay VAT)
- avoid publicity?
- repair family relationship?
- his costs?

ITEMS TO BE NEGOTIATED

1. the floor
2. the air lock
3. damage from broken air lock
4. payment of £30,000 to C

5. both parties' costs
6. publicity re: work/flower business?

CONDUCT OF NEGOTIATION—structure, strategy, etc

1. Explain D disappointment re contract—two major faults in contract, floor & air locks
2. Deal with air locks first as most NB (although not necessary reveal that—but do reveal that need fixing)
   - find out C position on this? what know? what prepared to do? his information on contacts with D re: fixing
   - be as amenable on this as possible > get agreement to fix asap
3. Floor—argue strongly that NO agreement—for C to prove variation
   - seek his version & evidence to support
   - reveal cost to D of fixing (show invoice)
   - try to get C to agree this BEFORE move to plants
4. Plants—argue strongly causation & forseeability easy to show
   - deflect from proof of amount
   - be prepared to reduce this sum for more on floor
5. £30,000 outstanding—clearly offset from this money above & our costs (probably NOT suggest reduce further if offer advertising for C as D say not allow family to become involved in my business again) Maximum pay on £30,000 (accept 1/2 of floor costs & 1/3 plants = £2,600) provided C fix air locks
6. Use costs/possible publicity as leverage

NOTES OF THE LAW—same for claimant and defendant

The floor: variation of contract:

- written contract; does oral promise suffice?
- what consideration for variation?

The air lock: contract for Supply of Goods & Services Act 1982

The air lock

- contract for transfer of goods (ie, one under which person transfers goods to another whether or not services are also provided)
- s 4(2) implied term where transferor transfers property in goods in course of business that goods supplied are of satisfactory quality (defined in s 4(2A) as meet the standard that a reasonable person would regard as satisfactory, taking account of any description of the goods, the price (if relevant) and all the other relevant circumstances)
- s 4(3) condition implied not extend to any matter

(a) specifically drawn to transferees attention before contract made

(b) where transferee examines goods before contract made which examination ought to reveal

(c) where transferred by sample which would have been apparent in sample

- s 4(4) where transferee expressly or impliedly makes known to the transferor any particular purpose for which goods are being acquired then by s 4(5) implied condition that goods supplied are reasonably fit for purpose whether or not that is the purpose for which such goods are commonly supplied. BUT s 4(5) not apply where circs show that transferee not rely or unreasonable for him to rely on skill/judgement of transferor

Installation of air lock

- s 12 SOGSA82—where supplier agrees to carry out a service
- s 13 implied term for supply of service where supplier acts in course of business that carry out service with reasonable care and skill

Damage flow from air lock?

- Legal Issues: causation; forseeability

SUGGESTED READING

Books

Fisher, R, Ury, W and Patton, B, *Getting to Yes—Negotiating Agreement Without Giving In*, 2nd ed (Penguin Books, 1991).

Gifford, D G, *Legal Negotiation: Theory and Applications* (St Paul, Min: West Publishing Co, 1989).

Ury, W, *Getting Past No: Negotiating Your Way from Confrontation to Cooperation* (Business Books Ltd, 1991).

Williams, G R, *Legal Negotiation and Settlement* (St Paul, Min: West Publishing Co, 1983).

Articles

Bergman, P, 'Is That a Fact? Arguments in Problem-Solving Negotiations' (1994) 1(1) *International Journal of the Legal Profession* 81–85.

Condlin, R, 'Cases on Both Sides: Patterns of Argument in Legal Dispute Resolution' (1985) 44 *Maryland Law Review* 64–136.

Condlin, R, 'Bargaining in the Dark: The Normative Incoherence of Lawyer Dispute Bargaining Role' (1992) 51 *Maryland Law Review* 1–104.

Goodpaster, G, 'Lawsuits as Negotiations' (1992) 8(3) *Negotiation Journal* 222–39.

Menkel-Meadow, C, 'Legal Negotiation: A Study of Strategies in Search of a Theory' (1983) 4 *American Bar Foundation Research Journal* 903.

Menkel-Meadow, C, 'Towards Another View of Legal Negotiation: The Structure of Problem Solving' (1984) 31 N4 *UCLA Law Review* 754–842.

Menkel-Meadow, C, 'Lawyer Negotiations: Theories & Realities—What We Learn From Mediation' (1993) 56(2) *Maryland Law Review* 361–79.

Priest, G L and Klein, B, 'The Selection of Disputes for Litigation' (1984) 13 *Journal of Legal Studies* 1.

Taylor, M, 'Teaching Negotiation: Changing the Focus from Strategy to Substance' (1999) 16(1) *Journal of Professional Legal Education* 23–52.

INDEX

A

accommodating behaviour 127
accuracy of information 104–105
acknowledgement 178, 179
admissions 118
advocacy 1
  comparison with negotiation 1–2, 37
  learning of skills 2, 3
agenda for negotiation 12, 136–137, 144
aggression 34, 72, 129–130, 146, 150
agreement 71
  checking on 174–175
  client's approval of 198–199
  contract or deed 192
  court orders 193–198
  draft agreements 145
  on facts 88
  form of 67
  letter setting out terms 191
  memorandum of agreement 193
  none reached 176
  partial 176
  recording 175–176
    methods 188–198
  as tactic 118
  on what is in dispute 140
allegations
  factual 88, 90–91
alternative dispute resolution 213–219
  court adjudication 217–218
  mediation 218–219
  negotiation 219
anchoring tactic 145
arbitration 213
argument 71
  application to case study 94–99
  argumentative style 72
  collaborative strategy 78–79
  competitive strategy 78
  cooperative strategy 78
  effective 167–168
  evaluation of 93
  formulating 83–99
    analysis of factual disputes 87–90
    consideration of evidence 90–91
    legal argument/dispute 87
    legal framework 85–87
    persuasive arguments 91–93
  meaning of 75
  merit-based 76–77, 79–82, 91–92
  norm/fairness-based 77
  persuasion and 7, 75–79, 158, 206
  practical 77
  purpose of 92
  response to opponent's arguments 93
  settlement standards and 76
  use of 78–79
  visual presentation 157
authority of client 32, 148–149, 162–163
avoiding behaviour 126, 129

B

backtracking 117
bargaining 6, 14, 134
  concessions and 114–117
  hard 18
  plea bargaining 24
  positional 18, 61, 64
  soft *see* **cooperative strategy for negotiation**
  strategic bargaining theory 26
barristers
  learning from 4
  mediation and 217
  negotiation and 1, 11, 24, 29–31, 200
  role of 1, 28, 32–33
behavioural aspects of negotiation 126–127
  communication and 152–154
  professional behaviour towards opponent 163–164, 209
Best Alternative to a Negotiated Agreement (BATNA) 21, 39, 73–74, 148, 177
bluffing 105
body language 153–154
bottom line 73–74, 103
Boulwarism 116
brainstorming 22
breaks 183–184
bridges, building 179
brief
  endorsement 187, 188–190
  instructions for negotiation and 58, 65–66
brinkmanship 148
bunching of demands 115
burden of proof 91

C

case studies of negotiation 41–53, 220–249
  concessions in 123–125
  context 58–59
  formulation of argument 94–99
  information exchange 109–110
  objectives 69–70
  planning structure 141–142
cause of action 85
checking on agreement 174–175
circumstances in which negotiation takes place 56–57
clarification 118
clarity 158

clients
approval of agreement from 198–199
authority of 32, 148–149, 162–163
benefits of out of court settlement 27
confidentiality 163
'day in court' 27, 64
future relationship with opponent 66
negotiation and
limitation on what client will accept 67–68
objectives 32, 38, 57, 64–68
present at meetings 56–57
priorities 68
role and influence of 31–33
priorities 68, 140
concessions and 122
coherence 158
collaborative behaviour 127
collaborative strategy for negotiation 17, 20–22
advantages 132
concessions and 114
information exchange 22, 103–104
limitations 132–133
measurement of success 21–22
objectives 60–63
persuasive techniques 73–74
principled negotiation 21
problem–solving 22
tactics 22–23
use of argument in 78–79
commercial disputes 216
common ground 183
communication 152–161
community disputes 216–217
competition
competing behaviour 127
increasing 147
competitive strategy for negotiation 16, 18–19, 128–130
advantages 129
concessions 18, 113
dealing with 180–181
information exchange 18, 19, 103, 104
measurement of success 19
objectives 60
persuasive techniques 72
risks and limitations 129–130
tactics 18–19
use of argument in 78
compromise 6, 16, 116
behaviour 127
as contract 187
see also **agreement; cooperative strategy for negotiation**
concessions 6, 111–125
application to case study 123–125
backtracking 117
bargaining and 114–117
client's priorities and 122
collaborative strategy 114
competitive strategy 113
conditional 170
cooperative strategy 113–114
distinguished from other tactics 117–118
early 115
evaluation of case and 120–121
information exchange and 106
lateral thinking 119–120
misleading 117
opening negotiation and 111, 113, 114, 121
overall package 117
planning of 39–40, 118–119, 121, 169, 203
psychological influences 111–112
recording 122–123
reopening 117
response 208
risks and limitations 130–131
slicing approach 116–117
staging 121
tactics 114–117, 143, 168–172
trade–offs 117, 122
use in negotiation strategies 18, 19, 20, 112–117
conciliation 73
conciseness 158
conclusion of negotiation 14, 174–176
conditional concessions 170
confidence 158–159
confidentiality 163
consent court order 195–196
context of negotiation 38, 54–59, 164–165
contract
compromise as 187
recording of agreement and 192
conviction 158–159
cooperative behaviour 127
cooperative strategy for negotiation 16, 19–20
advantages 130
concessions and 19, 20, 113–114
information exchange 19, 20, 103, 104
measurement of success 20
objectives 60
persuasive techniques 73
risks and limitations 130–131
tactics 20
use of argument in 78
coping
inability to cope 185–186
costs of litigation 67
course in negotiation 201–202
court adjudication
process 217
skills 217–218
courts
court orders 193–198
court–door negotiation 29–30, 55, 57, 67, 132
informing of settlement 199
credibility
concessions and 112
cross–cultural negotiations 101
culture
cross–cultural negotiations 101
negotiation strategy and 128

D

'day in court' 27, 64
deadlines 72, 148
deadlock 182–184
deal–making negotiation 54
argument, formulation of 83

use of merit-based argument 81–82
deed
recording of agreement and 192
defences 85
demands 146
bunching of 115
escalation of 116
false 115
opening 115
preconditions 115
tactics 143
differences
dealing with 127
difficulties 177–186
discussion phase 134
disputes
agreement on what is in dispute 140
analysis of 87–90
on facts 88
resolution of 8, 24, 54–55
formulation of arguments 83–84
use of merit-based argument 79–81
distortion of information 100–102, 104–105
distributive negotiation 9
divorce 216
draft agreements 145
dubious tactics 149–150

E

education of opponents 179–180
effective negotiation 34–35, 162–176
acting professionally 162–164, 208–209
context of negotiation 164–165
dealing with phases of negotiation 165–176
recognizing impact of stress 164
emotions 146–147, 178–179, 184–186
endorsement of brief 187, 188–190
escalation of demands 116
ethical issues
dubious tactics 149–150
information exchange and 103, 104–105
etiquette in negotiation 3
evidence
consideration of 90–91
expectations 100–101, 168
exploration 14, 134

F

face-to-face negotiation 12
facts
admission of 118
disputes over, analysis of 87–90
factual argument 76–77, 81
failure of negotiation 25
failure to move (deadlock) 182–184
fairness 131, 133
argument based on 77
false demands 115
family mediation 216
fax
negotiation by 11
final offers 148, 171, 182
flexibility 159, 207
forcing issue 148
form of agreement 67

G

game theory 34
gender
negotiation strategy and 128

H

hypothetical questioning 183

I

impersonal negotiation 9
inexperience 185
information
accuracy 104–105
checking information each side has 140
distortion 100–102, 104–105
exchange of 2, 7, 12, 100–110, 165–167, 206, 208
collaborative strategies 22, 103–104
competitive strategy 18, 19, 103, 104
cooperative strategy 19, 20, 103, 104
flow of information 105–106
strategies of negotiation and 102–104
tactics 104–106, 143
fear of revelation 102
filters 101–102
gaps in 92–93, 106, 108
visual presentation 157
injunctions 195
instructions for negotiation 58, 65–66
integrative negotiation 9, 21, 62
interests
negotiation and 6, 21, 61–62
interim court orders 195
interpretation
negotiation and 12
irritation 184–185
issues to be negotiated 11–13, 38–39, 92
items to negotiate 140–141, 203

J

judges
negotiation and 31
'just one more thing' tactic 144

L

language, use of 159, 206–207
lateral thinking
concessions 119–120
legal argument 76, 81, 87
legal negotiation 24–36
legal research 86
legal rights
as objective of negotiation 66
letters
exchange of 190–191
negotiation by 11

limitation on what client will accept 67–68
listening 156–157, 159–160, 178, 207
litigation 24
  costs 67
  reasons for 25
  uncertainties in 80–81
  which cases should go to trial 27–28
logrolling 117

M

manipulation 150
mediation 24–25, 213, 214–217
  barristers and 217
  commercial 216
  community 216–217
  evaluative 215
  face-to-face 214
  facilitative 215
  family 216
  procedures 214
  process 214–215, 218
  shuttle 214–215
  skills 218–219
  styles 215–216
  transformative 215–216
meetings 56–57
memorandum of agreement 193
merit-based argument 76–77, 79–82, 91–92
merits of case 2, 139–140
mirroring behaviour 113–114, 154, 181
misleading concessions 117
money
  as objective of negotiation 64, 66
  orders for payment of 195
  as part of claim 90
moral argument 77
'moving on' tactic 144
multiple issue negotiation 8–9, 62
multiple party negotiation 10–11
mutual gain *see* **win/win negotiation**

N

negotiation
  behavioural aspects 126–127
    communication and 152–154
    professional behaviour towards opponent 163–164, 209
  breakdown 14
  comparison with courtroom advocacy 1–2, 37
  comparison with mediation 219
  conclusion 14
  course 201–202
  criteria 202–209
  issues to be negotiated 11–13, 38–39, 92
  legal 24–36
  meaning of 6–7, 71
  phases of 134, 165–176
  process of 13–14
  skills
    assessment 200–212
    importance of 1–2
    learning 2–5, 200–201
  types *see* **individual topics**
no
  techniques for getting past 177–180
non-verbal communication 153–154
normative argument 77

O

objective standard 145
objectives of negotiation 7, 38, 60–70
  achievability 120–121
  clients 32, 38, 57, 64–68
  collaborative techniques and 60–63
  criteria 203
  opponent 68–69
  planning structure of negotiation and 138–139
  shared and opposing 69
offers
  final offers 148, 171, 182
  tactics 143
  see also **concessions**
omissions 172
one-off negotiation 10
opening negotiation 13–14, 134, 165
  concessions and 111, 113, 114, 121
  demands 115
  planning 135–138
opponent
  education of 179–180
  future relationship with 66
  objectives 68–69
  opening negotiation 138
  professional behaviour towards 163–164, 209
  responding to requests for information from 107–108
  response to arguments of 93, 207–208
  seeking information from 106–107
  techniques for getting past 'no' 177–180
  testing 160, 171
  weak/ill prepared 181–182, 208
overall package approach 117

P

pace 159
panic 186
partial agreement 176
performance criteria 200–201
personal issues
  negotiation and 9
  as objective of negotiation 66
  separation from problem 60–61, 63–64
personality
  clash of 184
persuasion 2
  argument and 7, 75–82, 158, 206
    persuasive arguments 91–93
  collaborative strategy 73–74
  competitive strategy 72
  cooperative strategy 73
  role in negotiation 71
  speaking and 155
  techniques 71–75
phases of negotiation 134, 165–176
planning and preparation 35–36, 37–41
  case studies 141–142

checklist for 209–211
concessions 39–40, 118–119, 121, 169, 203
dealing with weak/ill prepared opponent 181–182
formulating arguments 83–99
information exchange 106–108
opening negotiation 135–138
strategies 40, 126–133
structure of negotiation 40–41, 134–142
tactics 41
written plan 211
plea bargaining 24
poker face 160
positional bargaining 61, 64, 179
positive emotions 146–147
power
competitive strategy and 129
practical argument 77
preconceptions 100–101, 168
precondition demands 115
presentation 158–159, 205–207
principled strategy for negotiation 16, 20–22, 132–133
measurement of success 21
tactics 21
privileged discussion 163
problem-solving behaviour 127
problem-solving strategy for negotiation 16, 20–22, 133
information exchange 22
measurement of success 22
tactics 22
procedural law 86
process of negotiation 13–14
professionalism 162–164, 208–209
progress in negotiation 172–174
review of 183
proof
of allegations of fact 90–91
burden of 91
psychology
communication and 152–154
concessions and 111–112
tactics and 146–147

Q

questioning 155–156

R

rationality 160
reactions 127, 178
reasons 146
recapping 174
reciprocal (mirroring) behaviour 113–114, 154, 181
recording
agreement 175–176
contract or deed 192
court orders 193–198
letter setting out terms 191
memorandum of agreement 193
methods 188–198
concessions 122–123
reframing approach 145, 179
remedies 85
reopening 117
repeat negotiation 10, 33
representatives 148–149
negotiation by 10
requests 146
research 86
response 159–161, 171–172, 207–208
retaliation 129
review of conduct of negotiation 212
review of progress 183

S

seating 57
selection theory 26
settlement 14, 134, 204
letter setting out terms 191
out of court 1, 2
benefits of 27
reasons for 24–28
recognition that settlement may not be possible 184
standard of 12–13, 74, 76
silence as tactic 147, 178, 179
single issue negotiation 8–9, 62, 129
single offer approach 116
skills of negotiation
assessment 200–212
importance of 1–2
learning 2–5, 200–201
slicing approach 116–117
solicitors
negotiation by 28, 29
speaking 155
staging concessions 121
stereotypes 101
strategic bargaining theory 26
strategies for negotiation 13, 16–22
factors influencing choice of 128
planning 40, 126–133
underlying theories 16–18
see also **collaborative strategy for negotiation; competitive strategy for negotiation; cooperative strategy for negotiation**
stress 164
stroking tactic 146–147
structure of negotiation
planning of 40–41, 134–142
style of negotiation 15–16, 72, 74
success, measurement of
collaborative strategy 21–22
competitive strategy 19
cooperative strategy 20
principled negotiation 21
problem-solving negotiation 22

T

tactics for negotiation 13, 22–23, 143–151
agenda 144
anchoring 145
brinkmanship 148
collaborative strategies 21–22
competitive strategy 18–19
concessions 114–117, 143, 168–172
cooperative strategy 20

deadline 148
demands 143
drafts 145
dubious 149–150
forcing issue 148
increasing competition 147
information exchange 104–106, 143
objective standard 145
offers 143
planning 41
preparation 151
psychology 146–147
reframing approach 145
specific 143–149
structure of negotiation 144
teams 149
threats 150
teams
tactics and 149
test cases 27
testing opponent 160–161, 171
threats 150
time
time limits 67
use of 147–148, 171
tit-for-tat tactic 147
Tomlin orders 197–198
trade-offs 117, 122, 170
transactional negotiation 8
trust 73
two party negotiation 10–11

U

uncertainties 80–81
undertakings 196
unforeseen, dealing with 186

V

venue for meeting 56
visual presentation 157
vulnerability 185

W

walkout 72, 148, 182
weaknesses
dealing with weak/ill prepared opponent 181–182, 208
exposure of 160–161
win/lose negotiation 17, 18, 25, 112–113, 127, 130
win/win negotiation 18, 62–63, 64, 127, 179–180
'without prejudice' negotiations 33–34
written plan 211

Y

'yes but' tactic 146

Z

zero-sum negotiation 9, 18, 25, 62, 129